ONE WEEK LO

Across the Blocs
Cold War Cultural and Social History

Editors

RANA MITTER
PATRICK MAJOR

FRANK CASS
LONDON . PORTLAND, OR

First published in 2004 in Great Britain by
FRANK CASS AND COMPANY LIMITED
Crown House, 47 Chase Side, Southgate, London N14 BP, England

and in the United States of America by
FRANK CASS
c/o ISBS, Suite 300, 920 NE 58th Avenue, Portland, OR 97213, USA

British Library Cataloguing in Publication Data

Across the Blocs: Cold War Cultural and Social History
1. Cold War 2. Civilization, Modern – 20th century
I. Mitter, Rana, 1969– II. Major, Patrick
909.8'25

ISBN 0 7146 5581 3 (HB)
ISBN 0 7146 8464 3 (PB)

Library of Congress Cataloging-in-Publication Data

Across the Blocs: Cold War Cultural and Social History /
editors, Rana Mitter, Patrick Major.
   p. cm.
   ISBN 0-7146-5581-3 (Cloth) — ISBN 0-7146-8464-3 (Paper)
   1. Cold War. 2. Cold War—Social aspects—Europe.
3. Cold War–Social aspects–United States. 4. Cold War–Social
aspects–Soviet Union. 5. Popular culture–United States–History –20th
century. 6. Popular culture–Soviet Union–History–
20th century. 7. Anti-communist movements–United States–
History. 8. Mass media–Political aspects–United States–History– 20th
century. 9. Research institutes–United States–History–
20th century. 10. Research institutes–Soviet Union–History–
20th century. 11. Politics and culture–Soviet Union.
I. Mitter, Rana, 1969–. II. Major, Patrick. III. Title.
   D843.A383 2003
   909.82'5–dc21

                                      2003013159

This group of studies first appeared in a Special Issue of Cold War History (ISSN
1468-2745), Vol.4, No.1 (October 2003), [Across the Blocs: Cold War Cultural and
Social History].

Printed in Great Britain by Antony Rowe Ltd., Chippenham, Wiltshire

Contents

Foreword

This book attempts to set out a research agenda for a truly comparative approach to the cultural and social history of the Cold War. Although the international history of high politics still dominates the Cold War field, a good number of exciting and provocative books and articles have already tackled the cultural and, to a lesser extent, social impact of the Cold War on historical phenomena. Yet so far, such work tends to have been very largely focused on the United States. This issue proposes a number of themes – among them Cold War 'home fronts', nuclear fear, propaganda (reception as well as production), historical memory, and intellectual traffic – which might fruitfully be explored across the blocs, using sources from a variety of societies and cultures. It then showcases a number of essays designed to be indicative (though by no means exhaustively so) of the kind of cross-cultural and interdisciplinary comparisons that historians might develop further. Each pair of essays tries to illustrate one particular theme in Cold War socio-cultural history via first a Western, and then an Eastern bloc example. We hope that this may provide a fruitful complement to the existing studies of 'Cold war culture' from the standpoint of individual societies.

We have incurred many debts in the development of this special issue. First of all, we would like to express our gratitude to the board of *Cold War History* for inviting us to put together this set of essays and, in particular, to Odd Arne Westad for his advice and encouragement. An initial agenda-setting meeting in 2000 was funded by the Research Development office of the University of Warwick, and the small group meeting in 2002 which critiqued the papers before peer review was funded by the Research Fund of the Modern History Faculty of the University of Oxford. The initial meeting was helped immeasurably by the contributions of Pertti Ahonen, Susan Carruthers, Richard Fried, Akira Iriye, Simon Kuper, Scott Lucas, Philip Murphy, Christopher Read, Corey Ross, Detlef Siegfried, S.A. Smith, and Hugh Wilford; the second meeting benefited from the comments of Tom Buchanan, Rosemary Foot, Holger Nehring, David Priestland, and Eddy U. Anonymous peer reviewers also gave invaluable suggestions for the papers. We are most grateful to all the above, none of whom are responsible for errors, for which the editors naturally take responsibility.

Rana Mitter
Patrick Major

East is East and West is West?
Towards a Comparative Socio-Cultural
History of the Cold War

PATRICK MAJOR and RANA MITTER

> Oh, East is East, and West is West, and never the twain shall meet,
> Till Earth and Sky stand presently at God's great Judgement Seat;
> But there is neither East nor West, Border, nor Breed, nor Birth,
> When two strong men stand face to face, tho' they come from
> the ends of the earth!
>
> (Rudyard Kipling, 'The Ballad of East
> and West', 1889)

This introductory essay argues that it is time for a much more conscious change in our boundaries of what Cold War history means, and for us to organize the socio-cultural aspects of that era systematically and paradigmatically, rather than as an afterthought to the analysis of high politics. The phrase 'the new Cold War history', is often used to describe the wealth of recent work that has emerged since the fall of the USSR and Soviet satellite states in 1989–91, and the subsequent opening up of Eastern state archives. John Lewis Gaddis's *We Now Know: Rethinking Cold War History* has been among the most prominent of the works to marshal new evidence to reshape what we know, or thought we knew, about the conflict which dominated the second half of the twentieth century.[1] The 30-year rule is exposing key new periods of the Western experience, and the archival riches from the Soviet sphere continue to flow, if sporadically at times. Yet, the limitations of empirical, archive-only studies have also become apparent from the former Eastern bloc reading rooms, which have patently not yielded all the hoped-for answers. The Stalinist mindset, with communist leaders talking newspeak rather than brass tacks even behind closed doors, has nonetheless had the effect of forcing scholars to take culture seriously as a category. Western specialists have also taken a cultural turn and revisited the Western world's own rhetoric of freedom and democracy.[2] Cold War historians are thus being forced to spread their wings methodologically, and such diversification is only to be welcomed.

But in an important sense there are key elements of this 'new Cold War history' which are not so new. Broadly speaking, and with prominent exceptions which we shall address later, the subject matter itself has remained the field of international history.[3] Any newcomer opening a book at random from the Cold War shelf will, nine times out of ten, find that it deals with foreign policy. Yet, Kenneth Osgood has noted that 'the best of the "new" Cold War history need not be exclusively *international* history [but] must be balanced with questions addressing the propaganda, psychological, cultural, and ideological dimensions of the Cold War'.[4] However, this remains a challenge still to be taken up full-bloodedly. The admirable Cold War International History Project, for instance, has blazed the trail to the archival riches that have become available behind the former Iron Curtain, but has chosen to tap mainly the files of foreign ministries and party leaderships. New findings tend to illuminate the dealings of top leaders in both blocs, and any local excursions reach only as far as satellite leaders. Yet, the amount of Cold War work that transcends the diplomatic field is relatively small.

This is not necessarily surprising. Most histories of great wars start with diplomatic and military accounts, and only later, with increasing distance, move on to the wider social and cultural ramifications of those conflicts. Nevertheless, even within the field of 'hot war' studies, historians have gradually branched out into neighbouring subdisciplines, responding to broader historiographical trends. Thus, societal accounts of the First World War started to appear in the 1960s, when social history as a field was beginning to expand, just as gendered approaches to the world wars reflected the rise of feminist history from the 1970s onward.[5] It is now accepted that public opinion played an important role in shaping the mood of belligerence in 1914. Social and labour historians have examined mass mobilization on the home front. Cultural historians have reconstructed the gender roles imposed by propaganda, or the cultural messages of 'modern memory'.[6] An 'everyday history' of fascism has emerged which, rather than trivializing the subject matter, has in many ways revealed the true horror of the era. The study of 'ordinary Germans' has become mainstream, when once foreign policy dominated the field.[7] And indeed, the inter-war Soviet Union – but not yet the post-war – has begun to follow suit, exploring the experience of high Stalinism from a similar bottom-up perspective, using secret police reports and oral history, including a pathbreaking study by one of our own contributors.[8]

'Socio-cultural' is meant, therefore, as an umbrella term to encompass the mass experience of events – social history in its broad sense of the 'ordinary' and 'everyday', but often in extraordinary circumstances. Likewise, cultural does not necessarily imply the literary or artistic endeavour of high culture, but popular culture and general mentalities too. The *loci classici*, perhaps, are E.P. Thompson's declaration that his work was 'seeking to rescue the poor stockinger, the Luddite cropper ... from the enormous condescension of posterity', and Clifford Geertz's classic definition of 'culture' in anthropological terms as 'interworked symbols of construable signs': '[C]ulture is not a power, something to which social events, behaviors, institutions as processes can be causally attributed; it is a context, something within which they can be intelligibly ... described'.[9] We should stress at the outset, then, that we are hoping to define an agenda which is a logical extension of, but which transcends, the 'cultural Cold War' as recently applied to international relations and diplomatic history. Journals such as *Diplomatic History* and *Cold War History* have been pioneering in this regard, and case-studies of the rhetoric and values of world leaders such as John F. Kennedy have yielded important new insights.[10] Although we would not be so foolish as to deny that the Cold War was grounded in high politics, it is not primarily in the classic international relations/international history field that we seek to place the following essays. Encouraged by approaches such as Scott Lucas's, to expand horizons from the state to include state-private networks,[11] we wish to de-centre the focus of attention even more radically away from government and diplomacy, towards society and culture as autonomous spheres of historical interest, and to establish the Cold War 'home front' as a sub-field in its own right. In this way, post-war historical writing will find more common ground with the mainstream historiographical trends alluded to above. And if Geoffrey Barraclough claimed in 1964 that contemporary history began in 1914, 40 years on it is perhaps time to suggest that contemporary history now begins in 1945.[12] The immediate policy-driven concerns of political science and area studies, once devoted to Kremlinology, are now largely focused on post-Cold War issues. With growing distance, historians can now take a longer view and more even-handed approach, asking about the impact as well as the causes of the superpower confrontation.

We are not, of course, by any means the first to focus attention on Cold War home fronts. There has been a profusion of work recently on the American civilian population in the 1950s, dealing with what Tony Shaw has called 'the state's appreciation of the importance of culture as a weapon in the Cold War'.[13] The post-war US home front was, of course, a rather ambivalent concept – almost a contradiction in terms. The state was keen to maintain the momentum of public mobilization achieved during the Second World War, but even before 1945, stateside America had not experienced directly any of the horrors of the European or East Asian home fronts. But despite the remoteness of the shooting war to many Americans, it had been undeniably real, fought against two very tangible enemies: Germany and Japan. The armed truce of the Cold War, on the other hand, was far more of a virtual conflict and many citizens wanted instead to enjoy the peace dividend. The problem of convincing them to make the sacrifices necessary to wage this new kind of seemingly permanent war were all the more daunting for officialdom, despite the fact that, with the atomic bomb, the civilian population had become the potential front line of the next conflict. Yet, precisely because the main adversaries never came to blows directly, apart from notable and bloody proxy wars in the Far and Middle East, and because the Cold War remained very much a war of words, we need to pay special attention to the internal dynamics of the conflict. Clearly, the United States' political elites felt the need to keep a domestic consensus for Cold War going. The very ideological nature of the confrontation also placed a premium on conformity of ideas. The nexus between high politics and everyday society has thus been a vital factor in understanding the social disciplinary aspects of America's Cold War, even down to the local level.[14]

Nevertheless, there is something slightly isolationist about the scope of many of these studies. The titles often suggest that *only* America experienced a Cold War at home.[15] This is perhaps an inverse reflection of the USA's widely-held belief at the time in its 'manifest destiny' to lead the world to Christian salvation. Despite the political gulf between conservatives' retrospective pride in America's containment stand and liberals' self-flagellatory soul-searching about 'loss of innocence', both tend to cast the USA as chief hero or villain. Unlike the Second World War, which was perceived to have started as somebody else's war, this was America's contest. Yet, the current America-centric focus might have other, less obvious reasons. Its erstwhile partners in the Western camp are somewhat in denial about their own role, preferring a Cold War (and above all its McCarthyite, persecutory excesses) which only really happened 'over there', in a hysterical United States. Moreover, countries such as Britain and France felt themselves to be engaged as much in a

North–South struggle over decolonization, as in the classic East–West confrontation, which has tended to obscure the importance of anti-communism. Hitherto, considerations of the latter have been confined to the field of labour history,[16] or are told through the eyes of the US State Department.[17] Only very recently has a pioneering study been published on the British secret state's preparations for all-out war.[18] Other countries, such as Italy, also have a very interesting Cold War home front tale to tell, still in its infancy,[19] as does Germany.[20] Nevertheless, only rarely is the Cold War the central theme and therefore, just as the post-revisionist synthesis cast the diplomatic net away from the bipolar centres towards the periphery, we would encourage more regional studies within the Western camp.

Yet what of America's chief antagonist? Perhaps even more surprising is the paucity of studies on Russian society during the Cold War, despite one recent notable exception in the special edition of the *Journal of Cold War Studies* on 'High Culture and the USSR during the Cold War'.[21] Given the huge Anglo-Saxon literature on inter-war Russia, this deficit seems all the more stark. The Cold War appears at best as an epilogue to high Stalinism.[22] In part this is of course the result of availability of sources, linguistic barriers, and funding, but it would seem also that post-Soviet Russian scholars are perhaps unwilling to re-open this chapter of their history. Only very tentatively have some begun to tackle the view from the East, but often still through the lens of Western assumptions.[23] Publications are certainly more abundant for the former German Democratic Republic, which has seen a number of studies of East German society, notably from the Zentrum für Zeithistorische Forschung in Potsdam, or from a number of younger British scholars.[24] Yet, the rest of the Eastern bloc is heavily underresearched and focused on key isolated moments such as the Prague spring.[25] It would be a pity, therefore, if the cultural imperialism of which America was accused at the time were to be replicated in historical scholarship. Here we can perhaps learn from the Cold War International History Project, which consciously encouraged remedial research on the 'other side'. The editors' own current research falls on the Eastern side of the Iron Curtain, on East Germany and communist China respectively. In this volume, consequently, we have been keen to ensure a geographical balance between East and West. The fact that Eastern Europe witnessed a wholesale internal collapse in 1989 further reinforces the importance of the domestic arena for understanding the outcome of the Cold War. We, and the board of *Cold War History*, would therefore especially like to encourage new work on the *terra incognita* of Eastern Europe and beyond.

In the interests of focus, we had to narrow down the areas on which this collection would concentrate. First, the essays draw on sources within the Euro-American Cold-War world. While Eastern Europe is the major area of new exploration here, the intention was emphatically not to imply that this type of research is invalid for the history of the wider world in the Cold War, and references to that wider agenda will be suggested below. In addition, the topics of the papers centre on the role of media and popular culture, chiefly during the 'first' Cold War up to the 1960s. To this extent, the focus is more cultural than social, although Mark Pittaway's piece, for instance, engages squarely with the latter agenda. Nonetheless, as a starting point for this sort of comparative agenda, the media suggests itself for an important reason: this was as often as not a propagandistic, verbal war. Governments on both sides of the Iron Curtain sought to manipulate their media where they could, as Sarah Davies, Tony Shaw and Nicholas Cull demonstrate in this volume. Yet there were key differences between East and West: Eastern writers all faced strict censorship, unless they were prepared to engage in *samizdat*; Western journalists and filmmakers, on the other hand, enjoyed considerable autonomy, even if their products did reflect the dominant ideology in more subtle ways. The role of technology in the Cold War is also of great relevance, but especially so in the case of the media. The Iron Curtain was never a hermetic barrier, as Mark Pittaway shows us in the realm of radio broadcasting. Moreover, the fictionalized discussion of technology in the shape of science fiction revealed deeper truths about the respective societies' attitudes to science, which had liberated the atom, but potentially enslaved humanity to this new force of nature. David Seed shows us how the debate over civil defence was waged even in this popular medium, while in the Eastern bloc, in Patrick Major's complementary piece, utopian writing clung for longer to rationalist notions of progress, before succumbing to its own cultural pessimism.

Cold War 'Home Fronts': Ways Forward

Media was just one possible topic among many. Here, we suggest a number of other areas where Cold War home fronts could more systematically be brought into focus, as a stimulus to other potential themed volumes or collaborative projects. By placing Eastern and

Western experiences side by side, in an explicitly comparative, transnational, and cross-bloc framework, we can identify useful similarities and differences. Such an approach need not break down into a series of self-contained national histories. What follows is an attempt to chart tentatively, sometimes provocatively, what some of the common avenues of research might be. Cultures often define themselves by what they are *not*, and nowhere was this more so than in the Cold War. There has been a remarkable interest elsewhere in the past two decades in the concept of alterity, of the historical Other, particularly in post-colonial theory. An application to the Cold War of Saidian 'orientalism',[26] originally catering to nineteenth-century imperialism, would be highly instructive. Whereas previously alterity was often metaphorical, the Cold War literalized otherness. For instance, Stasi working documents regularly invoked 'the adversary', a protean, portmanteau term for omnipresent enemies within and without the German Democratic Republic (GDR).[27] Cold War orientalism would therefore have to be compared and contrasted with the other distorting mirror of 'occidentalism'. Such an approach will probably reveal surprising complexity. For instance, once the Soviet Union fell out with Mao's China in the late 1950s, Soviet propaganda was subject to its own orientalism, as Moscow fought a propaganda war on two fronts.

Some comparisons will yield similarities. East was sometimes strikingly like West, for instance in the paranoid search for fifth columns in the 1950s. This 'mirror imaging' was sometimes unwitting and ironic, but sometimes a deliberate decision to emulate a tactic in the opposite camp, for fear of one side stealing a march on the other. But in other encounters between East and West the twain never really did meet. Frequently, political leaders would justify an alternative course of action or set of values, precisely because difference legitimated the home side: they did not wish to be placed on the same moral plane as the opponent. We might call this the 'mirror opposite' and should be prepared to contrast East and West where there were genuine differences. Intellectual dissidents, on the other hand, conscious of the irony of national security states invoking discourses of freedom while applying ever greater controls, sought to avoid polarization and steer a middle course: the so-called 'third way'. This was always a precarious position given the fatal either/or logic of the Cold War. Neutralists frequently found themselves pushed willy-nilly into the opposite camp. Mirroring mechanisms were thus intimately connected in a dialectical relationship, partly as a result of the natural human proclivity to binary logic, as well as the competing claims to universalism of the two ideologies, but a dialectic which never achieved resolution. With the demise of fascist anti-Enlightenment thinking, both liberal democracy and communism pretended to the true mantle of scientific rationality. Both professed to embody modernity, and appropriated the word 'democracy ', but applied to it fundamentally different meanings. But the global conflict also created its own overarching logic, that of nuclear self-destruction and species preservation, which forced some to think outside the constraints of limited notions of national self-interest. Linguistic and discursive approaches are thus necessary for understanding both the texts and contexts of Cold War culture, as well as an important gateway into the analysis of class and gender identities *vis-à-vis* the 'master narrative' of system conflict.

The extension of these ideas will be of particular importance in sketching the still only partially understood context of the Cold War in the non-European world. East Asia in particular, as a faultline region in the era, would repay much closer examination of its socio-cultural history through a Cold War paradigm. A few topics, such as the importation of the nuclear theme into Japanese popular culture (discussed below), have already received critical attention. Yet, there are other themes that remain to be explored. It is only relatively recently that it has become possible to write the history of the Mao era in China using internal archival sources. So far, the history that has been written has primarily been focused on internal developments, and the international system tends to impact on grass-roots politics primarily as an absence: for instance, the growing dissension within the Sino-Soviet alliance as a stimulant for the disastrous self-reliant policies of the Great Leap Forward. Yet, the rhetoric of the era, shaped in substantial part by tropes that were Soviet- as well as Chinese-derived, again reflects the binary Otherness that marked the Cold War as a whole. Society and culture in Maoist China reflected obsessions with technology, paranoia, the pre-Cold War past, and other themes that marked it out as a product of a globalized Cold War cultural environment as much as a state newly independent of Western or Japanese imperialism. New Chinese scholarship and primary sources on previously taboo topics such as the Cultural Revolution have provided a way into this material in the last few years, presaging a potentially highly fruitful research agenda.[28] And just as East Asia must be considered as part of a wider socio-cultural system, regions in the rest of the world can also be rethought in terms not only of what made them different, but also what made them similar to systems elsewhere.

What are the other comparative themes that could be explored, and with which the authors in this collection have attempted to grapple? Since the Cold War was very much a war of words, propaganda is a prime suspect for investigation. Morale on the Cold War home front was clearly of vital concern to the authorities, as Nicholas Cull and Tony Shaw show in their respective pieces here on the United States Information Agency and the interpretation of George Orwell's *Nineteen Eighty-Four*.[29] Propaganda operates through hostile stereotypes which require an understanding of mass psychology and of local cultural prejudices.[30] The study of posters can be highly revealing.[31] We are beginning to see how the West constructed its enemy stereotypes, using a mixture of popular psychology, advertising techniques and even academic research.[32] There were, of course, also a number of hot wars during the Cold War which would be amenable to the same sorts of propagandistic analysis as the world wars. The civilian experience in Korea, Vietnam and Afghanistan immediately springs to mind. Nevertheless, just because there was no physical fighting elsewhere does not mean that other national publics were not mobilized too. Yet, whereas world war propaganda had a vested interest in demonstrating that the home side was winning, Cold War propaganda as frequently highlighted the shortcomings of the home front. Its tone is therefore less triumphalist. But no study of propaganda would be complete without reference to its reception on the ground. Although some of the techniques may have been similar, it has been mischievously suggested that the main difference between Western and Eastern propaganda was that only Westerners actually believed theirs. Was this true? We have begun to witness Western studies based on public opinion polls during crisis events,[33] but behind the Iron Curtain too, imaginative use of official reporting has been made to reconstruct 'popular opinion' there.[34]

Many attitudes towards war in general, but also towards anti-communism and anti-Americanism, were coloured by recent memories of the Second World War. Historical memory has been one of the dominant sub-fields of contemporary historiography in the last decade. Most oral historians would now accept that memories are a product of the present in which they are conceived, and evolve over time. The Cold War grew straight out of this epic conflict which, if bestsellers and school curricula are anything to go by, has provided the main identificational myth of the twentieth century for Anglo-American, but also for Russian and Chinese societies.[35] But historical memory of the Second World War was largely a product of the Cold War, attempting to manipulate its heroic status to legitimate a more ambivalent present. (Here, the dearth of official memorials to the Cold War, relative to the world wars, is telling.) Moreover, it is important to ask what was *not* depicted in official histories or on the cinema screen. Classic Hollywood wartime treatments, such as *The Longest Day* (1962), portrayed either the Western front, or, like *From Here to Eternity* (1953), the Pacific theatre.[36] The Eastern front, the most costly battlefield of the real Second World War, was conspicuously absent, although there had been attempts during the war itself to bridge this gap on the silver screen. In Soviet cinemas the airbrushing of the recent past also occurred, as Sarah Davies demonstrates here.[37] And in China too, the Communist regime reoriented portrayals of the war against Japan in film and fiction so as to cut out the awkward reality that the Nationalist government of Chiang Kai-shek, now a Cold War enemy, had been instrumental to the Allied victory.[38] The direction of scholarly research on the war was also influenced by Cold War propaganda needs. For instance, Britain broke its own Official Secrets Act to sanction research into the Special Operations Executive, to counter the wave of communist-sponsored accounts of partisan heroics.[39] The English love affair with the upper-crust cloak and dagger began with Virginia McKenna in *Carve Her Name with Pride* (1958) and is still evident in novels such as Sebastian Faulks's *Charlotte Gray* (1998). Yet, personal memories were always in danger of cutting across authorized versions, harking back to alliances which had seen East and West work together. In the special case of the defeated nations of Germany and Japan, some former foes (in the West) had become allies, while other former enemies (in the East) remained such.[40] At certain points of *détente* it was also possible for much more sympathetic views of the Russians as former comrades-in-arms, for instance in Jeremy Isaacs' monumental television history of the early 1970s, *The World at War*.[41]

The atomic destruction which had ended the Second World War became another key aspect of the Cold War home front. From 1949, the bomb held the world in a global balance of terror, unleashing a nuclear fear which had to be either managed or repressed.[42] One growth area of study, but still confined to the United States, has been civil defence, including Kathleen Tobin's study, as well as Andreas Wenger's and Jeremi Suri's links between nuclear diplomacy and social protest.[43] The psychology of mass terror is of particular interest in a period which was rather self-consciously exploring its Freudian unconscious, in the West at least. Yet, the Soviet Union's preparations are still a largely unknown quantity. We know of only one book on the subject, now over 40 years old.[44] Moreover, comparative studies of the peace movement in both Cold War camps would reveal how much, or little, 'third ways' had in common with each other.[45] The Eastern bloc promoted its own official 'peace camp', but how did this interact with unofficial initiatives? How did political pragmatists in the West fare with the fundamentalist religious stands within the movement against the bomb? The culture of Japan, in particular, as the only country to have experienced nuclear war first-hand, is of particular relevance here, and the atomic theme in Japanese high and popular culture (Kurosawa's *Record of a Living Being*, the *Godzilla* films, manga such as *Barefoot Gen* and *Akira*) deserves further comparative study.[46] As well as the immediate issue of survivalism, the bomb raised other questions about the nature of science and progress in general. The Cold War, encompassing the atomic and space ages, represented the high watermark of scientific rationalism. Yet, rational means appeared to be serving irrational ends. Was technology getting out of control and beginning to take on a momentum of its own, providing a common enemy against which East and West would have to cooperate to avoid self-destruction? Nevertheless, the space race in some ways saved science from total cultural pessimism, offering a means of escape, but also a symbolic 'new frontier' which captured the popular imagination.[47] Science, and science fiction, can moreover be read as social maps of the future, of how capitalist and communist societies were supposed to develop or deal with disaster, as the pieces by David Seed and Patrick Major suggest here.[48]

These issues also stress the importance of understanding the origins of Cold War culture; Soviet and US techniques of the post-1945 period owe huge debts to what was learned in the 1930s, but were adapted to circumstances as well. Techniques of propaganda production in both the US and USSR, as the pieces by Nicholas Cull and Sarah Davies suggest, owed a great deal to technical and political developments in the pre-war era. Separating what was new and what was adapted is important: the Cold War was, unlike the Berlin Wall, a permeable sphere of definition. So for example, in Japan, the threat of nuclear war might have been a product of the end of the Second World War, but the particular type of paranoia it engendered owed a great deal to feelings of international isolation which had entered political culture from the Meiji era (1868–1912) onwards. The obsession Mao's China showed with scientism stemmed in part from the wider Cold War fascination with technology as a panacea, but also derived from the era of the 'May Fourth' New Culture movement of the 1910s and 1920s, when 'Mr Science' and 'Mr Democracy' were touted as the duumvirate who were going to bring about national salvation.[49]

As working historians of countries which were divided – into an East and West Germany; a mainland, communist and an offshore, nationalist China – we are keenly aware that there was perhaps more interaction between East and West than the finality of the Iron Curtain would suggest. In some countries a cold civil war was being waged, whereby international confrontations were simultaneously domestic conflicts, often with inter-war roots.[50] The number of countries which were physically divided is striking. Besides Germany and Korea, China and Vietnam are obvious examples. But in Cold War France and Italy too, the memory of real civil strife during the Second World War was fresh, but both reinforced and cut across Cold War battlelines. Greece moved straight from German occupation to civil war, drawing in great power sponsors. In other countries too, not physically divided, metaphorical cold civil wars raged. As Zhdanov claimed in 1948, the border cut not only through Germany, but across the entire capitalist world. Republican America wreaked its revenge on pre-war New Dealerism. In Germany, too, East German communists relived the political battles of the Weimar years, now transposed to a geopolitical level, but often trapped in the political vocabulary of the 1930s. The Cold War was a conflict constantly in search of 'enemies within', but questions need to be asked about whether these were always fifth columns in league with an outside sponsor, or to what extent many of the internal rivalries started indigenously, only to have the geopolitical dimension grafted on at a later stage.

Fear of internal subversion led to a number of political witch hunts, most famous of which was of course, McCarthyism, or 'Hooverism' as it should perhaps more properly be called.[51] But relatively little comparative work has been done on the parallel show-trials in the Eastern bloc of 1948–54, or about the Chinese Hu Feng and other mass campaigns of that period.[52] The understandable interest in Stalinist purges has focused almost exclusively on those of 1937–38, while the post-war wave has been curiously ignored. Cold War 'surveillance society', we would suggest, would be another common item to place on the research agenda. Political denunciations reveal the levels to which ordinary citizens were co-opted into global crusades, be it against 'commie' infiltration or the capitalist 'class enemy'. The Cold War could be an empowering tool for ordinary people, if they chose to deploy it, and we are seeing the beginnings of comparative studies in this field, across countries and time.[53] Studies of the secret police in the Eastern bloc have proliferated especially for the former GDR, which has had a unique policy of openness of access to Stasi files. It must be said, however, that these have remained largely institutional, and do not yet give a particularly good 'feel' for the experience of police persecution, which should be another socio-cultural aim.[54] In the West too, 'subversives' were kept under surveillance, including icons of the counter-culture.[55] And in the realm of popular publishing, revelations about espionage, as well as the spy thriller, were staples of popular consumption. If any one idea became imprinted on the public mind, it was that the Cold War was about secrecy. Yet, in the West, surveillance society came to mean much more than just spooks and bugging devices. Much of the New Left's anger in the 1960s was directed against what was seen as an increasingly manipulative society, using consumerism as a more subtle form of totalitarian control,[56] employing the 'hidden persuaders' of advertising as an alternative form of mind control.[57]

A clever poster by Coca-Cola once showed various world leaders, from Caesar to Lenin and Hitler, beside a bottle of Coke. The caption read: 'Only one launched a campaign that conquered the world'.[58] With the hindsight of 1989, it has become a truism that the Cold War was won not so much at the negotiating table, as in the shopping basket. Indeed, consumerism and commercialism have been another pair of historiographical buzzwords of the 1990s which have obvious applications for the Cold War. It is possible to argue that all paths of Cold War social and cultural history lead, either positively or negatively, to a consideration of consumerism. In the 1950s, the Americans had seen affluence as one of their main weapons against political radicalism behind their own lines in Western Europe. A growing literature on European anti-Americanization has thus emerged, revealing how overt Cold War concerns overlay pre-existing cultural fears of modernity and mass society, as well as the mass media's supposed oversexualized pandering to the pleasure principle.[59] But alarm bells began to ring even inside America. Affluence was a double-edged sword, in danger of turning the

stateside home front 'soft', vulnerable to the Spartan vigour of the
Soviet interloper. (Part of the 'remuscularization' of system conflict
occurred, of course, in the Olympics).[60] Nevertheless, as the potential
military confrontation stabilized with *détente* in the 1960s, the
Eastern bloc too, realized that socialist consumerism was a useful
means of maintaining a depoliticized society. This is, however, a key
area where difference can be measured in explaining the outcome of
the Cold War. However hard they tried, Eastern bloc states never
convincingly managed to fulfil consumer aspirations in the East.[61]
The glamour and allure of foreign products remained strong,
providing a counterpoint to spheres where indigeneity was offered as
the source of authenticity and legitimacy. But we should not perhaps
overstate this factor. American values might be welcomed in a soft
drink, but not necessarily in a radio broadcast. For some countries,
such as China, periodization is key: consumer culture became much
more of an issue during the Second Cold War of the 1980s, when
Deng Xiaoping's reforms led to disputes over the availability and the
significance of Japanese and Western consumer goods, and the state
became at least in part accountable in terms of its ability to provide
them.

The shop window politics of consumer competition were at their
most evident in divided Berlin. Yet, the inner German frontier was
remarkably porous in the 1950s, and even after the Berlin Wall was
built in 1961, did not provide a hermetic seal.[62] East Germans could
regularly watch the acquisitive society in the West on television.
Another important question, especially concerning media and
popular culture, is how much West–East, and even East–West,
transmission of ideas occurred across the Iron Curtain. Some media,
such as film, were more susceptible to border controls and audience
surveillance. Paperbacks and magazines, on the other hand, could be
readily secreted. Port cities such as Leningrad, or on the Baltic,
became centres of illicitly smuggled records.[63] It is well known that
rock music forged a West–East passage through the ether, but was
also capable of erupting into an indigenous semi-public sphere at
Eastern bloc concerts.[64] Popular music later became a conscious
medium of *détente* in the 1980s, with tours of the Eastern bloc by
Western artists.[65] Moreover, radio and television could penetrate the
Iron Curtain in both directions, subject only to jamming, and
furthermore could be consumed in private, as Mark Pittaway shows
in the current collection.[66] As Frances Stonor Saunders has also
reminded us, we do not have to descend to kitsch in order to observe

the politicization of art.[67] Artists, in the East at least, were a group who were keenly aware of what was happening on the other side of the Iron Curtain, and whose commitment to universal truth often conflicted with the partisan demands of the Cold War. Through international organizations such as the association of writers (PEN), it was also possible for leading intellectuals to exchange ideas face to face, since neither Cold War combatant was willing to expose itself as philistine, and thus encouraged a certain artistic *rapprochement*.

The relationship between artists and the national security state was always a difficult one. Censorship is another historical dimension which can be added to existing literary and cultural studies by archival research. In the Eastern bloc the various ministries of culture held a tight rein on their writers.[68] Cultural products there reflected the propaganda needs of the state. Yet, even in the West, publishers and public taste imposed a less formal censorship. Governments also exerted a form of patronage, as Tony Shaw has shown for British cinema, and Sarah Davies demonstrates in her piece below.[69] Nor was Her Majesty's Government averse to clapping injunctions on what it regarded as offensive publications, most famously in the *Spycatcher* case of the mid-1980s.[70] On both sides of the Iron Curtain, however, we might ask how censors wished the other side to be portrayed, but also where they were sensitive to 'subversive' criticisms of the home side. The relative autonomy of Western commercial popular culture meant that film studios and publishing houses were on a looser rein. Moreover, the formulaic demands of many Cold War *noir* films and pulp novels, designed to sell, already encouraged a certain level of parody, which threatened to rebound on the national security state. With Stanley Kubrick's *Dr Strangelove* in 1963, Cold War absurdism seemed to have found its authentic voice.[71]

Here there are also interdisciplinary boundaries to be considered. Naturally, historians are not the only ones interested in the evolution of media culture. In fact a large part of the existing literature on Cold War culture has been written by scholars in other disciplines, notably literary and film studies.[72] Nevertheless, what could be a fascinating interdisciplinary field is in practice still multidisciplinary, with some linguists and cinematologists engaged in what seem to outsiders to be narrow debates about genre and style, in which the text can become an end in itself. As historians, we can and should take notice of these. Much of the joy of studying cultural artefacts lies in appreciating their 'intertextuality', that is, the dialogue occurring between specific works in the coded language of the particular genre, rather than in construing

clumsy links to the high politics of the day. The latter approach often
relies on guilt by association to explain the relationship between art
and politics. But we can ask historical questions of cultural productions
too. The Cold War witnessed the rise and domination of the mass
media, so that it would be possible to analyse shifting reading patterns
in the age of the paperback, as well as changing viewing habits from
cinema to television. For instance, how widespread were televisions,
paperbacks, but also comics in Russia, compared with America?[73]
Historians should analyse the medium as well as the message. Besides
being conduits of information, these media were themselves measures
of consumerist success, initially resisted in the East, but then recognized
as means of collective agitation. Film had a new potency in this period
too, arguably rivalling that of books and pamphlets in the eighteenth
and nineteenth centuries.

The links between social reality and popular cultural construction
were exceedingly close in the Cold War. Even the KGB apparently
realized the danger of James Bond winning the thriller war,
commissioning their own fictional hero, Avakum Zakhov, to fight 007
on the printed page.[74] Stasi recruits also reported that one of their
motivating factors had been the fictional East German spy, Achim
Detjen, star of the 1973 GDR television series, 'The Invisible Visor'.[75]
The vast majority of those who lived through the conflict probably
derived their images of it from such popular imagery. A large part of
the task of the socio-cultural history of the Cold War will thus consist
in disentangling fiction from reality, but also in realizing where fiction
took on a momentum of its own, and became the effective reality.
These simplified cultural representations, pitting man against man, in
film car chases, across the chess board, or on the ice-hockey rink,
reflected the bipolarity of the conflict. But they also unwittingly
revealed the incapacity of the individual to grasp what had become a
conflict without an overview, a wilderness of receding mirrors, to use
a popular contemporary metaphor. The scope and secrecy of global
conflict was bound to make the individual feel excluded. The military
worst-case scenario had metaphysical implications for the survival of
the human race, and was for many literally unthinkable.

We should also raise the question of periodization. The half-
century conflict is often divided into a First Cold War, from 1947
until the 1960s and *détente*; then a Second Cold War in 1979 with
the Afghan invasion, followed by another miniature *détente* under
Gorbachev. This at least was how high politics influenced the Cold
War chronology. But were these ebbs and flows at the top shared by

the general public below? Did popular culture and the mass media simply reflect the diplomatic timetable, or were they driving forces in creating sea-changes of public opinion? Future research will reveal whether this was true of the 1980s, which witnessed a mass loss of faith in the system, especially in the East, but we hope to provide some of the answers for the earlier period. The 'high' Cold War productions of the 1950s, be they flying saucer movies or Stalinist spy thrillers, are viewed today with a certain amount of tongue-in-cheek amusement, as 'Cold War camp'. Whether they achieved the requisite suspension of disbelief at the time would be interesting to know. Yet, the very fact that they became dated so quickly, and that, for instance, Ian Fleming felt compelled in 1959 to replace the Soviet-backed SMERSH with the 'neutral' criminal syndicate of SPECTRE as Bond's arch-enemy, hints at a changing ground swell of opinion from the 1950s to the 1960s.[76] The Cold War home front was bored with austerity and nuclear doom and gloom, and the media turned superpower conflict into a form of entertainment and compensation for consumerist conformity. Hysteria gave way to hilarity, in the West at least, only to return in the 1980s. Consequently, the very longevity of the Cold War, which spanned several generations, created a number of different constituencies within Cold War society, some of whom could remember real war, but others who had known nothing but this static confrontation. Cultural products too, spawned imitators and sequels, some of which were reshaped to suit the changing needs of the Cold War. When Nigel Kneale's 1950s' television adaptation of *Quatermass and the Pit*, which carried a very strong pacifist message, was transferred to the cinema screen in the 1960s, Hammer studios quietly dropped what they saw as its intrusive politics.[77] These changes suggest that the Cold War was not merely an era of conflict, but also of accommodation and restraint in which both sides were at times at extreme pains to avoid provoking the other, and it is worth acknowledging those differences in analysing the dynamic between the Cold War actors. It was, after all, the continuing acknowledgement of boundaries that meant that the Cold War remained 'cold' while still being meaningfully, if ambiguously, a 'war'.

A Final Caveat

We should add a note of caution here, before others add it for us. As with other paradigms – class, gender, modernity – there is a danger that socio-cultural interpreters using a Cold War framework might read the

Cold War into every issue, every event. *Quatermass* was about a host of other things, not the least of these being the debate over evolutionary biology. James Bond was arguably as much about upward social mobility within the British class system as he was about the realities of espionage. 'Grand narratives' should not be so grand that they can cover everything and nothing. In that sense, we are willing to concede clear limits to the usefulness of the Cold War as an interpretative framework for socio-cultural issues, not least since that strengthens its power where it is genuinely explanatory. One of the most damaging consequences of an overdetermination of the evidence would be to make a bland and mushy equivalence between 'post-war history' or 'late twentieth-century history' and 'Cold War history'. Our criteria above seem to us usefully analyzable under a Cold War rubric, remaining broadly political and able to relate the domestic to the international, the home front to the diplomatic front. But for those used to finding smoking archival guns, the socio-cultural Cold War will clearly be as much about misperceptions and self-interest as about uncovering 'the truth'. The process of interpreting narrative and counter-narrative cannot have the exactitude that documenting diplomatic decision-making can hope for. We can only move towards an impressionistic collective view, consolidating where others have made a start, borrowing from other periods and disciplines, and encouraging new collaborative initiatives, such as the 'Cold War cultures' network of which this collection is a part.[78] But by making concerted use of outlets such as the journal *Cold War History* and, to use a Cold War metaphor, establishing a 'critical mass', we can at least raise a common set of questions, for a better chance of a coherent set of answers.

NOTES

1. John Lewis Gaddis, *We Now Know: Rethinking Cold War History* (Oxford: Oxford University Press, 1997).
2. Lynn Boyd Hinds and Theodore Otto Windt, *The Cold War as Rhetoric: The Beginnings, 1945–1950* (Westport, CT: Praeger, 1991); Martin J. Medhurst *et al.*, *Cold War Rhetoric: Strategy, Metaphor and Ideology* (Ann Arbor: Michigan State University Press, 1997); Shawn J. Parry-Giles, *The Rhetorical Presidency, Propaganda and the Cold War, 1945–1955* (Westport, CT: Praeger, 2001).
3. But see Christian G. Appy (ed.), *Cold War Constructions: The Political Culture of United States Imperialism, 1945–1966* (Amherst: Massachusetts University Press, 2000); Peter J. Kuznick and James Gilbert (eds.), *Rethinking Cold War Culture* (Washington, DC: Smithsonian Institute Press, 2001).
4. Kenneth A. Osgood, 'Hearts and Minds: The Unconventional Cold War', *Journal of Cold War Studies* 4/2 (2002), p.107. See also Tony Shaw, 'The Politics of Cold War Culture', *Journal of Cold War Studies* 3/3 (2001), pp.74–5. A pathbreaking new

examination of links between social protest and global diplomacy is Jeremi Suri, *Power and Protest: Global Revolution and the Rise of Detente* (Cambridge, MA: Harvard University Press, 2003).

5. For instance, Arthur Marwick, *The Deluge: British Society and the First World War* (London: Bodley Head, 1965), and Joanna Bourke, *Dismembering the Male: Men's Bodies, Britain and the Great War* (London: Reaktion Books, 1996).

6. Among the notable works are Paul Fussell, *The Great War and Modern Memory* (Oxford: Oxford University Press, 1975), and Jay Winter, *Sites of Memory, Sites of Mourning: The Great War in European Cultural History* (Cambridge: Cambridge University Press, 1995).

7. Christopher Browning, *Ordinary Men: Reserve Police Battalion 101 and the Final Solution in Poland* (New York: HarperPerennial, 1993); Robert Gellately, *Backing Hitler: Consent and Coercion in Nazi Germany* (Oxford: Oxford University Press, 2001).

8. Sarah Davies, *Popular Opinion in Stalin's Russia: Terror, Propaganda and Dissent, 1934–1941* (Cambridge: Cambridge University Press, 1997); see also Robert W. Thurston, *Life and Terror in Stalin's Russia, 1934–1941* (New Haven and London: Yale University Press, 1996); Sheila Fitzpatrick, *Everyday Stalinism: Ordinary Life in Extraordinary Times: Soviet Russia in the 1930s* (New York: Oxford University Press, 1999); Catherine Merridale, *Night of Stone: Death and Memory in Twentieth-Century Russia* (London: Granta, 2000).

9. E.P. Thompson, *The Making of the English Working Class* (London: Penguin Press, 1991, original edn. 1963), p.12; Clifford Geertz, *The Interpretation of Cultures* (London: Hutchinson, 1975, original edn. 1973), p.14.

10. Robert D. Dean, 'Masculinity as Ideology: John F. Kennedy and the Domestic Politics of Foreign Policy', *Diplomatic History* 22 (1998), pp.29–62. See also idem, *Imperial Brotherhood: Gender and the Making of Cold War Foreign Policy* (Amherst: Massachusetts University Press, 2002).

11. Scott Lucas, *Freedom's War: The US Crusade against the Soviet Union, 1945–56* (Manchester: Manchester University Press, 1999). Although covering the whole of the twentieth century, rather than being specific to the Cold War, an agenda-setting approach to bringing 'culture' into the study of international society is Akira Iriye, *Cultural Internationalism and World Order* (Baltimore: Johns Hopkins University Press, 1997).

12. Geoffrey Barraclough, *An Introduction to Contemporary History* (London: Watts, 1964).

13. Tony Shaw, 'The Politics of Cold War Culture', *Journal of Cold War Studies* 3/3, p.74.

14. Philip Jenkins, *The Cold War at Home: The Red Scare in Pennsylvania* (Chapel Hill: University of North Carolina Press, 1999). See also Richard Fried, *The Russians are Coming! The Russians are Coming!: Pageantry and Patriotism in Cold-War America* (New York: Oxford University Press, 1998) One of the pathbreaking works linking the Cold War and American social history was Elaine Tyler May, *Homeward Bound: American Families in the Cold War Era* (New York: Basic Books, 1988); innovative recent examples include Lee Bernstein, *The Greatest Menace: Organized Crime in Cold War America* (Amherst: Massachusetts University Press, 2002) and Daniel Horowitz, *Betty Friedan and the Making of The Feminine Mystique: The American Left, the Cold War, and Modern Feminism* (Amherst: Massachusetts University Press, 2000).

15. For an excellent discursive overview: Stephen J. Whitfield, *The Culture of the Cold War* (Baltimore: Johns Hopkins University Press, 2nd edn., 1996).

16. For example, Peter Weiler, *British Labour and the Cold War* (Stanford, CA.: Stanford University Press, 1988).

17. Irwin M. Wall, *The United States and the Making of Postwar France, 1945–1954* (Cambridge: Cambridge University Press, 1991); James E. Miller, *The United States and Italy, 1940–1950: The Politics and Diplomacy of Stabilization* (Chapel Hill: University of North Carolina Press, 1986).

18. Peter Hennessy, *The Secret State: Whitehall and the Cold War* (London: Penguin, 2002).

19. Christopher Duggan and Christopher Wagstaff (eds.), *Italy in the Cold War* (Oxford: Berg, 1995).

20. Christoph Kleßmann and Georg Wagner (eds.), *Das gespaltene Land: Leben in Deutschland 1945 bis 1990: Texte und Dokumente* (Munich: Beck, 1993).

21. *Journal of Cold War Studies* 4/1 (Winter 2002).
22. One of the few exceptions is Jeffrey Brooks, *Thank you, Comrade Stalin!: Soviet Public Culture from Revolution to Cold War* (Princeton, NJ: Princeton University Press, 2000), pp.210–32, though the primary focus is on the earlier years.
23. Eric Shiraev and Vladislav M. Zubok, *Anti-Americanism in Russia: From Stalin to Putin* (New York and Houndmills: Palgrave, 2000).
24. A good cross-section of the ZZF's work is available in English in Konrad H. Jarausch (ed.), *Dictatorship as Experience: Towards a Socio-Cultural History of the GDR* (New York and Oxford: Berghahn, 1999); see also Mark Allinson, *Politics and Popular Opinion in East Germany, 1945–68* (Manchester: Manchester University Press, 2000) and Corey Ross, *Constructing Socialism at the Grass Roots: The Transformation of East Germany, 1945–65* (Basingstoke: Macmillan, 2000).
25. Kieran Williams, *The Prague Spring and Its Aftermath: Czechoslovak Politics 1968–1970* (Cambridge: Cambridge University Press, 1997).
26. Edward Said, *Orientalism* (London: Routledge and Kegan Paul, 1978).
27. Jens Gieseke, *Die Hauptamtlichen Mitarbeiter der Staatssicherheit: Personalstruktur und Lebenswelt 1950–1989/90* (Berlin: Links, 2000).
28. A notable journal in the Chinese academic trend of examining the post-1949 Chinese experience as history rather than as contemporary politics is *Dangdai Zhongguoshi yanjiu* (Research in Contemporary Chinese History), though the journal's focus is primarily on high politics. One particularly valuable collection of primary sources, though in this case not authorized by the Chinese government, is the *Chinese Cultural Revolution Database* (Hong Kong: The Chinese University of Hong Kong, Universities Service Centre for China Studies, 2002). A major new contribution is Charles K. Armstrong, 'The Cultural Cold War in Korea, 1945–1950', *Journal of Asian Studies* 62/1 (Feb. 2003), pp.71–100.
29. On Britain's Information Research Department, see Paul Lashmar and James Oliver, *Britain's Secret Propaganda War, 1948–1977* (Thrupp: Sutton, 1998). Also on the US, see Lucas, *Freedom's War: The US Crusade against the Soviet Union, 1945–56.*
30. For a Freudian take, using much visual imagery, see Sam Keen, *Faces of the Enemy: Reflections of the Hostile Imagination: The Psychology of Enmity* (San Francisco, CA: Harper & Row, 1986).
31. Deutsches Historisches Museum (ed.), *Deutschland im Kalten Krieg 1945 bis 1963* (Berlin, 1992); James Aulich and Marta Sylvestrova, *Political Posters in Central and Eastern Europe: 1945–1995: Signs of the Times* (Manchester: Manchester University Press, 1999).
32. Ron Robin, *The Making of the Cold War Enemy: Culture and Politics in the Military-Industrial Complex* (Princeton, NJ: Princeton University Press, 2001).
33. Benjamin I. Page and Robert Y. Shapiro, *The Rational Public: Fifty Years of Trends in Americans' Policy Preferences* (Chicago: Chicago Univesrsity Press, 1992).
34. Allinson, *Politics and Popular Opinion in East Germany*, and Ross, *Constructing Socialism at the Grass Roots.*
35. Studs Terkel, *The 'Good War': An Oral History of World War Two* (New York: Ballantine, 1984); Nina Tumarkin, *The Living and the Dead: The Rise and Fall of the Cult of World War II in Russia* (New York: Basic Books, 1994); Rana Mitter, *The Manchurian Myth: Nationalism, Resistance and Collaboration in Modern China* (Berkeley, CA: University of California Press, 2000).
36. For a handy overview, see John Whiteclay Chambers and David Culbert (eds.), *World War II, Film, and History* (New York and Oxford: Oxford University Press, 1996).
37. See also Carola Tischler's project on Soviet film at the Zentrum für Zeithistorische Forschung in Potsdam, aired at the 2002 American Historical Association conference.
38. Although not dealing with the Cold War framework directly, an intriguing analysis of how films about the Sino-Japanese War were oriented during the 1946–49 Civil War in China is Paul G. Pickowicz, 'Victory as Defeat: Postwar Visualizations of China's War of Resistance', in Wen-hsin Yeh (ed.), *Becoming Chinese: Passages to Modernity and Beyond* (Berkeley, CA: University of California Press, 2000).
39. See Christopher Murphy's doctoral work at Reading University, UK.

40. John W. Dower, *Embracing Defeat: Japan in the Aftermath of World War II* (London: Allen Lane, 1999).
41. We are grateful to Philip Murphy of Reading University for raising this point at our initial gathering.
42. Spencer R. Weart, *Nuclear Fear: A History of Images* (Cambridge, MA: Harvard University Press, 1988); Robert J. Lifton and Greg Mitchell, *Hiroshima in America: A Half Century of Denial* (New York: Putnam's, 1995).
43. Kathleen A. Tobin, 'The Reduction of Urban Vulnerability: Revisiting 1950s American Suburbanization as Civil Defence', *Cold War History* 2/2 (2001), pp.1–32; Andreas Wenger and Jeremi Suri, 'At the Crossroads of Diplomatic and Social History: The Nuclear Revolution, Dissent and Détente', *Cold War History* 1/3 (2001), pp.1–42, especially, 10–15. See also Guy Oakes, *The Imaginary War: Civil Defence and American Cold War Culture* (New York and Oxford: Oxford University Press, 1994); Paul Boyer, *By the Bomb's Early Light: American Thought and Culture at the Dawn of the Atomic Age* (Chapel Hill, NC: University of North Carolina Press, 1994); Andrew D. Grossman, *Neither Dead Nor Red: Civilian Defence and American Political Development during the Early Cold War* (New York and London: Routledge, 2001); Kenneth D. Rose, *One Nation Underground: The Fallout Shelter in American Culture* (New York: New York University Press, 2001).
44. Leon Gouré, *Civil Defense in the Soviet Union* (Berkeley, CA: University of California Press, 1962).
45. For the East–West gulf, see Václav Havel, 'Politics and Conscience', in Václav Havel, *Living in Truth*, ed. Jan Vladislav (London: Faber, 1987), pp.136–57.
46. For the reshaping of Japanese culture and society in the early Cold War, see Dower's monumental *Embracing Defeat*. On popular culture, see John Whittier Treat, *Writing Ground Zero: Japanese Literature and the Atomic Bomb* (Chicago: University of Chicago Press, 1995), and Mick Broderick, *Hibakusha Cinema: Hiroshima, Nagasaki and the Nuclear Image in Japanese Film* (London and New York: Kegan Paul International, 1996).
47. James L. Kauffman, *Selling Outer Space: Kennedy, the Media and Funding for Project Apollo, 1961–1963* (Tuscaloosa: Alabama University Press, 1994); Howard E. McCurdy, *Space and the American Imagination* (Washington, DC: Smithsonian Institution Press, 1997).
48. See also David Seed, *American Science Fiction and the Cold War: Literature and Film* (Edinburgh: Edinburgh University Press, 1999).
49. This is a relatively new area, but a fascinating recent work that explores the damage to China's environment caused by the technological obsession of Maoism, is Judith Shapiro, *Mao's War Against Nature: Politics and the Environment in Revolutionary China* (Cambridge: Cambridge University Press, 2001).
50. Patrick Major, *The Death of the KPD: Communism and Anti-Communism in West Germany, 1945–1956* (Oxford: Oxford University Press, 1997), pp.294–304. On the shaping of the Chinese civil war by the Cold War, see Odd Arne Westad, *Cold War and Revolution: Soviet–American Rivalry and the Origins of the Chinese Civil War, 1944–1946* (New York: Columbia University Press, 1993).
51. Ellen Schrecker, *Many Are the Crimes: McCarthyism in America* (Princeton, NJ: Princeton University Press, 1998).
52. However, see Georg H. Hodos, *Show Trials: Stalinist Purges in Eastern Europe, 1948–1954* (New York: Praeger, 1987); Merle Goldman, *Literary Dissent in Communist China* (Cambridge, MA: Harvard University Press, 1967).
53. Sheila Fitzpatrick and Robert Gellately (eds.), *Accusatory Practices: Denunciations in Modern European History, 1789–1989* (Chicago: Chicago University Press, 1997).
54. A notable exception, but with a necessarily specific remit, is Timothy Garton Ash, *The File: A Personal History* (London: Harper Collins, 1997).
55. Herbert Mitgang, *Dangerous Dossiers* (New York: Donald J. Fine, 1988); Jon Wiener, *Gimme Some Truth: The John Lennon FBI Files* (Berkeley, CA: University of California Press, 1999).

56. Herbert Marcuse, *One-Dimensional Man: Studies in the Ideology of Advanced Industrial Society* (London: Routledge, 1964).

57. Vance Packard, *The Hidden Persuaders* (New York: McKay, 1957).

58. Eric Hobsbawm, *The Age of Extremes: The Short Twentieth Century, 1914–1991* (London: Michael Joseph, 1994), ill. 64.

59. Most recently: Heide Fehrenbach and Uta Poiger (eds.), *Transactions, Transgressions, Transformations: American Culture in Western Europe and Japan* (New York and Oxford: Berghahn, 1999). France tends to dominate the literature: see Richard F. Kuisel, *Seducing the French: The Dilemma of Americanization* (Berkeley, CA: University of California Press, 1993).

60. Derek L. Hulme, *The Political Olympics: Moscow, Afghanistan and the 1980 US Boycott* (New York: Praeger, 1990).

61. Susan E. Reid and David Crowley (eds.), *Style and Socialism: Modernity and Material Culture in Post-War Eastern Europe* (Oxford: Berg, 2000).

62. Patrick Major, 'Going West?: The Open Border and the Problem of *Republikflucht*', in Patrick Major and Jonathan Osmond (eds.), *The Workers' and Peasants' State: Communism and Society in East Germany under Ulbricht, 1945–71* (Manchester: Manchester University Press, 2002), pp.190–208.

63. Artemy Troitsky, *Back in the USSR: The True Story of Rock in Russia* (London: Omnibus, 1987), p.4.

64. Timothy W. Ryback, *Rock Around the Bloc: A History of Rock Music in Eastern Europe and the Soviet Union* (New York: Oxford University Press, 1990).

65. Michael Rauhut, *Schalmei und Lederjacke: Udo Lindenberg, BAP, Underground: Rock und Politik in den achtziger Jahren* (Berlin: Schwarzkopf and Schwarzkopf, 1996).

66. Walter L. Hixson, *Parting the Curtain: Propaganda, Culture and the Cold War, 1945–1961* (Houndmills: Macmillan, 1997).

67. Frances Stonor Saunders, *Who Paid the Piper?: The CIA and the Cultural Cold War* (London: Granta, 1999). See also Christine Lindey, *Art in the Cold War: From Vladivostok to Kalamazoo, 1945–1962* (London: Herbert Press, 1990), and more recently Volker R. Berghahn, *America and the Intellectual Cold Wars in Europe* (Princeton, NJ and Oxford: Princeton University Press, 2001).

68. Simone Barck *et al.*, *Jedes Buch ein Abenteuer: Zensur-System und literarische Öffentlichkeiten in der DDR bis Ende der sechziger Jahre* (Berlin: Akademie, 1997).

69. Tony Shaw, *British Cinema and the Cold War* (London: I.B. Tauris, 2000).

70. Malcolm Turnbull, *The Spycatcher Trial* (London: Heinemann, 1988).

71. Margot A. Henriksen, *Dr. Strangelove's America: Society and Culture in the Atomic Age* (Berkeley: University of California Press, 1997).

72. Disaster novels and movies have attracted more than their fair share: Martha A. Bartter, *The Way to Ground Zero: The Atomic Bomb in American Science Fiction* (New York: Greenwood, 1988); Nora Sayre, *Running Time: Films of the Cold War* (New York: Dial, 1982); Jack G. Shaheen (ed.), *Nuclear War Films* (Carbondale: Southern Illinois University Press, 1978).

73. For the 1980s see Ellen Mickiewicz, *Split Signals: TV and Politics in the Soviet Union* (New York and Oxford: Oxford University Press, 1988). There are also the beginnings of a fascinating application of popular culture to Cold War studies, but again, so far only for the US. See Bradford C. Wright, *Comic Book Nation: The Transformation of Youth Culture in America* (Baltimore: Johns Hopkins University Press, 2001); Woody Haut, *Pulp Culture: Hardboiled Fiction and the Cold War* (London: Serpent's Tail, 1995).

74. Andrei Gulyashki, *The Zakhov Mission* (London: Cassell, 1968, original Russian edition 1963).

75. Personal communication of Jens Gieseke, at Federal Commission for the Stasi Records.

76. Andrew Lycett, *Ian Fleming* (London: Weidenfeld and Nicolson, 1995), p.350.

77. Peter Hutchings, '"We're the Martians now": British SF Invasion Fantasies of the 1950s and 1960s', in I.Q. Hunter (ed.), *British Science Fiction Cinema* (London and New York: Routledge, 1999), pp.36–46.

78. We would encourage any readers who would care to be involved in this agenda to contact the editors, on p.major@warwick.ac.uk or rana.mitter@Chinese.ox.ac.uk.

'The Man Who Invented Truth': The Tenure of Edward R. Murrow as Director of the United States Information Agency During the Kennedy Years

NICHOLAS J. CULL

The international cultural history of the Cold War should begin with the most obvious point of contact between the realms of culture and politics: state-sponsored propaganda.[1] For the United States the key propaganda agency of its Cold War campaign was the United States Information Agency (USIA). Accounts of this agency – particularly those written by USIA insiders – typically select one particular period in its history for particular valediction: the tenure of the best-known director from its career covering five decades: the former Columbia Broadcasting System (CBS) journalist, Edward R. Murrow.[2] The story of Murrow's time at USIA is made doubly relevant by Murrow's own significance as an icon of domestic American Cold War culture. Murrow had a reputation for objectivity and truth in reporting. He had covered the Second World War and the war in Korea; he had been instrumental in turning the tide of public opinion against Senator Joseph McCarthy.[3] Then, in 1961, at the invitation of President John F. Kennedy, he assumed the directorship of the most extensive public relations machine in the world. Murrow's initial statements about his new job traded on his reputation for straight talking. He would display the United States 'warts and all'. Much in Murrow's new job must have been familiar: he certainly knew about the clash between journalistic ethics and the needs of national policy, but now, as USIA director, Murrow found himself on the policy side of the fence: news poacher turned gamekeeper. Although the USIA staff relished the kudos that flowed from their new celebrity chief, many of his new staff at the agency's radio arm – Voice of America – were bitterly disappointed by his attitude towards journalistic freedom. It seemed that Murrow cared less about the substance of truth, but rather focused on its appearance. Truth seemed to be a matter of style rather than content. Disillusioned, one of the journalists in the VOA newsroom, Bernie Kamenske, coined a bitterly ironic nickname for Murrow: 'The man who invented truth.'

Murrow's tenure at USIA, and indeed the whole history of the agency, serves as a valuable reminder that the images which were so much a part of the Cold War were not disseminated by accident. Vast areas of the world knew about the Berlin Wall, Soviet nuclear testing or Soviet missiles in Cuba because the USIA told them, and distributed the photographs and data to prove their case. Those audiences also saw images of prosperity in the United States, shared insights into the everyday life of a particularly photogenic president and watched America openly engaging its problems, be they the technical headaches of failed rocket launches at Cape Canaveral or, racial tensions on the streets of Alabama. Their views of the USA and the Cold War developed accordingly.

This account of Murrow's tenure at USIA builds on three biographies and a small number of monographs on the agency, most of which were written by agency 'insiders'.[4] It seeks to expand and add nuance to the existing account rather than to correct it, though in places correction is necessary.[5] The sources of this piece are recently declassified papers in the Kennedy library and extensive interviews with USIA and Voice of America veterans conducted in the course of research for a complete history of USIA from its foundation in 1953 to its dissolution in 1999.[6]

US Propaganda to 1961

The United States of America had been relatively slow to enter the world of international propaganda. The vast Committee on Public Information structure created in the First World War had been hastily dismantled in 1919, and the inter-war period had seen only the most tentative initiatives. The late 1920s saw the beginnings of a network of 'bi-national' cultural centres in Latin America operated by American expatriates in conjunction with the local community; a Cultural Division of the State Department to manage academic and scientific exchange followed in 1938. The Second World War accelerated such development beginning with the Office of Inter-American Affairs, a propaganda bureau for Latin American audiences directed by Nelson Rockefeller from 1940. US belligerence brought the Office of War Information with its network of United States

Information Service offices around the world, and Voice of America short wave broadcasting. Propaganda played a key role both on the battlefield and off, laying the foundations for a liberal international order founded on Franklin Roosevelt's 'Four Freedoms'.[7]

At the end of the Second World War, Republicans in Congress pressed to dismantle the global network. The official in charge of overseas information programmes, the Assistant Secretary of State for Public Affairs and acknowledged Madison Avenue genius, William Benton, managed to build a case for preserving international information as an element in the normal running of US foreign policy. The widening fissures in the Soviet–American relationship provided a convenient logic for Benton's appeal to Capitol Hill. In January 1948 he won massive appropriations for State Department propaganda activity under the so-called Smith-Mundt act. Other initiatives in the period including the re-education of occupied Japan and Germany, while the Marshall Aid programme also had information activities attached. Eventually the US government developed a 'grey' propaganda capacity by covertly subsidizing the creation of Radio Free Europe (and later Radio Liberty). These stations were staffed by refugees from the Communist bloc organized under the ostensibly private auspices of the National Committee for a Free Europe. This allowed a more aggressive approach to propaganda than would be seemly from an official outlet like Voice of America. By 1950 the Truman administration had embraced all-out ideological warfare with the Soviet Union. William Benton (by this time a Democratic Senator for Connecticut) called for a Marshall Plan of Ideas while Truman pledged a 'Campaign of Truth'. Despite Soviet jamming, the radio sets of the Eastern bloc hummed with the rhetoric of liberation.[8]

Although the Republican party had strong connections with members of the National Committee for a Free Europe, the incoming Eisenhower administration of 1953 took a rather more circumspect approach to propaganda. Eisenhower moved away from the idea of liberating Eastern Europe, and rationalized the structure of US information overseas into a single agency: the United States Information Agency (USIA), created in August that year. USIA absorbed the various programmes established during the Truman years. It included press offices at US embassies; it administered libraries; it taught English; it made and distributed documentary films; it ran Voice of America radio; it printed and distributed books, leaflets and magazines about American life and ideas; it created magnificent exhibitions that showcased American technology, some of which toured behind the 'Iron Curtain' and, as Murrow pointed out on more than one occasion, it cost rather less than a single Polaris missile every year. USIA played a central role in presenting the major foreign policy initiatives of the period: depicting the US economic system as 'people's capitalism.' Radio Free Europe and Radio Liberty remained outside the USIA fold, but – like the 'bad cop' in the classic police interrogation technique – their existence allowed Voice of America to develop along less aggressive lines, as a news-based international radio station comparable to the BBC World Service. In 1960 the journalists at VOA obtained a charter, which underlined their responsibility to present balanced news. Murrow's pledge to display the US 'warts and all' was in fact rather behind the times as far as VOA was concerned. He arrived promising freedom to people who already felt free and instead, as director of USIA, found himself attempting to rein in that freedom, as the Kennedy administration attempted to inject ideological vigour back into an American foreign policy which owed more to Truman's approach in 1950 than the later Eisenhower years.[9]

Recruiting Murrow: The Kennedy Administration and Propaganda

Images mattered to the Kennedy administration. John F. Kennedy – and his family political machine – was acutely image conscious. He successfully manipulated his image in his 1960 election campaign against Richard Nixon. More than this, the issue of the international image of the United States *vis-à-vis* the Soviet Union became a recurrent issue in the campaign. Kennedy insisted that he had poll evidence, collected by USIA, showing that the Soviet Union was ahead in terms of international image.[10] On winning the election, Kennedy immediately created a set of foreign policy task forces to investigate the key areas of foreign policy, including a task force dedicated to the USIA. In a little over a month the USIA Task Force consulted 22 leading academics, journalists and experts in international affairs, including Edward R. Murrow.[11]

    Kennedy gave careful consideration to the post of director of USIA. Kennedy's first choice was the President of CBS, Frank Stanton. Stanton declined but nominated arguably the best-known journalist of the era and a legendary figure in liberal America, a man with a reputation for probing journalism, Edward R. Murrow. Stanton and Murrow were not on good terms at this point, and

Stanton's suggestion may have been double-edged, but Murrow offered the Kennedy administration both glamour and liberal credibility (lacking in appointees like Dean Rusk or McGeorge Bundy).[12]

Kennedy sweetened the job offer by promising Murrow access to National Security Council (NSC) meetings and a voice in policy-making.[13] Murrow accepted on that understanding. He made clear in his confirmation hearing statement that he intended to tell the truth about the USA. But Murrow's tenure at USIA proved much more complicated than either he or the staff of Voice of America could have expected. The problems began even before Murrow had been confirmed. During the confirmation hearings, enemies of the administration had drawn attention to Murrow's last major CBS documentary, *Harvest of Shame,* an exposé of the treatment of migrant labour in the US. Then a press leak revealed that Murrow had attempted to halt a screening of the film on British television. He had asked his friend at the British Broadcasting Corporation (BBC), Sir Hugh Carlton Greene, to pull the film from the schedules as a 'personal favour' to avoid offending the farm lobby. The BBC refused and Murrow's attempt to censor his own journalism became a brief scandal. For some of the VOA staff, Murrow's reputation never quite recovered.[14]

The Bay of Pigs

If Murrow's attitude disappointed the VOA, he too had reason to feel betrayed. On the morning of 5 April the new deputy director, Don Wilson, stopped in Georgetown for a casual breakfast with his old journalist friend Tad Szulc of the *New York Times.* Szulc had travelled up from a mysterious assignment in Miami, and was staying at the home of his uncle, former Ambassador John C. Wiley. Over toast and coffee he alluded to the Kennedy administration's plans to support an invasion of Cuba by an army of American-trained, anti-Castro exiles. Szulc was just about to publish a story on the build up to the invasion. He estimated that it would take place on 19 April, and wondered how USIA would be supporting press coverage. Szulc realized from Wilson's expression that this was the first he had heard of the plan. Wilson dashed over to Murrow's office to confirm the story. Murrow was equally astonished and the two men raced to a hastily scheduled meeting with Allen Dulles at the Central Intelligence Agency (CIA). Dulles refused to confirm the plan and merely sat nonchalantly smoking his pipe. Twenty minutes later, Murrow received a summons to the White House from the special assistant to the President for National Security Affairs, McGeorge Bundy, who set out the entire background to the story. The plan appalled Murrow. He predicted a psychological disaster, but the wheels were already in motion. Ed Murrow and the USIA had been left 'out of the loop' on one of the biggest American foreign policy decisions of the decade: the landings at the Bay of Pigs.[15]

Murrow did not pass the details of the plan over to his own staff. The director of VOA – a Republican appointee named Henry Loomis – learned of the Bay of Pigs invasion over his car radio on the way to work. Within two hours he rallied the Voice to expand their Spanish language broadcasting to Latin America, from an hour of programming a day to a marathon 19 hours, which VOA maintained until the final defeat of the landings on 22 April.[16]

The Voice struggled hard to find the hard facts of the invasion. Loomis noted: 'While there was a wild outpouring of stories and items, there was a dearth of hard items and confirmable detail – thus complicating the Voice's problem of providing accurate and credible information.'[17] The Voice attempted balanced coverage. It reported Fidel Castro's claim that aircraft from the US had bombed Cuba, but gave a little more weight to Adlai Stevenson's statement to the United Nations that these bombers were actually defecting pilots from Castro's own air force. Unfortunately, Stevenson had been misinformed.[18] The News Analyses (VOA's unofficial editorials as cleared by USIA policy officials) were similarly as confused and compromised by rumour as any other American report or commentary. The News Analysis by Ronald Dunlavey carried on 17 April castigated Castro for implicating the United States in an *invasion* as the word 'implies an attack by a foreign power. The invaders in this case appear to be Cubans returning to their homeland ... The United States is not intervening'. The analysis recycled CIA wishful thinking and reported sympathetic revolts elsewhere in Cuba.[19] Soon the true scale of the disaster emerged. Castro's army had slaughtered the exiles on the beaches. On 20 April, Kennedy addressed the nation, publicly taking the blame for the fiasco.[20] Despite the achievement of the Spanish Language branch in expanding their output virtually overnight, this was not the VOA's finest hour. Loomis and his team resented the way they had been fed misleading material by the State Department and the USIA policy office.[21]

Linguistic Adjustments

Murrow spent much of the next three years recovering from the implications of the Bay of Pigs. This was not the approach to propaganda that Kennedy's team had planned or that the new President had promised. More than this, the entire administration now needed to restore US prestige and confront Soviet propaganda. Here Murrow began the task of reshaping the international profile of the USA along lines that reflected the renewed confrontation with the Soviet Union seen in Kennedy's inaugural address. On 8 June 1961, Murrow and Secretary of State Dean Rusk announced an American slogan to compete with 'Peaceful Coexistence', the theme around which the Soviets had based their propaganda since 1956. America's response would be the concept of 'peaceful world community'. The phrase promised to provide a context for Kennedy's attempts to advance disarmament. Murrow instructed all USIA media to use the phrase as appropriate.[22] At the White House, Arthur Schlesinger, Jr was unimpressed by the phrase because of translation problems. He reported that the Russian adjectives for peaceful and world-wide were the same (*mirnoye*) and added that in many languages the word *community* is rendered as either *village* or *communism*. The United States, naturally, needed to avoid the suggestion that it wanted 'peaceful worldwide communism'.[23] Murrow took the point. A luncheon meeting of the principal figures in US foreign policy, including Murrow, held on 29 June, generated an alternative: 'world of free choice' and commissioned Murrow to 'spread this phrase and its full meaning around the world'. The first major use of the phrase came in a speech to the Press Club by the Secretary of State, Dean Rusk, on 10 July, characterizing the international situation as a choice between 'the world of free choice and free cooperation' and 'the world of coercion'. Kennedy added his blessing to what became 'National Security Action Memorandum 61' (NSAM 61) and instructed the White House staff to make use of the concepts as necessary.[24]

NSAM 61 whetted the appetite of USIA for linguistic sensitivity. Murrow instructed his staff to drop such terms as 'under-developed' and 'backward countries' from their lexicon and use positive terms like 'developing countries' or 'modernizing countries' instead. He also requested suggestions as substitutes for such Truman/Eisenhower-era clichés 'East–West', 'Cold War' and 'pro-American'.[25] From the White House, Arthur Schlesinger Jr., who now characterized his role as 'hand-holder for USIA' added that 'Free World' was perhaps not the best way to describe Spain, Portugal, Paraguay, Haiti or Taiwan and suggested that USIA 'begin to recapture the word "democracy" from the enemy.'[26] Murrow saw the irony of USIA 'puffing' a dictator like Chiang Kai-shek, and ended the agency's glorification of the regime in Taiwan.[27]

The discussions of the early summer of 1961 reveal that Murrow, and the Kennedy administration, had a genuine sense of the sort of values that the United States should project to the world. The nature of his tenure at USIA was such that he seldom had the chance to initiate, and more often steered Agency reactions to domestic or international events. Such events burst upon the agency with full force in August 1961.

The Berlin Wall and Nuclear Testing

August and September 1961 saw two set-piece propaganda confrontations: the Berlin Crisis and the resumption of Soviet nuclear testing. In the first instance the USIA swiftly mobilized its global network to make political capital from the daily haemorrhage of refugees from East Berlin.[28] In mid-August Murrow himself visited Berlin to inspect USIA facilities. While he watched, the East Germans began to build the Berlin Wall.[29] The Wall proved to be an enduring gift to agency propagandists. USIA distributed a stream of images of East German escapees, including the famous shot of a frontier guard in mid-air as he leapt to freedom across barbed wire. These pictures formed the backbone of *The Wall,* a photographic exhibition devised by the United States Information Service in Berlin (USIS Berlin), ten copies of which toured USIS posts world-wide. A selection of images of the Berlin Wall reached as far as Kathmandu and the winter fair in Udorn, a small Thai town, only 50 miles from the Laotian border. The television services produced documentaries with titles like *Anatomy of Aggression* and *Focus Berlin: Barbed Wire World.*[30] The agency understood that the best propaganda came from the independent witnesses and hence assisted the German government in bringing 750 foreign journalists to Berlin to view the wall for themselves. The British helped with a parallel effort. The agency placed particular emphasis on journalists from the 'Afro-Asian' world, where interest in the crisis had been limited. For similar reasons a segment called 'Berlin through African eyes' reached the 30 million viewers of USIA's monthly African film magazine *Today.* The USIA intended to make full use of the most potent images since Soviet troops crushed Hungary in 1956.[31]

Then, on 31 August 1961, the United States Atomic Energy Commission detected the first Soviet nuclear test since 1958. The world press, including numerous left-wing papers, immediately objected in the greatest surge of anti-Soviet sentiment since the suppression of the Hungarian Rising of 1956. The *Manchester Guardian* went so far as to draw a parallel with the Nazi-Soviet pact of 1939. To stoke the outrage USIA produced a map showing the location of the Soviet test site and an ugly black stain representing the fall-out zone, which spread from Japan, the Pacific and the United States to a bulb over Britain and Northern Europe. Versions of this map made the front page of newspapers around the world.[32] The Voice of America beamed news of world indignation back to the Russian population, still unaware that the testing had begun again. Exposing this obsessive secrecy gave an additional propaganda value to VOA broadcasts on the subject to both the USSR and the rest of the world.[33]

Murrow played a key role in devising the US response. Even before the Soviet move, the military pressed for the US to resume its own atmospheric nuclear test programme. Murrow stressed the importance of the US commitment to disarmament. In a secret memo of 24 June, Murrow called the US commitment to a nuclear test ban 'a key, conceivably *the* key, to our Cold War posture'. Any new American nuclear tests would take six months to prepare. Murrow proposed filling this time with a massive information effort to establish Soviet bad faith and the US commitment to a test ban. Suggestions included a co-ordinated effort with the Macmillan government in London and even a CIA rumour campaign to suggest that any earthquakes or trinitrotoluene (TNT) explosions detected in the USSR were actually illicit nuclear tests.[34]

On 31 August he noted that a delay in resuming testing could 'be used to isolate the Communist Bloc, frighten the satellites and the uncommitted, pretty well destroy the *Ban the Bomb* movement in Britain, and might even induce sanity into the SANE nuclear policy group in this country'.[35] Developing his argument, on 1 September he wrote to the President:

> It is obvious that the longer we can delay our announcement, the greater the international political benefit. Our surveys of foreign press and radio indicate that the Soviet decision has

been a tremendous political warfare windfall. Khrushchev has become the focus of fear. The United States is, for the time being, the repository of hope. Our posture should be a combination of restraint, reluctance, plus a determination to exhaust all possibilities before resorting to a competition, which may turn out to be uncontrollable.[36]

For the time being, at least, Kennedy followed Murrow's advice. It would be his only decisive contribution to Kennedy's foreign policy-making.

The immediate audience for America's display of restraint was the Conference of the Twenty-Four Non-Aligned States, then meeting in Belgrade. Nehru obliged with a ringing denunciation of the Soviet tests. Murrow noted a general acceptance of the view expressed in the White House statement of 31 August that the new nuclear tests served no useful military purpose and amounted to 'atomic blackmail'. He referred Kennedy to Joseph Goebbels' dictum: 'He who speaks the first word convinces much of the world.'[37] Although the US resumed underground tests on 15 September, before the end of the month USIA followed up with news that the United States had, in contrast, established a Disarmament Administration, the world's first government agency dedicated to disarmament and peace.[38]

On 31 October Russia detonated a 50-megaton device. At the NSC meeting of 2 November, Secretary of Defence Robert McNamara demanded that the USA also resume immediate atmospheric testing. Murrow again insisted that Kennedy's best option would be to milk the propaganda value of the situation. He noted that the United States 'had a tremendous propaganda advantage' and 'should make the most of it as long as possible'.[39]

VOA provided the centrepiece of the USIA's response to the nuclear tests with a one-hour documentary called *Have You Been Told?*, designed to present the Soviet people with the facts of the tests and the danger of fall-out entering the food chain. The Talks and Features section of VOA knew that the USA would soon resume its own tests and disliked the element of hypocrisy in the project. The section did its best to write a balanced script for the programme in keeping with the VOA's charter of 1960. Murrow and his deputies insisted on a revised script with increased ideological content and music to 'hold an audience'. The second draft pulled no punches. Now the programme began with an explosion noise followed the ominous question: *Have You Been Told?* VOA spiced the whole piece with impassioned editorials from around the globe about the issue of poisonous fall-out.[40] On Sunday 5 November the VOA cancelled all of its regular programming to the USSR and, again using newly-acquired authority to commandeer other agencies' transmitters, let rip with 4,331,000 watts of primetime propaganda over eight hours and 80 frequencies, the combined output of 52 transmitters. The programme could be heard in Russian, English, Ukrainian, Georgian, Armenian, Latvian, Estonian, and Lithuanian, on short wave and over the one kilowatt medium wave transmitter at Munich. USIA believed that the broadcast was audible on at least half of the frequencies used, even in the most heavily jammed areas. Some listeners even reported hearing the programme on car radios.[41] The programme had shown the power of radio propaganda, but role of the USIA director in shaping its content did not sit well with the staff at VOA, especially after reaction reports from the field noted that Russian audiences preferred broadcasts with a less strident tone. Loomis and his team felt that their initial concern had been justified. USIA and VOA had shifted onto a collision course.[42]

On 20 November the test ban talks reopened in Geneva. By February the Kennedy administration had resolved to resume its own tests. Kennedy handled the announcement perfectly. In a television and radio address to the nation on the evening of 2 March 1962, he presented a detailed argument to support the American intention to resume atmospheric tests unless the USSR signed a test ban. The US tests recommenced on 25 April 1962, but the image of the United States remained substantially intact. Despite the absolute supremacy of the United States in nuclear weapons, a USIA survey of global media reaction suggested that the world accepted Kennedy's decision as the act of a moderate man doing the minimum to keep pace with an aggressive opponent.[43] Other trends in world opinion caused USIA concern. Although polls suggested growing Western European confidence in America's world leadership and 'dedication to peace', the same nations also believed that the USSR was militarily stronger than the USA and ahead in the 'space race'. Moreover, an 11-country Gallup survey in October 1961 found that in nine countries a majority of respondents placed the USSR ahead in the Cold War.[44] Murrow still had much work to do.

The Cuban Missile Crisis

The next major Cold War challenge came in October 1962: the Cuban Missile Crisis. The issue was not only the obvious strategic threat to the United States inherent in missiles just 90 miles from the Florida coast but, as McGeorge Bundy made clear in a top secret pre-crisis memorandum dated 31 August 1962, a substantial psychological threat to the US regional and global standing.[45] On 16 October President Kennedy assembled an Executive Committee of the National Security Council – this 'ExCom' became the central forum in which the administration pondered its response to this latest and boldest gambit from Khrushchev. The ExCom did not originally include a representative from USIA. Three days into the crisis Murrow's deputy, Don Wilson, joined ExCom to represent the agency, Ed Murrow being sick with a lung condition. His first task was to ensure that the Cuban people could hear Kennedy's forthcoming speech on the Crisis.[46]

USIA performed well during the crisis: triumphs included their publication of the actual photographs of the Soviet missile sites.[47] But there were costs. The key to the Cuban missile crisis lay in ensuring that the world understood the US position. There could be no room for equivocation or mixed signals. For this reason the USIA decided to take the unprecedented step of taking direct control of the Voice of America. On the morning of Sunday 21 October, Wilson called his policy chief, the old USIA hand Burnett Anderson, into his office and instructed him to 'go down to the Voice of America now, and stay there until further notice ... You are personally responsible for every word said on the air'. Anderson took a desk in the 'mouth' of the Voice of America: the VOA News Room. From that point until the end of the crisis, nothing went on the air without his approval. He had no hesitation killing stories that he felt likely to be counterproductive.[48] Concerns included not only misrepresenting the American position to the Soviet Union but also encouraging the Cuban people into an incautious rising. The USIA remembered the lessons of Hungary in 1956.[49]

As the crisis developed, the USA and USSR used their respective radio stations as a channel for carrying correspondence between the two leaders, a role that passed in the aftermath of the crisis to the much needed innovation, the 'hot line'. But VOA resented the ease with which the administration had taken control of their output. In the aftermath of the crisis, VOA director Henry Loomis broached his concern over the level of USIA control in a letter to Murrow. Despite personal respect for Burnett Anderson, and acceptance that news had been largely unaffected during the crisis, Loomis regretted the degree to which VOA commentaries had been variously killed, altered or not written as a result of USIA control. This left little room for the VOA to discharge its charter obligation to present 'responsible discussion and opinion on these policies'. Murrow's compromise response was to reaffirm both the charter and the existing USIA guidance procedures. He confirmed that Loomis was obliged to follow instructions from the Director, Deputy Director and Deputy Director for Policy. Finally he added a new paragraph to the VOA charter, laying down further ground rules for commentaries. Loomis read the revised charter suspiciously. It contained three sentences. The first, that 'VOA should not mislead our friends or foes' was unobjectionable. The second, that 'Commentaries should reflect nuances and special emphasis as well as the main thrust', seemed to confirm that in the future the VOA would not be barred from the sort of discussion that had been prohibited during the missile crisis. But the third worried Loomis: Commentaries should give 'as accurate a picture of US public policy *as can most persuasively* be presented'. For Loomis the emphasis on persuasion flew in the face of Murrow's pledge to his confirmation hearing that 'USIA would seek to make US foreign policy everywhere intelligible *and wherever possible* palatable'. He now wanted something other than 'the US – warts and all'.[50]

Projecting Civil Rights and the March on Washington

Murrow's notion of showing 'the US – warts and all' could be seen in the matter of Civil Rights, but USIA still added its own 'spin'. As Murrow explained: 'USIA policy has been to stick to hard news, playing down the violence and emphasizing Federal action to protect the civil rights of Negro citizens.'[51] An observer relying only on USIA sources for their picture of the African American Civil Rights movement would have the impression that the hero of the Civil Rights era was the American system to which the protestors appealed, and the Federal Government which came to the aid of the distressed Black citizens. Although the USIA's analysts recorded a massive wave of international revulsion against incidents like the beating of Freedom Riders in Alabama in early 1962, the agency drew satisfaction from evidence of widespread understanding of the Kennedy administration's position on the matter.[52]

Murrow knew the prestige value of the space programme and urged Kennedy to open the space programme to black astronauts. When NASA argued that it only trained qualified test pilots, Murrow pressed Kennedy to begin training black test pilots as well.[53] While NASA dragged its feet, USIA led the way in hiring African Americans.[54] Between 1960 and 1963 the number of black Americans in USIA's foreign service doubled. By the end of the Kennedy years, black people held one in ten of all senior and middle grade USIA career posts.[55] USIA used these officers extensively in African work. The presence of black staff enabled the agency to give a positive racial dimension to otherwise 'white' subjects like the space programme. USIA hired two black 'special lecturers' to present the space programme to schools and universities around Africa. The English-language lecturer John Twitty, recruited in 1962, had previously worked as a journalist for the African American press, including *Ebony* magazine and a spell as city editor for *Amsterdam News*. As Twitty recalled, after six months' training with NASA, he spent two years on the road in Africa with a selection of models, diagrams and other visual aids, presenting a one-hour lecture on the space programme. He even appeared on children's television in Nigeria. His skin colour added another level to the operation, although he soon discovered that his audiences knew little of black American life. Nigerian schoolchildren regularly asked whether he was a slave and applauded when he told them that he was free. A group of Muslim pupils asked him to sing a spiritual. Twitty obliged them with an appropriate song, before beginning his usual lecture.[56]

There were limits to the agency's willingness to represent African American culture overseas. As a legacy of the McCarthy inquiries of the 1950s, USIS cultural facilities around the world remained somewhat jumpy about distributing African American authors. Blacklisted books included Ralph Ellison's *The Invisible Man*, which was 'not being purchased by the Agency'.[57] Murrow left the issue un-challenged. It changed only when Richard Nixon's director of USIA, Frank Shakespeare, instituted a review of book purchasing procedures, ironically to ensure that the conservative position was properly represented.[58]

USIA concern over the Civil Rights issue peaked in the spring of 1963 when Black protests in Birmingham, Alabama produced a backlash of white police violence. While the news cameras rolled, the Birmingham Police Department used high-pressure fire hoses and dogs to disperse demonstrators. The world press recoiled in horror. In Paris the usually sympathetic Socialist paper *Populaire* proclaimed:

'Violence in Alabama, a dishonour for the US.'[59] As violence escalated with the murder of Civil Rights activist Medger Evers, and mass gaoling of protestors, Communist bloc propaganda went into overdrive. Radio Moscow devoted an estimated 20 per cent of its coverage to the story, and reported that 'racist ... storm troop detachments' marched through the streets and African Americans were being 'herded into concentration camps of the Buchenwald and Auschwitz pattern' where 'barbed wire cordons, starvation rations, and brutal beatings ... drive the inmates to suicide'.[60] Chinese sources warned the Asian and Pacific world to heighten their 'vigilance against the sweet words of the United States Imperialists' and take note of 'their filthy deeds'.[61] The President's address on the issue on 11 June, disseminated internationally by USIA, attracted more positive reporting. The *Morning Post* of Nigeria praised Kennedy as 'one of the greatest champions of the rights of man that ever lived'. A Singapore paper dubbed the President 'the most enlightened President of the United States since Lincoln'.[62]

With this background, Murrow worked hard to ensure maximum publicity for Martin Luther King's march on Washington in August 1963. The march fitted easily into the USIA approach to Civil Rights as a child of Federal policy. VOA built up to the event with interviews. Coverage of the march itself included on-the-spot running reports in English and Swahili, and coverage took over the entire East Africa service for the day. The Indian service stressed the triumph of Gandhian non-violence, while the Chinese service paid particular attention to the radical speaker, James Farmer, who pointedly rejected an offer of aid from Mao Zedong.[63] USIA supported this coverage with written reports and photographs. The agency immediately shipped film of both the event and follow-up discussions with participants. But a half-hour 35 mm documentary film formed the centrepiece of USIA's coverage. George Stevens assembled a team of his own interns and contracted cameramen from Hearst to film the event under the direction of James Blue. The film would not be ready until early 1964. It would become a focus for controversy in the early weeks of the Johnson administration.[64]

Vietnam

In the matter of Vietnam, Murrow attempted to act as a voice of moderation. He was generally ignored. He unsuccessfully urged Kennedy to avoid defoliant operations. His suggestion that the US rationalize its media operations in Vietnam by creating a 'single press relations Tsar' at the Saigon Embassy was not implemented till 1965 (arguably too late to make much difference). But frustration at the chaotic Vietnam policy-making ground him down in the summer of 1963. A White House minute of 10 September reflected Murrow's frustration: 'Mr. Murrow asked that he be relieved of writing press guidance until after tomorrow's meeting in view of the fact that the guidance could not be written until our policy was clear.'[65] Murrow's feelings over Vietnam had been shaken by the events of August 1963. The crisis bears relating in some detail.

During the course of 1963 the US government became increasingly unhappy with its Vietnamese proxy Ngo Dinh Diem and his repression of the Vietnam's Buddhist population. On 20 August Diem launched a series of violent raids on Buddhist pagodas around the country in search of communist propaganda and weapons. The VOA, which was now the news source of first resort for most urban South Vietnamese, initially followed the initial Embassy and CIA understanding of events and blamed units of the South Vietnamese army. The Vietnamese army protested its innocence. Evidence mounted that the true culprits were forces under the control of Diem's 'wicked brother' Nhu, including secret police disguised as Vietnamese regular soldiers. It seemed that a nudge from the US might encourage key Generals to overthrow Diem. On 24 August the Saigon mission sent a memo setting out these points. At the State Department the Assistant Secretary of State for Far Eastern Affairs, Roger Hilsman, drafted a response. He obtained the approval of other officials including the Under-Secretary, George Ball (over whose signature the memo was sent). This cable proposed a dramatic and blunt ultimatum: press Diem to remove Nhu and if he refuses 'we must face the possibility that Diem himself cannot be preserved'. The cable promised the Ambassador to Saigon (Lodge) that State would 'have Voice of America make a statement' on the Pagoda raids 'whenever you give the word'.[66] Hilsman believed that the best way for VOA to correct the story was for the State Department to place a revised version with the wire services, which could then be reported as news. He tracked down the UPI State Department correspondent, Stewart Hensley, at his home and read the unclassified portions of the memo dealing with the events of 20 August.[67] VOA then reported the planted wire story as news, ending with the sentence that sources in Washington 'say that America may cut its aid to Vietnam if President Diem does not get rid of the police officials responsible'.[68]

In South Vietnam this last sentence seemed like a green light for a coup. But none followed. Instead Kennedy re-convened the ExCom, and for the rest of the week the pro-coup and anti-coup factions in Washington argued over the future of Diem. VOA carried an official denial of any US plan to revise aid to Vietnam, but the damage to the delicate relationship between the US government and both Diem and the South Vietnamese army had been done.[69] Ambassador Lodge in Saigon wrote a stiff note attacking the Voice. Secretary of State Rusk apologized for the broadcast, blaming the 'failure of machinery here over the weekend to carry out policy instructions'. Rusk saw the broadcast as an extension of the existing issue of VOA carrying negative American press stories relating to Vietnam: 'VOA will broadcast only hard news coverage for the next few days', he wrote, adding that they 'will refrain from relaying press speculation as they did on this occasion'.[70]

Like Rusk, Roger Hilsman, blamed the Voice for the broadcast. He claimed that journalists had failed to check their copy of the relevant guidance cable.[71] The Voice staff disputed this. They reported that Hilsman had himself called the Voice to direct them cover the story in the first place, and the Voice had even called back to confirm the story. The news room concluded that a pro-coup clique within the American government had manipulated VOA. Their view of the incident was born out by General Maxwell Taylor, who spoke of the incident in football terms as a botched 'end-run' by a free-wheeling faction of Hilsman, Harriman and Forrestal. Murrow accepted that the VOA had 'been had' but told the news room to 'be good soldiers' once again, and take the rebuke 'in the national interest'.[72] In a secret memo Murrow warned McGeorge Bundy that VOA should not be used in this way:

> I also suggest that 1) VOA can be used tactically to incite only once, and therefore that this weapon be held until the right moment; 2) in the event of a change in the US public position on Viet-Nam that such a change be announced publicly (e.g. by the President, the Secretary, Hilsman or Phillips) rather than backgrounded anonymously and therefore ambiguously.[73]

At the State Department the incident became another argument for increased control over the VOA. At the Voice, the story underlined the need for an enhanced VOA charter to further separate the government from the news.

While the VOA felt irritated by Murrow, the Director himself felt increasingly ill at ease with the Kennedy administration. He felt uneasy about the influence of Robert Kennedy on policy, which he saw at close quarters as a representative on USIA on RFK's Counter Insurgency Group and anti-Castro 'Operation Mongoose' committee. Murrow felt instinctively mistrustful of a man who had been close to his old enemy, Joe McCarthy: 'Thank God there is little of Bobby in the President', he said, 'that man could be dangerous in a position of authority.' Murrow saw little distinction between the intrusive behaviour of J. Edgar Hoover and his line manager, Robert Kennedy. Once, when unexpectedly coming into his office at USIA, Murrow found a strange man rifling through his desk. Murrow slammed the drawer shut on the man's hand and threw him out of his office yelling: 'Tell Bobby if he wants to know something, he can ASK JACK.' Vietnam – with which Bobby Kennedy was associated through his chairmanship of the Counter Insurgency Group – merely deepened his sense of unease. Privately, Murrow approached ABC News in search of a job. He never made the move. That autumn Murrow – a chain-smoker – learned that he had lung cancer. Within months the disease first required the removal of one of his lungs and then forced his retirement.[74]

The USIA at the End of 1963

There was some cause for satisfaction as Murrow's tenure at USIA drew to a close. In the early summer of 1963, a survey of world opinion showed renewed sympathy for the United States. The USSR suddenly stopped jamming VOA broadcasts and Kennedy's sustained pressure on the Soviet Union in the matter of the nuclear test ban finally bore fruit with an atmospheric test ban treaty. The agency had a string of flourishing new initiatives, the most obvious being the film division run by George Stevens Jr. The news network maximized the distribution for US news and pictures, which always made an eloquent contrast with the terminally laconic and secretive USSR. Ironically the greatest testament to this came in November 1963 with the USIA's news management of the Kennedy assassination. Murrow acted swiftly. He rose from his sick-bed and hauled himself up the steps into the Congressional office building to personally demand an emergency budget of $8 million from the obstructive House appropriations chair, John Rooney of New York.[75] The result, from coverage of the state funeral to memorialization of Kennedy's life proved exactly what a well-funded propaganda agency with a winning story could achieve. The Soviets did not attempt to swim against the tide, but merely to divert it a little by promoting rumours of a right-wing conspiracy, which proved a perennial problem for Murrow's successors.

Murrow, who did not get on well with Lyndon Johnson, left the agency in January 1964. He died in the spring of 1965. The USIA immediately took his memory to heart. Key institutions took his name including the agency's new short-wave transmitter in Greenville, North Carolina, an agency distinguished service award and a centre established at the Fletcher School for Diplomacy at Tufts University in Massachusetts to train USIA staff in what was now called not propaganda but *public diplomacy*. The drawback was that Congress did not necessarily accept that public diplomacy was a necessary dimension to modern international relations. Appropriations in the 1960s continued to be justified by the Cold War and later by the publicity needs of the Vietnam conflict. *Détente* would render USIA vulnerable.

At the VOA his legacy was somewhat more mixed. Murrow was seen as remote, too political and too influenced by his politically-appointed deputies. The disputes which had simmered in his era boiled over in the Johnson years when Murrow's successor, the hapless Carl Rowan, attempted to strong-arm the VOA over both the deepening war in Vietnam and the US intervention in the Dominican Republic. Henry Loomis, the VOA director, resigned, and in an embarrassed aftermath Johnson essentially sacked Rowan. The issue of VOA autonomy was only resolved when in 1976, in the aftermath of Nixon administration attempts to play down Watergate, the VOA charter was written into law.[76]

It is notoriously difficult to evaluate the effect of propaganda, and the Murrow period at USIA is no exception. There were set-piece triumphs, such as the successful dissemination of images of the Berlin Wall or news of the Soviet atomic tests, but USIA was much more than a tool of crisis management. Murrow's network included much day-to-day work performing unglamorous duties such as teaching English, screening documentary films, meeting writers around the world and developing links with the United States. USIA acted as the 'in-country' end of US educational exchange programmes and the schemes to enable potential leaders in particular countries to visit the United States (later in the decade the young Margaret Thatcher made her ideologically-formative first pilgrimage to the USA as part of such a joint USIA/State Department scheme). Hence the success or otherwise of USIA must be judged across decades and in broad trends rather than solely through attention to the spikes. The Murrow period saw a growth of institutional pride within the agency that played into the long-term development of its work. The agency did well in communicating the Kennedy administration's special message of hope to the developing world, and the international outpouring of genuine grief seen at the time of the Kennedy assassination was testament to that success. The operation of the commercial media alone would not have elicited such a response because there would in previous years have been no commercial reason to ensure that Thailand or the Philippines received news of Kennedy's latest speech or films in the appropriate language of Jackie Kennedy touring India. This work created a tremendous resource of goodwill for the Johnson administration, which was largely squandered by the excesses of Vietnam.

USIA veterans present Murrow's tenure at USIA as a glorious pinnacle of his career. Murrow's biographers have tended to skate over the period, finding little to enhance the picture of an American hero. We find politicking, compromises and weakness in Murrow's tenure at USIA, but there are undeniable flashes of principle too. An apologist would say that Murrow's health was not good enough for more, but realistically many of the same failings could be found in the better-known periods of Murrow's media career. One must remember that the man who brought *See it Now* to the screen also fronted the scripted celebrity interview show *Person to Person*. Murrow's greatest triumphs were always in the realm of images and his tenure at USIA proved no exception. Whatever the reality his initial pledges to 'portray the US warts and all', remained in the imagination of the USIA and (with justice or irony) became a benchmark for dealing with the troubled years ahead.

Murrow's tenure at USIA must also be seen as an expression of the bureaucratic truth that behaviour tends to flow from position; the poacher will be a zealous gamekeeper once he sees the world from that end of the field. Murrow's transformation was not as astonishing as it might seem today. In the pre-Vietnam War, pre-Watergate era there was less of a sense of an oppositional media in the United States. Many journalists shared in the broad outlines of the Cold War project, and Murrow had always felt at home at gatherings of the transatlantic foreign policy elite at events like the Ditchley seminars in England.

In terms of the wider 'cultural Cold War', Murrow's work and the operation of the USIA serve to underline the degree to which the hand of government directed and assisted the international flow of ideas and images during the period. Some of the best-known words and images of Kennedy's Cold War circulated as a matter of policy, following the intervention of, and via the channels created by the USIA. Much of the world saw the Berlin Wall and the missile sites in Cuba because USIA made it possible. The Russian people and much of the rest of the world learned about resumption of nuclear testing because of USIA and VOA. Cumulatively such initiatives undermined the foundations of Soviet Communism, while the cultural apparatus associated with the agency – the film and book programmes, the educational exchanges, and even the support provided to American Studies courses at universities around the world – assisted the extension of American culture. This story carries within it an irony. The USIA helped the win the Cold War *for* the 'free market' but it did not win it *through* the free market. The USIA and VOA were agencies of state intervention, but without the Cold War to justify spending on 'public diplomacy' or propaganda the budgets for such programmes withered, and the United States increasingly came to look to commercial media channels to 'tell America's story to the world'. Like their forebears in 1919 and 1945 the Congress of 1999 judged an international information agency to be a necessity of war only. The USIA had, by its own success, put itself out of a job. Hence, at the end of September 1999 the agency was dissolved and its personnel and activities transferred to the State Department. VOA became independent under a Broadcasting Board of Governors.[77]

The underlying structural problems remained. In the wake of the terrorist attacks of 11 September 2001, as the Bush administration looked now to the State Department to win back the hearts and minds of the Arab world, the State Department made strenuous attempts to prevent Voice of America from broadcasting an interview with the Taliban leader Mullah Omar. VOA stuck to its guns and insisted on maintaining objectivity. It would have all seemed very familiar to Ed Murrow.[78]

NOTES

1. For introductions to the role of information in international relations see Philip M. Taylor, *Global Communications, International Affairs and the Media since 1945* (London: Routledge, 1997); Jarol B. Manheim, *Strategic Public Diplomacy and American Foreign Policy: The Evolution of Influence* (New York: Oxford University Press, 1994).
2. For accounts by USIA staff see Thomas Sorrenson, *The Word War: The Story of*

American Propaganda (New York: Harper & Row, 1968); Allen C. Hansen, *USIA: Public Diplomacy in the Computer Age* (New York: Praeger, 2nd edn. 1989); Hans N. Tuch, *Communicating with the World: US Public Diplomacy Overseas* (New York: St. Martin's Press, 1990); and Fitzhugh Green, *American Propaganda Abroad: From Benjamin Franklin to Ronald Reagan* (New York: Hippocrene Books, 1988).

3. For biographies, see Alexander Kendrick, *Prime Time: The Life of Edward R. Murrow* (Boston: Little, Brown and Co., 1969); A.M. Sperber, *Murrow: His Life and Times* (London: Michael Joseph, 1986); Joseph E. Persico, *Edward R. Murrow: An American Original* (New York: McGraw-Hill, 1988).

4. Ibid. Monographs dealing with this period include Gary D. Rawnsley, *Radio Diplomacy and Propaganda: The BBC and VOA in International Politics, 1956–64* (London: Macmillan, 1996); and the accounts by USIA staff: Sorrenson, *The Word War*; Hansen, *USIA*; Tuch, *Communicating with the World*; and Green, *American Propaganda Abroad*. Interviews cited below include: from VOA: Cliff Groce and Bernie Kamenske; from USIA: Burnett Anderson, Alex Klieforth, Don Wilson, John Twitty and Frank Shakespeare.

5. This is particularly so in the Bay of Pigs and Vietnam material below.

6. Files consulted at the John F. Kennedy Presidential Library, Boston (hereafter JFKL) include. National Security Files (NSF), Oral History collection, Pre-presidential papers (PPP), President's Office Files (POF), Salinger papers, Schlesinger papers, USIA director files microfilm, Voice of America microfilm, White House Central Files (WHCF); the Edward R. Murrow papers at Tufts University, Boston; and records held at the United States Information Agency Historical Branch in Washington, now the State Department's Public Diplomacy Historical collection.

7. On US international information to 1945 see Frank A. Ninkovich, *The Diplomacy of Ideas: US Foreign Policy and Cultural Relations, 1938–1950* (Cambridge: Cambridge University Press, 1981); Allan M. Winkler, *The Politics of Propaganda: The Office of War Information, 1942–1945* (New Haven: Yale University Press, 1978); Holly Cowan Shulman, *The Voice of America: Propaganda and Democracy, 1941–1945* (Madison: University of Wisconsin Press, 1990).

8. Sidney Hyman, *The Lives of William Benton* (Chicago: University of Chicago Press, 1969); David Krugler, *The Voice of America and the Domestic Propaganda Battles, 1945–1953* (Columbia, MO: University of Missouri Press, 2000); Scott Lucas, *Freedom's War: The US Crusade Against the Soviet Union, 1945–1956* (Manchester: Manchester University Press, 1999); Walter Hixson, *Parting the Curtain: Propaganda, Culture and the Cold War, 1945–1961* (Basingstoke: Macmillan, 1997).

9. For overviews of the Eisenhower period see Lucas, *Freedom's War*, and Hixson, *Parting the Curtain*.

10. Theodore H. White, *The Making of the President, 1960* (London: Jonathan Cape, 1961), p.304; Mark Haefele, 'John F. Kennedy, USIA and World Opinion', *Diplomatic History* 25/1 (2001), p.69.

11. JFKL Pre-presidential papers, box 1074, Summary of Recommendations, 31 Dec. 1960.

12. JFKL Salinger papers, box 132, 1961 file USIA, Robert Oshins (DNC) to Salinger, 21 Dec. 1960. Other candidates included Sig Mickelson and Fred Friendly of CBS and Phil Graham, publisher of the *Washington Post*; Sperber, *Murrow*, p.611; Persico, *Murrow*, p.465; Interview: Frank Stanton.

13. Sperber, *Murrow*, pp.614–19; JFKL NSF, Meetings and Memoranda, box 313, folder 2, NSC meeting 475, 1 Feb. 1961.

14. Kendrick, *Prime Time*; Sperber, *Murrow*, p.629; Interview: Clifford Groce, 30 Nov. 1995; also Frank Cummins and Bernie Kamenske; 'TV: Defence for Murrow', *New York Times*, 28 March 1961.

15. Interview (telephone) Tad Szulc, 30 Oct. 2000, and Donald Wilson, 2 July 1996; *Foreign Relations of the United States (FRUS), 1961–1963*, Vol.X, *Cuba, 1961–1962*, doc. 231, Memo 1; Cuba Study Group to President, 13 June 1961, items 39, 40; Peter Wyden, *Bay of Pigs: The Untold Story* (New York: Touchstone, 1979),

pp.144–5. Wilson has on several occasions (including JFKL oral history interview) misdated these events to Saturday 15 April, only two days before the invasion, hence the error in Sperber, *Murrow*, pp.623–4, and Persico, *Murrow*, p.475. Szulc's story appeared in the *New York Times* in much eviscerated form on 7 April 1961.

16. *FRUS, 1961–1963*, Vol. X, doc. 231, Cuba Study Group to President, 13 June 1961, item 40; Sperber, *Murrow*, pp.623–4; JFKL USIA director files, reel 7, Loomis to Murrow, IBS Monthly Report, 5 May 1961.

17. JFKL USIA director files, reel 7, Loomis to Murrow, IBS Monthly Report, 5 May 1961.

18. Bernie Kamenske to author, 28 Nov. 2000; Wyden, *Bay of Pigs*, pp.185–90.

19. JFKL VOA microfilm reel 1, News Analysis 1647; Ronald Dunlavey, 'The Invasion of Cuba', 17 April 1961.

20. Murrow was profoundly impressed by this, and stopped his practice of referring to Kennedy as 'that boy in the White House'. Hereafter it was 'the President'. Interview: Donald Wilson, 2 July 1996.

21. Interview: Kamenske, 6 Dec. 1995.

22. JFKL NSF, Meetings and Memoranda, box 330, NSAM 61, Rusk and Murrow to President, 8 June 1961.

23. JFKL NSF, Meetings and Memoranda, box 327, Staff memoranda, Schlesinger to McGeorge Bundy, 9 June 1961.

24. JFKL NSF, Meetings and Memoranda, box 330, NSAM 61: Minutes of lunch meeting, 29 June 1961, McGeorge Bundy; Murrow to McGeorge Bundy, 30 June 1961; McGeorge Bundy to Rusk/Murrow, 14 July 1961.

25. JFKL POF, Depts. and Agencies: USIA, box 290, General, Murrow to Sorenson, 19 July 1961.

26. JFKL Schlesinger papers, White House files, box WH-23, USIA. Schlesinger to Murrow, 1 Aug. 1961; the 'hand-holder' quote comes from NSF, Meetings and Memoranda, box 327, Staff Memoranda, Schlesinger, Memo to Salinger, 7 June 1961.

27. Sperber, *Murrow*, p.659.

28. JFKL USIA director files, reel 4, Wilson to Rusk, secret, 'USIA Berlin Program', 2 Aug. 1962.

29. Sperber, *Murrow*, p.644.

30. USIA HB, USIA 17th Review of Operations, 1 July–31 Dec. 1961, pp.5–7.

31. Ibid.; JFKL, NSF, CO Germany, Berlin, General, box 81, Murrow to Rusk, 10 July 1961: 'USIA Planning and Action on Berlin'; Salinger papers, box 132, 1961 file, USIA, Murrow to President, Weekly Report, 22 Aug. 1961. The death of a refugee on the Berlin Wall was featured in the 1963 USIA film *The American Commitment* directed by Leo Seltzer and narrated by Howard K. Smith) (see National Archives sound and motion picture branch, Washington DC, RG 306 387). The film shows the USIA sending news of the death around the globe. Memorable images include scenes of a Public Affairs Officer in Central America driving past a wall decorated with the slogan: 'Castro Si, Yankis Non!'

32. USIA HB, USIA 17th Review of Operations, 1 July–31 Dec. 1961, p.15; JFKL POF, Depts. and Agencies USIA, box 91, Murrow to President, 31 Aug. 1961. The *Daily Express* version, 2 Sept. 1961, showed only the site and relative location of Western Europe, but associated articles dealt with the risk of fall-out.

33. JFKL VOA, reel 1, News Analysis, 1847, Raymond Swing, 'The Soviet People are not told', 6 Sept. 1961.

34. JFKL USIA director file, reel 6, Murrow to Bowles, 24 June 1961, secret, 'The Nuclear Test Ban Issue'.

35. *FRUS 1961–1963*, Vol.VII, *Arms Control and Disarmament*, doc.59, Murrow to President, 31 Aug. 1961; Considerations regarding nuclear testing. SANE (the National Committee for a Sane Nuclear Policy) had been founded in 1957 by Norman Cousins and Clarence Pickett as a non-partisan pressure group for restraint in nuclear policy. Early objectives included a nuclear test ban treaty and the US

disarmament administration. The organization's papers are held in the Swarthmore College Peace Collection.

36. JFKL USIA director file, reel 4, Murrow to President, Confidential, 1 Sept. 1961.
37. JFKL POF, Depts. and Agencies: USIA, box 91, Murrow to President, 1 Sept. 1961 and undated 'reactions to nuclear tests'. For text of White House statement of 31 August see *Public Papers of the Presidents: John F. Kennedy, 1961*, pp.584–5.
38. JFKL WHCF Subject file: FG296 USIA, box 184, Executive, Murrow to all posts, 27 Sept. 1961.
39. Richard Reeves, *President Kennedy: Profile of Power* (New York: Simon and Schuster, 1993) p. 251; Persico, *Murrow*, p.476.
40. Interviews: Len Reed, 12 Dec. 1995; Cliff Groce, 30 Nov. 1995; Alex Klieforth, 7 Jan. 1997.
41. USIA HB, USIA 17th Review of Operations, 1 July–31 Dec. 1961, pp.16–18; JFKL VOA microfilm, reel 5, Loomis to Murrow, IBS Monthly Report, 18 Dec. 1961; On extent of jamming see NA RG59, State CPF 1960–63; box 1064, Moscow 1455, 522.604/11–561, Thompson to USIA, 5 Nov. 1961.
42. Interview: Cliff Groce, 30 Nov. 1995; JFKL VOA microfilm, reel 5, Loomis to Murrow, IBS Monthly Report, 18 Dec. 1961.
43. JFKL POF, Depts. and Agencies USIA, box 91, USIA Research and Reference Service, 'Reaction to the Presidential Announcement on Nuclear Testing', R-21–62, 6 March 1962; Murrow to President, 3 Aug. 1962; *Public Papers of the Presidents: John F. Kennedy, 1962*, pp.186–93.
44. JFKL Salinger papers, box 132, 1961 file, USIA, Wilson to President, Weekly Report, 17 Oct. 1961. The average split was 29 per cent for Russia winning, 14 per cent for the West, 22 per cent for neither and 35 per cent with no opinion. The other countries surveyed were US, UK, Ireland, Vietnam, West Germany, Holland, France, Finland and Uruguay.
45. JFKL NSF, Meetings and Memoranda, box 338, file on NSAM 181, Bundy to Kennedy, Top Secret and Sensitive, 31 Aug. 1962 (reproduced in *FRUS 1961–1963*, Vol. X, document 331 m).
46. JFKL Interview: Don Wilson, 2 Sept. 1964; Interview: Don Wilson, 2 July 1996; Persico, *Murrow*, p.484.
47. Interview: Don Wilson, 2 July 1996; Robert Smith Thompson, *The Missiles of October: The Declassified Story of John F. Kennedy and the Cuban Missile Crisis.* (New York: Simon and Schuster, 1992), pp.298–9. USIA distributed some 50,000 prints around the world. As White House Press Secretary, Pierre Salinger later recalled, the distribution of these pictures 'was the best thing that ever happened. Those pictures played a major role in persuading foreign opinion that the President was justified in taking action'. The photograph also featured on a leaflet, which USIA prepared to be dropped over Cuba. The US Army's psychological warfare team at Fort Bragg produced six million copies, which were ready for delivery at just 12 hours' notice from the White House by the middle of the crisis week. President Kennedy never gave the order for the drop. JFKL Interview: Donald Wilson, 2 Sept. 1964, pp.22–3.
48. Interview: Burnett Anderson, 14 Dec. 1995; ADST Oral History, Anderson; Interview: Bernie Kamenske, 6 Dec. 1995. Anderson and Loomis worked well together during the crisis and, in later years, Loomis invited Anderson to serve as his deputy at the Corporation for Public Broadcasting.
49. Rawnsley, *Radio Diplomacy and Propaganda*, p.119.
50. For Loomis' account of this see USIA Alumni Association, 'The US – Warts and All': *Edward R. Murrow as Director of the USIA, Presenting the US to the World: A Commemorative Symposium* (Washington DC: USIAAA/Public Diplomacy Foundation, 1992), pp.19–22.
51. JFKL Salinger papers, box 132, 1961 file, USIA, Murrow to President, 23 May 1961.
52. JFKL USIA director's papers, reel 6, Murrow to Adam Clayton Powell, 21 June 1961, with attached 'report summary world-wide reaction to racial incidents in

Alabama'.
53. Persico, *Murrow,* p.483, Sperber, *Murrow,* p.657.
54. JFKL WHCF subject file FG 296 USIA, box 184, Executive, Wilson to Frank D. Reeves, 9 May 1961.
55. LBJM, Panzer papers, box 469, USIA, summary memo: 'United States Information Agency', 1 Oct. 1963.
56. Interview: John Twitty, by telephone, 15 Nov. 2000.
57. Interview: Pistor; NA RG 59 State CPF 1960–63, box 1061, Prague-A-50, 511.492/1–8 63, Rusk to Prague (drafted by Squires, USIA, ICS), 8 Jan. 1963.
58. Interview: Frank Shakespeare, 11 Jan. 1997.
59. NA RG 59 State CPF 1960–1963, box 3269, INF France, Embassy Paris to State Department, 8 May 1963.
60. JFKL POF, Depts. and Agencies: USIA, box 91, Sorenson to President, 'Reactions to your Civil Rights Speech', 14 June 1963; Salinger papers, box 132, USIA 1963, Wilson to President, 14 May 1963.
61. NA RG 59 State CPF 1960–1963, box 3271, INF 11 PAK, Embassy Karachi to Dept. of State, 22 June 1963.
62. JFKL POF, Depts. and Agencies: USIA, box 91, Sorenson to President, 'Reactions to your Civil Rights Speech', 14 June 1963.
63. JFKL VOA reel 11, Loomis to Murrow, 24 Sept. 1963, IBS Monthly Report, Aug. 1963. For News Analyses of the march see reel 4.
64. Nicholas J. Cull, 'Auteurs of Ideology: USIA Documentary Film Propaganda in the Kennedy Era as Seen in Bruce Herschensohn's *The Five Cities of June* (1963) and James Blue's *The March* (1964)', *Film History* 10/3 (1998), pp.295–310.
65. Persico, *Murrow,* p.487; Reeves, *President Kennedy: Profile of Power,* p.597; Sperber, *Murrow,* p.681.
66. For context see David Kaiser, *American Tragedy: Kennedy, Johnson and the Origins of the Vietnam War* (Cambridge, MA: Harvard University Press, 2000), pp.226–31; JFKL, NSF, Meetings and Memoranda, box 316, Vietnam, Ball to Lodge, Top Secret, 24 Aug. 1963.
67. Roger Hilsman, *To Move a Nation* (New York: Doubleday, 1967), pp.484–90.
68. *FRUS, 1961–1963,* Vol.III, doc.287, Voice of America broadcast, Saigon, 26 Aug. 1963. Hilsman's notes record the broadcasts as 12:35 am: 'The officials in Washington indicated there may be a sharp reduction in the US aid program for the Republic of Viet-Nam unless President Diem gets rid of Secret Police officials responsible for the attacks against the Buddhists', and 8:30 am 'The American officials indicated the US may sharply reduce its aid to Viet-Nam unless President Diem gets rid of Secret Police officials responsible for the attacks.' JFKL Hilsman papers, box 3, Countries, Vietnam, 'VOA Vietnamese Broadcasts re. US Aid', 26 Aug. 1963.
69. *FRUS, 1961–1963,* Vol.III, doc.289, Minutes of Meeting at White House, 26 Aug. 1963.
70. JFKL NSF, Countries: Vietnam, box 198, State Cables, Rusk to Lodge, 26 Aug. 1963.
71. Hilsman, *To Move a Nation,* pp.489–90.
72. *NYHT,* 27 Aug. 1963, 'In Viet, we absolve, while we blunder: Our Voice', pp.1, 10; Interview: Bernie Kamenske, 6 Dec. 1995; Alex Klieforth, 7 Jan. 1997; JFKL VOA, reel 11, Loomis to Murrow, 24 Sept. 1963, IBS Monthly Report, Aug. 1963; Maxwell Taylor, *Swords into Plowshares* (New York: Norton, 1972), pp.292–4. Klieforth visited Vietnam shortly after this incident and explained the VOA version of events first to Lodge (with whom he had worked in the 1950s) who accepted the VOA version and then, on the return journey, to Ambassador Edwin Reischauer in Tokyo, who had been alarmed by the story.
73. JFKL Hilsman papers, box 3, Countries, Vietnam, Murrow to Bundy, Secret, 28 Aug. 1963.
74. Persico, *Murrow,* p.485, Sperber, *Murrow* pp.659, 681.

75. Sperber, *Murrow*, p.685.
76. Prime movers in getting the VOA charter into law included the now head of News,
    Bernie Kamenske. For a narrative see Laurien Alexandre, *The Voice of America: From
    Détente to the Reagan Doctrine* (Norwood, NJ: Ablex Publishing Corp., 1988).
77. Murrow's equivalent in the George W. Bush administration is the Undersecretary of
    State for Public Diplomacy and Public Affairs, Charlotte Beers, a former advertising
    executive best known for her work selling 'Uncle Ben's Rice'. Elizabeth Becker and
    James Dao, 'Bush will keep wartime office promoting US', *New York Times*, 20 Feb.
    2002; Naomi Klein, 'Brand USA', *Los Angeles Times*, 10 March 2002.
78. For comment on this dispute see William Safire, 'State out of Step', *New York Times*,
    1 July 2002.

Soviet Cinema and the Early Cold War: Pudovkin's *Admiral Nakhimov* in Context

SARAH DAVIES

Although the comparative socio-cultural history of the Cold War has received some attention, it is striking, as the editors of this volume point out, how little has been paid to the eastern bloc, including the USSR, one of the chief protagonists.[1] In the case of the USSR, this is partly because of deeply entrenched historiographical assumptions that the post-war Soviet Union can be understood simply through the lens of 'Stalinism' or 'totalitarianism'. Recent studies of the *inter-war* period have begun to try to situate the USSR within a broader European and international, comparative framework. While not denying the unique features of the Soviet Union, these studies argue persuasively that we can only fully comprehend this uniqueness if we are also aware of the similarities with other powerful twentieth-century states emerging from the shadow of the First World War. Such similarities include a strong impulse towards social control through surveillance, reproduction politics, and the use of technologically sophisticated mass media.[2] A comparative approach to the post-war USSR would be equally valuable. Just as it had following the First World War, and indeed during the Second World War too, the Soviet Union after World War Two confronted a series of challenges, which were faced to a greater or lesser extent by many other states. These common challenges, profoundly shaped by the international context of the Cold War, propelled some of these states along often strikingly similar trajectories.

The following study of Soviet cinema in the crucial transition period of 1944–46 does not pretend to offer a truly comparative approach. However it does address this research agenda in at least two respects. First, when read in conjunction with other papers in this volume, it sheds some light on how the emerging Cold War inclined the Soviet Union towards increasing state intervention in cultural policy, censorship and so on, just as it did in the 'democracies' of Britain and the USA. It would be possible to interpret the post-war authoritarianism of cultural policy associated with Zhdanov as simply a continuation of Stalinist norms,[3] and indeed in many ways the Soviet state was better prepared than most for such a strategy with thirty years' experience of the political control of culture. Yet we should not forget that during World War Two Soviet cultural policy had been considerably relaxed, with many assuming that the liberalization would continue after victory.[4] The post-war crackdown was undoubtedly related directly to the imperatives of the Cold War, which confronted others, including America and Britain, all of whom had to face the prospect of mobilizing war-weary populations against a distinctly intangible foe.[5] Secondly, the study also points towards the existence of an ongoing 'dialogue' between the USSR and the West, and more particularly the USA. The Soviet Union continued to borrow American ideas and adapt them for their own purposes, confirming Major and Mitter's hypothesis 'that there was perhaps more interaction between East and West than the finality of the Iron Curtain would suggest'.[6]

If, as some have argued, the Cold War was presented as a cultural and ideological battle, as a contest of values,[7] then cinema was surely one of the key battlefields. By the 1940s film technology, especially sound and colour, was becoming increasingly sophisticated, making films ever more attractive to pre-television era audiences. Because films had the potential to reach huge domestic and international audiences, a flourishing film industry was a matter of prestige for both the main combatants in the Cold War. In the post-war years the Soviet leadership became possibly more preoccupied by cinema matters than ever before or after (ironically this coincided with the *malokartin'e*, or dearth of films – the period from the mid-1940s until Stalin's death when Soviet film production fell to dramatically low levels[8]). The most notorious example of leadership 'concern' in this period came in the form of the Central Committee resolution of 4 September 1946 which savaged four films: Lukov's *Bol'shaia zhizn'* (A Great Life) part 2, Eisenstein's *Ivan Groznyi* (Ivan the Terrible) part 2, Kozintsev and Trauberg's *Prostye Liudi* (Simple People) and Pudovkin's *Admiral Nakhimov* – with devastating repercussions for the industry as a whole.[9] This article will focus on the story of *Admiral Nakhimov*, which, unlike the other three films, survived the critique, even going on to win a prestigious Stalin Prize after its release in 1947.

The story of the making of the film, and of its survival, cannot be fully understood without an appreciation of contemporary Soviet thinking on cinema and its role. The first section of the study is therefore devoted to an exploration of the origins and development of Soviet ideas of, to paraphrase Tony Shaw, the importance of film as a weapon in the emerging Cold War.[10] In this respect, the USSR's relationship with Hollywood was crucial. The USSR was engaged in a permanent 'dialogue' with American cinema, which served as a primary point of reference and a source of self-definition. The wartime alliance had seen considerable interchange between Soviet cinema and Hollywood, with the Soviets often aspiring to emulate the Americans. However, with the growing sense of an ideological war from the end of 1945, the Soviet leadership attempted to turn away from the hugely influential American model towards a national cinema capable of attracting those disenchanted with American cultural hegemony. Yet there remained an ambiguity in Soviet perceptions: even as they aspired to a distinctive national cinema (framed in Russian as much as Soviet terms), they continued to define their own cinema in terms of the powerful American model. In this context, it should be no surprise that Zhdanov and others explicitly described *Admiral Nakhimov* as the Soviet counterpart to Alexander Korda's wartime epic about Lord Nelson, *Lady Hamilton* (1941).[11]

The Context: Soviet Cinema and Hollywood from World War to Cold War

Cooperation and Competition in the Second World War

The uneasy wartime military alliance was mirrored by a similarly ambivalent relationship between Soviet cinema and Hollywood characterized by both wary cooperation and a sense of acute competition. In this period the USSR was exposed to American cinema to a degree unprecedented since the late 1920s.[12] Although the Hollywood model had exerted a strong hold over the Soviet film industry in the 1930s with the establishment of the 'Red star' system, the creation of Grigorii Aleksandrov's musicals, and Boris Shumiatskii's plans to build a Soviet Hollywood in Crimea,[13] American cinema itself had generally been dismissed as bourgeois, and very few American films were actually shown in the USSR.[14] During the war, they enjoyed a partial rehabilitation. For instance, in August 1942 as the USSR desperately sought the opening of a Second Front, the Kinokomitet (Committee for Cinema Affairs – the state body which ran the Soviet film industry) and VOKS (All-Union Society for Cultural Relations with Foreign Countries) organized a conference on 'The War and the Cinema of the Allied Countries' at which speaker after speaker acknowledged their debts to American cinema and portrayed it in a democratic light. Eisenstein, for example, described American cinema as 'of the people, by the people, for the people'.[15] In this period Soviet delegations visited Hollywood to study the American experience and there was a new openness towards American films, some of which were shown in the USSR, including, of course, Hollywood Russophile epics such as *Mission to Moscow* (1943).[16] The Soviet leadership also expressed interest in producing films which might appeal to American audiences.[17] Film was regarded partly as a way of promoting greater understanding between the two countries as well as a means of exporting Soviet ideological values.

There was clearly a sense amongst at least some of the filmmaking establishment – leading directors and creative workers as well as party and state officials involved in running the film industry – that this spirit of cooperation would continue after the war, that film could be used as a medium for encouraging international peace. In May 1945 Pudovkin argued that during the war the 'cultured people' of the world had united to defeat the general enemy, and that after the war 'the advanced progressive sections of various nationalities' would want to develop this *rapprochement*. He suggested that cinema could play a great role in this process and that it was necessary to make films which could reach wide audiences, in the same way that silent movies had done in the past.[18] Director Mikhail Romm shared this understanding. Looking back from the rather different perspective of late 1946, he recalled this period as one in which creative workers believed that there would be quite a long period of peace, and that as Soviet films would be shown in the West, they should be intelligible to and popular with westerners. He believed that there had even been a special directive to this effect.[19] It is certainly true that several Soviet films of this period, such as *Bliznetsy* (Twins, 1945), *Bespokoinoe khoziaistvo* (Anxious Management, 1946) and *Nebesnyi tikhokhod* (The Celestial Sloth, 1945), exhibit characteristics more typically associated with Hollywood – a lightness of tone, humour and a focus on relationships and private life.

However this spirit of *rapprochement* with Hollywood always coexisted with a more competitive tendency. In 1944 the Soviet Union was already concerned about post-war competition for world, and particularly European cinema markets. Mikhail Kalatozov, the Kinokomitet's representative in the USA, produced a report in April

1944 which analyzed the future influence of the USA upon international markets. His report highlighted American ambitions to monopolize these markets, including that of the Soviet Union, and noted that the Americans were already embarking upon a large-scale programme of dubbing films for European countries. In this period American ambitions tended to be understood in narrowly economic terms – Kalatozov suggested that the film studios and financiers were motivated primarily by the desire to maximize their profits.[20]

Clearly some felt that the USSR must respond to what Kalatozov, using a characteristically military metaphor, described as this 'cinematographical attack' led by Hollywood. In particular, the head of the Kinokomitet, Ivan Bol'shakov, could not ignore the opportunity simultaneously to promote his institutional interests. In May 1944 he alerted Molotov to the fact that the British and Americans were preparing to show films in liberated Europe.[21] He reiterated this at a meeting with film-workers in June arguing that along with the Allies, the Soviet Union must also take the initiative to show Europeans 'the truth for which our people struggled'.[22] On the eve of victory, in April 1945, an important meeting was convened by the Central Committee to discuss how to improve the work of the film studios of the Soviet republics. In his introductory speech to the meeting, Bol'shakov stated even more emphatically that the Soviet Union must compete with Hollywood. He informed the assembled audience of directors, screen-writers and others connected with the industry that the USSR must increase its level of production from the current rate of 35–40 films per year to 60, primarily in order to compete on the world cinema market, and he specifically mentioned the popularity of Soviet films in many European countries, especially the Balkans. Bol'shakov presented this new line as a response to American initiatives: 'American papers write openly that after the war there'll be great competition between American and Soviet film industries.' Like Kalatozov, Bol'shakov suggested that the Americans were motivated by commercial interests, while for the Soviet Union it was a political issue: 'We have to strengthen our influence through cinema.'[23]

The discussion which followed Bol'shakov's speech is interesting, revealing the range of Soviet perspectives on Hollywood in this period. There are echoes in the debate of the discussions of the 1920s between 'cinema-westernizers', who favoured learning from the hugely popular American movies, and their opponents, who regarded them as a malign influence.[24] While many of those present were full of admiration for American achievements, others were much keener to minimize their successes and to promote a distinctive national approach. Some participants openly praised Hollywood – its ability to produce several hundred films every year, its superior technology, its professionalism, its more rational organization, and the quality of its actors. Many at the meeting obviously felt they could learn from the American experience, indeed that they would have to learn if they were to keep up. Romm argued that although currently the Soviet Union was very fashionable, this would pass in a couple of years, and unless there was a serious change in the structure of and investment in the Soviet film industry, there would be no chance of competing with the USA.[25] While some of those who praised Hollywood were also quick to defend the ideological superiority of Soviet films, a few rejected any kind of 'abasement' before the US. The Georgian director M. Chiaureli, who became one of the chief architects of the Stalin cult in movies, attacked all this 'grovelling before American cinema ... I don't like bragging. The great Stalin said that a devil is never as terrible as when people pray to him, and we need films of quality, and as far as quality is concerned, some of ours were literally as good as the American ones if not better.'[26]

In this period the quite strident anti-Americanism of Chiaureli was far from universal. During the last years of war and its immediate aftermath Soviet perceptions of American cinema were relatively positive, characterized by some cooperation and a desire to learn from the American experience, as well as by a growing sense of competition. At this stage the Americans' desire to monopolize world film markets was usually understood in economic terms rather than as part of a grand strategy for ideological hegemony. However with the escalation of tension between the two sides towards the end of 1945 a new discourse of 'ideological war' developed in which the views of those like Chiaureli came to predominate. In this period the Soviet Union increasingly began to represent the American threat in ideological terms and to develop a more coherent notion of ideological counter-attack based on the superiority of Soviet national morality.

Mobilizing for Ideological War

On 9 February 1946 Stalin made his famous election speech, which, although certainly not a declaration of war as it was interpreted in some American circles, did appear to hint at a hardening foreign policy line. Stalin continued to refer to the Allies as 'freedom-loving'; however he also reaffirmed the superiority of the Soviet system and suggested that war was a logical consequence of capitalism.[27] Within the Soviet Union the speech does indeed seem to have marked a turning point, coinciding as it did with deteriorating US–Soviet relations and also the growing Soviet perception of an ideological attack from the West. From the end of 1945 Sovinformburo (Soviet Information Bureau) had been reporting constantly on the 'Anglo-American propaganda attack' directed at both Eastern and Western Europe, much of which was based on criticism of Soviet foreign and domestic policy. As V. Pechatnov points out, although this attack was ostensibly the work of private media organizations rather than governments, in Soviet eyes all the leading media were viewed as to some degree dependent on governments.[28]

While in 1946 the Soviet Union did not appear to be fanning the flames of ideological war in public,[29] in private the tone was becoming more belligerent. Following Stalin's 9 February speech the language of 'ideological war' soon started to be promulgated within the film industry, and with it the vilification of American film. One of the last organized demonstrations of approval for Hollywood was a meeting of the cinema section of VOKS on 13 February held to discuss the work of John Ford. Among the contributions to this meeting was a speech by the influential director Ivan Py'rev, who praised Ford's work, arguing that such films as *How Green Was My Valley* and *The Grapes of Wrath* raised universal human values.[30] However, a week later, when the Kinokomitet's Artistic Council (*khudozhestvennyi sovet*) – a group of directors, creative workers, and political figures set up in 1944 to oversee film production[31] – met to discuss the 1947 plan for film scenarios, a new more militant tone was in evidence among some of its members. General Talenskii referred explicitly to 'the ideological front', arguing that the USSR must approach the West skilfully and subtly, and present herself as victor, saying 'Follow this path, win victory this way!' He added that the Soviets had a great advantage in their art, and that they should show it to the world.[32] Py'rev continued to applaud John Ford, arguing that they should not be 'red patriots' and reject everything positive and interesting about US cinema, such as Ford's films, but it was clear that he was now on the defensive, and that 'red patriotism' was rapidly becoming the new state orthodoxy.[33]

At this Artistic Council meeting and at a subsequent meeting devoted to discussing Stalin's speech held by the party organization of the Kinokomitet on 5 March (the same day as Churchill's Fulton speech), Bol'shakov and others made it clear that a new *dirigiste* approach was required in the light of Stalin's pronouncements.

Bol'shakov interpreted Stalin's speech as implying that the war was
far from over, arguing that cinema had a role to play in developing 'a
sense of patriotism, a sense of courage and bravery in the battle for
the motherland'. He called for greater concentration on the
ideological aspect of films, and gave precise instructions about the
kinds of themes which were necessary. Films were now required to
show the superiority of the Soviet order over bourgeois democracy.
The powerful weapon of cinema could no longer be wasted on
entertainment films.[34]

The new strategic importance of cinema as a key weapon in the
ideological war was affirmed by the creation of an entire Ministry of
Cinematography (MK), decreed by a CPSU (Communist Party of the
Soviet Union) plenum on 14 March 1946. In Stalin's words, a
Ministry was necessary because cinema 'is a very great matter in the
sense of propaganda and agitation. It's a hugely important matter ...
No radio, nor press can speak as films can.'[35] The creation of the
Ministry signalled the start of escalating state intervention. In April
1946 Zhdanov called a meeting of film-workers to 'discuss' the 1946
thematic plan for films, at which he announced the exclusion of some
'unnecessary' themes (historical films, especially those about the non-
Russian republics, screen adaptations of classic novels) and the
introduction of new 'useful' subjects. Zhdanov confirmed that the
central task of cinema was now propaganda rather than
entertainment, and that this could be achieved through more careful
planning: 'Our plan should have a clearly expressed propagandistic
character: to propagandise and confirm those characteristics of
Soviet people that we need to develop and inculcate at the moment.'[36]

Zhdanov was a key spokesman for this line, but its inspiration was
Stalin who had a strong personal interest in film, and who was
evidently now particularly sensitive to the impact of Soviet film
abroad. In a speech to the Orgburo (Organisational Bureau) on 9
August he lambasted three films: Eisenstein's *Ivan Groznyi* part 2,
Pudovkin's *Admiral Nakhimov* and Lukov's *Bol'shaia zhizn'* part 2.
The films were criticized for distorting history, and, in the case of
Bol'shaia zhizn', for depicting the Soviet Union as backward and
Russians engaged in excessive drinking, dancing, and singing of gypsy
songs, rather than working. Stalin stressed that directors had a duty to
project the correct image of Russia's past and its Soviet present, partly
because these films would be shown internationally – 'the eyes of the
world' would be upon them.[37] The Central Committee resolution of 4
September mentioned above (p.50) followed shortly after this.

Over the course of 1946 the role of filmmaker was thus increasingly defined as one of state servant in the ideological war. How did the professionals respond to the new measures? Although in February it was still possible for directors such as Pudovkin and Aleksandrov to speak out against the policy of ideological directives from above, and to criticize the absence of discussion about the artistic aspects of film,[38] following Stalin's intervention most appear to have publicly endorsed the new line. For example, at an Artistic Council meeting on 22 August, the director Sergei Gerasimov declared that the central aim of all creative work should be to help the state in its domestic and foreign policy. Konstantin Simonov reported from his recent travels in the USA that probably the world had never seen such an intense ideological conflict as that currently taking place – 'a real ideological war which is developing in the biggest and the smallest matters, every day and every hour'. According to Simonov artists should be constantly aware of this intense war, and 'mobilise all [their] spiritual, physical and creative forces for this most severe war of ideas which [was] taking place throughout the world'.[39]

Soviet Morality and the Ideological War

But just how was the USSR to win this war of ideas? What messages should Soviet film project? An overriding preoccupation throughout the many discussions held in 1946 was the need for film to highlight the moral superiority of Russian/Soviet man over his American counterpart. Rather than just an economic or geopolitical battle, the Cold War was to be presented above all as a contest of moral values. Russian/Soviet socialist morality was to be credited with producing a new, more noble kind of person and a more humane civilization; the Soviet victory over fascism was confirmation of the superiority of its moral values. As Zhdanov expressed it at the April meeting: 'The point is not to be ashamed to introduce into films those ideas which we consider necessary to transmit to the Soviet public. We don't have any reason to be ashamed of our ideology, and from the point of view of moral ideology we sustained victory.'[40]

Soviet morality was defined in explicit opposition to what were perceived as American moral values, particularly those allegedly glorified in American films, such as sex, violence, lawlessness and materialism. Thus when Chiaureli criticized colleagues who turned up to watch American films at Dom Kino (House of Cinema) he particularly attacked those films which showed 'flibbertigibbets', with 'sexy little songs, with young girls ... with shaped eyebrows'.[41]

Zhdanov attacked the violence and lawlessness of an American cowboy film which made no real distinction between the bandits and the sheriffs and judges: 'The judge and sheriff, in general terms, are not quite assistants, not quite best friends of the bandits.' He suggested that the point of the film was clearly to show smart guys, but that a Soviet viewer would feel pity for the judge who was under the thumb of not only the bandit but also the sheriff, who was portrayed as a crook in this so-called civilized country. 'Where's the civilization here?', asked Zhdanov. In his view, American 'civilization' was based on crude materialism, which he contrasted with Soviet morality: 'In America you can buy everything – women, the title of mayor, respect ... We are ashamed to preach to our country and the world the most progressive ideas of humanity, the blood-stained truth.'[42]

Pyr'ev was equally adamant that as Soviet films would be shown abroad they should display the correct image of Soviet morality in order to attract sympathizers. Unlike Zhdanov and Chiaureli, he argued that American films often propagated an image of the American way of life as very appealing, an image which did not correspond to the reality of most Americans' existence. He even advocated learning from American experience:

> Look how skilfully they agitate to the world with their films, how thoughtfully they propagandise their ideas! Take any American film ... the people in it are courageous, noble, exalted, pure ... But is it really the case that the mass of American people are like that? No – far from it. Over there there are more smart operators, brokers, pharmacists. People of small souls, greedy for profit, free-and-easy, boorish. Only take Byrnes who virtually puts his feet on the table when he's chairing the Paris peace conference! And I assure you that these people do not have the great internal culture and nobility of soul which our people have. Look at the screen! How great the standard American 'hero' is! How noble he is when poor ... how 'simple' when rich, how nicely he talks to girls, how finely he kisses ... and you think: 'My God! What rare human examples of humankind live in that America!' And that's what everyone who watches American films thinks.

Py'rev went on to argue that while the Americans were propagating this image of the noble American, Soviet films tended to portray their protagonists as morally dissipated: 'a bit drunk, out-of-control, boorish, rude, unthinking'. In films such as *Bespokoinoe khoziaistvo* or *Nebesnyi tikhokhod* Soviet man was shown stuffing himself with pancakes and dancing in a repulsive way; in *Bol'shaia zhizn'* drinking and behaving rudely; in *Prostye liudi* being too familiar with comrades and older people, without respect for noble feelings. Py'rev maintained that at a time of ideological struggle when reactionaries were trying to portray Soviet people as wild, uncultured and boorish people, it was surely wrong for Soviet filmmakers to present them in this light too. He also pointed out that when foreign critics commented on Russian films they observed that: 'Russians are good at dying, they work hard and self-sacrificially, that's their elementalism (*stikhiinost'*). But clearly noble feelings, elevated human culture, duty, friendship and love are alien to them.' Or they wrote that Russians were good at depicting mass scenes, revolution, and elementalism, as in Eisenstein's films, or labour as in Vertov's. They could show the hatred and heroism of their people, but they could not show elevated human feelings, nobility of thought.[43]

Pyr'ev suggested that filmmakers learn not only from the Americans, but also from the example of Russian and Soviet writers who portrayed great images of Russian people. This idea of a national cinema drawing on the classics of Russian literature and their posing of moral questions had earlier been proposed at the April 1946 meeting with Zhdanov by the writer V.A. Solov'ev who argued that Russian cinema should follow a different path from Hollywood. Russian art from Pushkin, Dostoevsky and Tolstoy had always focused on penetrating the profundities of human nature and Soviet cinema should try to approach this tradition to create a Russian national cinema (*kino russkogo naroda*).[44] In this respect there was at least a partial convergence of interests between filmmakers such as Pyr'ev who were keen to promote Russian cultural values, and party and military leaders such as Zhdanov and Galaktionov who were primarily intent on strengthening the power of the Soviet socialist state.

In this period Soviet cinema underwent a process of redefining itself and its role. The wartime *rapprochement* with Hollywood was jettisoned as film came to be regarded as a political weapon in the emerging Cold War. As part of this process Soviet cinema quite deliberately tried to distance itself from the Hollywood model. It was to be a cinema characterized by a high moral seriousness and drawing inspiration from the Russian classics. The accent on morality was more pronounced in Soviet propaganda than it had been before the war, partly because in this very international fight for the allegiance of the European peoples in particular, the issue of morality was not insignificant. After all this was a period in which anti-Americanism was quite rife in Europe, and when some European intellectuals were vocal critics of what they perceived as the shallow, crass materialism of American culture.[45] From the Soviet perspective, by claiming the moral high ground they imagined they might win over those disenchanted with the 'American way' more successfully than if they had simply focused on the economic and political advantages of Soviet socialism. As Py'rev had noticed, the Soviets were not alone in this presentation of the ideological war in terms of a moral contest. The Americans were of course equally concerned to present attractive moral messages. As the Motion Pictures Producers' Association head, Eric Johnston, told screenwriters in 1946: 'We'll have no more *Grapes of Wrath*, we'll have no more *Tobacco Roads*, we'll have no more films that deal with the seamy side of American life. We'll have no more films that treat the banker as a villain.'[46] In the early years of the Cold War both sides used cinema to sell their moral messages to domestic and international audiences.

Pudovkin's *Admiral Nakhimov*

One of the first Soviet films to be affected by the new climate of ideological war was Pudovkin's *Admiral Nakhimov*, which was conceived in 1943, but did not appear on public screens until January 1947. The idea for a film about Nakhimov, one of Russia's great Admirals who led the Russian fleet to victory over the Turks at the battle of Sinope (1853), and presided over the defence of Sevastopol until his death in 1855, was a logical stage in the development of Soviet wartime propaganda. The cult of Russian heroes in film had begun even before the war, with epics devoted to Aleksandr Nevskii, Peter the Great, and Suvorov. This trend continued during the war, especially from 1943 with *Kutuzov* (1943) and *Ivan Groznyi* part 1 (1944). In 1943 a new Order of Nakhimov was instituted, and *Admiral Nakhimov* was one of ten proposed historical and biographical themes included on 13 August 1943 in the Kinokomitet's thematic plan of films to be commenced in 1943–44.[47] On 14 August the committee's Scenario Studio agreed that work on the script should be maximally speeded up, and that the scriptwriter, Konstantin Paustovskii, should be consulted on his progress.[48]

Paustovskii obviously had problems with the script – several sources confirm that he found little of interest in Nakhimov's biography. It was then given to Igor' Lukovskii, author of a 1939 play about Nakhimov. He produced various versions of the script, and with considerable assistance from Pudovkin, a final version was agreed and published in 1944. In October 1944 Pudovkin began filming. The first complete version of the film was ready in early 1945, and in January the Artistic Council recommended that it be released. Then, after a series of interventions from on high – a CPSU Secretariat decree in May followed by Stalin's August speech – the film was fundamentally reworked and completed towards the end of that year.

The Hero and Villain in Nakhimov

Because of its political sensitivity, the film was subjected to quite close monitoring even before 1946. Particular attention was paid, first, to the representation of Nakhimov and secondly, the portrayal of the international conflict and image of the enemy. A debate quickly emerged on how to represent Nakhimov. As Paustovskii had discovered, he was a difficult character to represent artistically. Single, with little or no private life, he was entirely devoted to his work. But unlike Suvorov, for example, he had only one victory – Sinope. Lukovskii's approach was to reveal the human side of Nakhimov through his interactions with a variety of other people: sailors, officers, women and children. In the early versions he comes across as democratic – enjoying friendly, informal relations with people from a range of backgrounds. He behaves paternally, not only with his many godchildren, but also with his sailors. He encourages relationships between an officer, Burunov, and Tania, the daughter of a retired Captain Lavrov, and between Vassa – a sailor's widow's daughter – and the popular sailor Koshka. The inclusion of women (and the private sphere they represented) in a scenario for a film of this type was in itself quite a striking new departure. Most of the recent historical-biographical films had ignored this aspect   – *Kutuzov* and *Suvorov* contained no female roles.

Even at this stage, the excessive democracy and familiarity (*panibratstvo*) of Nakhimov and the stress on the private sphere was criticized. A consultant, Sergeev-Tsenskii, found Lukovskii's Nakhimov too vulgar.[49] Mosfil'm's direction advised that Nakhimov should not be depicted as too familiar and undisciplined with his subordinates, that the Vassa–Koshka story was unsuccessful, and that the rather saccharine depictions of his involvement in weddings, christenings and so forth could be reduced.[50] In the scenario revised by Pudovkin and Lukovskii some of these criticisms were addressed, for example the Vassa plot was removed. However the 'human element' which Pudovkin and Lukovskii both considered so important was retained. Several times in 1944–45 Pudovkin justified the stress on the human angle, at the expense of showing Sevastopol more fully. He argued that it was important to show the Admiral's humanity, his fatherly qualities. Nakhimov's humanity was part of his greatness – he cared about strategy, but he also cared about the everyday problems of his people. This was what made him a Russian patriot.[51]

This understanding of what constituted a great Russian leader was bound to be controversial. Unlike their Hollywood equivalents, Soviet biographical films rarely encroached upon their heroes' everyday lives and relationships. However, the more relaxed wartime climate and the influence of American films evidently encouraged Lukovskii and Pudovkin to take this unusual step. By 1945, such an approach was encountering growing disapproval from the authorities. At a meeting of the Artistic Council on 5 April 1945, while some of its members supported the decision to show Nakhimov as a human being, including the actor Okhlopkov, who argued that Shakespearean heroes are great because they are multi-faceted, and that it was equally important to show Nakhimov's personal life,[52] others disagreed. Among them was *Pravda*'s military editor, General Galaktionov, who insisted that the focus should be on Nakhimov as Admiral. According to the General, to show him as a patriot it was not necessary to show his complex psychology and so on – it was more important to emphasize his power. Bol'shakov too maintained that he wanted more of the Admiral and less of the man. Betraying the inescapable influence of Hollywood on Soviet thinking, he stated quite explicitly that the film should be different from its Hollywood equivalent, Korda's *Lady Hamilton* (1941), which focused on Nelson's private life.[53] It is significant that, despite these criticisms, Pudovkin was still relatively free to develop his own interpretation at this stage. Only in 1946 did a much firmer line emerge.

The other big controversy concerned the international conflict and the image of the enemy. How much attention was to be paid to the historical context – the conflict with Turkey and the Western powers over Russia's influence in the Black Sea and Turkish straits? In the earliest versions, foreign policy was present rather as a backdrop – its significance and the nature of the enemy seem to have been kept deliberately vague, given the wartime alliance, and the importance of not offending allies and potential allies. In the 1941 version of Lukovskii's original play, the enemy was defined as the

Turks lined up with the British and French.[54] Likewise the first of Lukovskii's versions of the film script from 1943 identified the British as backing Turkey. However, this script also included a lot of admiration for British naval prowess, and pointed praise for Lord Nelson – Nakhimov was even described as the Russian Lord Nelson.[55]

By 1944 the climate had changed again, with the opening of the Second Front. There appears to have been a deliberate decision to keep the British out of the film. In Lukovskii's 1944 revised version of the play, the enemy was always depicted as French.[56] So too in the 1944 published film scenario, the British were barely mentioned, and the attack on Sevastopol came from a vague 'numerous enemy' or 'huge enemy fleet'. From time to time the French substituted for the British. The Turks were mentioned but only briefly. In a conversation between Nakhimov and a group of old sailors it was observed that Russia and Turkey had fought many times, and they should now realize that they should not be conspiring with others, but live in peace and friendship with Russia.[57] But the general lack of a convincing foreign policy context was striking. This approach was criticized by director Yu. Raizman at a meeting of the Mosfil'm Artistic Council in June 1944. Wondering why the film did not explain why the British and French had attacked Russia and laid siege to Sevastopol, he surmised, no doubt correctly: 'Perhaps it's a bit of bashfulness, that France and Britain were once our enemies on the Black Sea.'[58]

The War Scare and its Impact

As we have seen, throughout its making, the film was subject to constant discussion and intervention, although the director continued to exercise considerable discretion in his interpretation. In 1946, as the film was complete, this intervention reached the highest levels, namely the Secretariat and Stalin himself. Changing international circumstances completely altered the leadership's attitude to the film, which now became caught up in the first 'war scare' of the emerging US–Soviet conflict, the conflict over the Turkish Straits.[59] From 1945 the Soviets had begun pushing for a revision of the 1936 Montreux Convention on the neutrality of the Straits, for joint Soviet-Turkish defence of the Straits and for cession to the USSR of Kars and Ardahan (once conquered by Tsarist Russia and ceded by Lenin to Atatürk in 1922). They got nowhere with this, but in 1946 tried to intimidate Turkey and the West by amassing troops in areas bordering on Turkey. The USA, mindful of the Iran crisis, feared possible Soviet invasion. Matters reached a head in

August, when the USA sent warships to the Eastern Mediterranean. In September the Soviets appeared to be concentrating more troops in the Balkans, but then Stalin seemed to back down, without abandoning the principle of his claims.

Against this backdrop, the film assumed even greater political significance. The contemporary relevance of Russian ambitions to control the Straits and of Turkey's manipulation by Western powers depicted in *Admiral Nakhimov* was self-evident. Although the Artistic Council had recommended that the film come out in its current form in January 1946, a different line evidently emerged from within the Soviet leadership sometime between February and April. It is possible that Stalin saw the film, as he saw all films before their general release, and demanded changes.[60] At his 26 April meeting with film-workers, Stalin's spokesman Zhdanov, while criticizing the excessive number of historical films in the 1946 plan, did nevertheless defend the usefulness of *Nakhimov*, while also stressing that it would require substantially reworking. Once again the film was compared explicitly with *Lady Hamilton*: 'It will be one of the best films and in order that it will be our *Lady Hamilton*, it's best that it should be reworked so that it's a masterpiece. *Admiral Nakhimov* has the chance of being finished in such a way that it can stand on a level with the classic productions of Soviet cinematography.'[61]

In April Pudovkin and Lukovskii produced a plan of four additional scenes, which were sent to Molotov on 17 April by the Agitprop Department along with a draft decree on the reworking of the film. He sent it to the Orgburo, who confirmed the draft and forwarded it to Stalin on 8 May. Stalin approved it,[62] paving the way for the Secretariat to issue the decree on 11 May.[63] The devotion of an entire decree to the film is indicative of its unusually great importance. The decree criticized several aspects of the film, particularly its failure to pay sufficient attention to issues of military and foreign policy, and it specified necessary changes based in part on the Pudovkin/Lukovskii proposals. There was to be much greater emphasis on the battle of Sinope and its impact, and on the defence of Sevastopol and Admiral Nakhimov's role within it. Clear injunctions were given about the portrayal of the Turks and the British.

Even as Pudovkin was working on these changes the film was dealt another crushing blow by Stalin himself in his Orgburo speech of 9 August. At the height of the war scare over the Straits, Stalin accused Pudovkin of resting on his laurels, of not taking the film sufficiently seriously, of focusing 'on trifles, a few paper boats and dances, meetings, episodes to amuse the viewer'. He said: 'It's not actually a film about Nakhimov, but a film about any old thing, with some episodes about Nakhimov.' Stalin, obviously concerned about the international impact of the film, and the messages it transmitted about Russia and the Soviet Union, referred to Pudovkin's 'unconscientious attitude to work, to a work which will be demonstrated throughout all the world'.[64]

Pudovkin made the necessary revisions. The interpretation of Nakhimov was completely revised. The focus shifted from Nakhimov as a man to Nakhimov as an Admiral, issuing orders, taking decisions, educating and inspiring. Unlike those around him he was always a calm presence, sometimes shown smoking a pipe. The personal stories in which Nakhimov was involved were completely eliminated. The scenes with godchildren and the whole Tania-Burunov story were excised. Indeed, all female roles were eliminated. The entire cast was now male (apart from a few crowd scenes in which women figured). This was consistent with the new stress on serious matters of state. Women were identified with a 'soft' private sphere, which had no place in the hard male world of politics and war. 'Trivial' scenes, such as a ball scene, could not be entirely removed, but were relegated to the background.

These changes allowed more space for concentration on the required military and political aspects. Much more attention was paid to the battle of Sinope and its effects, and many new scenes of fighting in Sevastopol were introduced to highlight the bravery and determination of the Russians. The Turks were depicted more concretely, shown as 'backward' – naïve and religious, and under the influence of the real culprits – the British. A new scene showed the Turkish Admiral Osman-Pasha's speech before the battle of Sinope in which he claimed that Allah had ordained that they should be masters of this land and quoted the Koran. Throughout the speech, he was carefully watched by the British Captain Slade. At the start of the battle, two British officers were shown on the Turkish boat. They passed on advice from Slade, and asked in cowardly fashion if they could leave for Slade's boat. Osman-Pasha refused this request, claiming he needed their advice.

After Sinope, the Turks were portrayed primarily as victims. One scene depicted Russian sailors rescuing Turkish civilians from a burning Sinope. A wounded but noble Osman-Pasha was brought to Nakhimov, who behaved very graciously towards him. In turn Osman-Pasha asked that the Russian sailors who rescued the Turks be rewarded and contrasted the attitude of the Russians with that of his

so-called British 'friend' Slade who had abandoned him. At this point
Nakhimov made it quite clear who his real friends were, saying that
Turkey had been betrayed, and that throughout history as long as she
had maintained good relations with Russia things had gone well.

The real enemies were now identified unambiguously as the
British who manipulated the Turks at Sinope, and, along with the
French and the Turks, laid siege to Sevastopol. They were cowardly
and perfidious and objects of derision. When captured by the
Russians, the two British advisers (dressed in Turkish uniforms)
demanded that they should not be treated as prisoners since they
were serving in the British fleet, and had just happened to be on the
Turkish boat! One of them then reappeared during the battle for
Sevastopol – this time he was made to look ridiculous – captured by
the popular hero Koshka in a basket and rolled down a hill before
being presented wild and dishevelled to an amused Nakhimov.

In a further new scene of a conversation between a French
General and Lord Raglan, Raglan was depicted as ill and ineffectual.
The Anglo-French alliance was clearly under strain, and Raglan
fainted when the French General became hysterical about his
defeatist response to the Russians' brave defence of Sevastopol. This
innuendo about the instability of foreign alliances would not have
been lost at this stage of the Cold War. The film contained nothing of
the earlier admiration of British naval prowess. Instead, Raglan was
depicted praising the Russians' fighting abilities and calling Russia a
'great nation'.

Reception

The result of these revisions was almost an entirely new film. As
Romm pointed out at a meeting of the Artistic Council, whilst earlier
versions had focused on Nakhimov's relations with other secondary
characters, in this it was the Turks, English and French against
Nakhimov. Romm and some other members of the Council expressed
support for the changes which they thought had made the film much
more relevant to current political concerns in the region. Not
surprisingly Galaktionov was pleased that Nakhimov was now
portrayed primarily as an Admiral.[65] But the response of other
Council members was not entirely enthusiastic (it is noteworthy that
even at the end of 1946 genuine disagreements and discussions
among Council members still continued). The writer Leonov and the
actor who played Nakhimov, Dikii, argued that the human stories –
Tanya and Burunov, the scene between Nakhimov and the child –

should remain. Py'rev also thought that the latter should be retained since it served to warm the image of the Admiral. Aleksandrov complained that the captured Osman-Pasha was shown as too noble and disliked the implication that 'The Turks were good little boys, and it was the bastard British who wormed their way into this affair. Maybe it was a bit like that, but I would not like to see the Turks as more sympathetic than they deserve'.[66] Yu. Raizman criticized the new version for having too much in common with the contemporary situation – he felt that a sense of historicism should have been maintained.[67]

What about the general public? Did all these changes have the required effect? Did audiences view the films in the way they were intended to, focusing on the foreign policy issues and their contemporary significance, and on Nakhimov as Admiral? Unfortunately we have little evidence of audience reactions. What is clear is that large numbers did see the film. Over a million viewers went to see it in Moscow when it was released in January 1947 which made it the most popular adult film of the first half of the year (the second most popular was a German 'trophy' film, *Girl of My Dreams*, which attracted 900,000 viewers).[68]

Published reviews can perhaps capture something of wider audience reactions and the early reviews of the film are particularly interesting in this respect. Several did in fact focus on what remained of the multi-faceted image of Nakhimov and his relationships, and the bravery of the soldiers and sailors, while almost ignoring the foreign policy significance of the film.[69] This was criticized sharply in *Pravda* of 6 January in a response to a review in *Krasnaia zvezda* on 4 January. The *Pravda* article, primarily the work of Galaktionov, accused the reviewer of failing to highlight the identity of the enemies – it referred only to the Turkish fleet, not the Anglo-French coalition, appearing to ignore the fact of British aggression. It also ignored the military aspects of Nakhimov – rather than as a great Russian Admiral, he was described as a 'man of a bright soul', like a 'good daddy' in relation to his subordinates. His military, patriotic qualities, his sense of duty, his role as an outstanding teacher and leader who could be harsh and demanding when circumstances dictated were ignored by *Krasnaia zvezda*.[70] After *Pravda* had presented this official interpretation, all subsequent reviews toed the line, including a new review printed by *Krasnaia zvezda*. However, it is possible that like the early reviewers, many ordinary viewers continued to ignore the Cold War significance of the film.[71]

With increasing tensions between the Soviet Union and their former allies over the course of 1945–46, attitudes towards the role of Soviet cinema underwent significant revision. As films came to be regarded as powerful weapons in what was understood to be a new global *war of ideas*, the notion of a national cinema quite distinct from Hollywood in its tone and preoccupations was promoted not only by party-state officials, but also by some directors themselves. Soviet films were now to focus on profound themes and to project the superiority of Soviet morality. The making of *Admiral Nakhimov* illustrates this evolution in Soviet attitudes towards film. If in 1944, and even in 1945, Pudovkin was able to pursue his own particular interpretation of Nakhimov, by 1946 the film had become a matter of the highest state importance, subject to detailed interventions from even Stalin himself. *Nakhimov* had to be virtually remade to resonate with contemporary foreign policy concerns. In the process it abandoned most of its Hollywood-like features, and acquired a suitably serious high moral tone.

The development of Soviet thinking on the role of cinema after 1945 was obviously not determined exclusively by the imperatives of Cold War. Since 1917, the Bolsheviks had sought to control culture. However the extent of this control, and the form it took, varied from period to period. The war saw significant liberalization, which might have continued but for the escalation in tension between the USA and the USSR. The new more interventionist policy obviously had precedents in recent Soviet history, but it also had parallels with developments in the West, where governments, especially the American government, were concerned about their reputations abroad, and adopted similarly interventionist measures: prescribing the content of movies, refusing export licences to 'un-American' films and so on.[72] More systematic comparative research will shed further light on the similarities and differences of these measures, and will help us not only to understand better trans-national tendencies in the culture of the Cold War, but also to reinterpret post-war Soviet cultural history itself.

NOTES

1. See Patrick Major and Rana Mitter in the Introduction to this volume.
2. Peter Holquist, '"Information is the Alpha and Omega of Our Work": Bolshevik Surveillance in its Pan-European Context', *Journal of Modern History* 69/3 (1997); David Hoffman, 'Mothers in the Motherland: Stalinist Pronatalism in its Pan-European Context', *Journal of Social History* 34/1 (1999); Stephen Kotkin, 'Modern Times: The Soviet Union and the Inter-war Conjuncture', *Kritika* 2/1 (2001).
3. For a recent study of Soviet cinema under Stalin which sees post-war developments

primarily in terms of domestic politics, see Natacha Laurent, *L'Oeil du Kremlin: Cinema et Censure en URSS sous Staline* (Toulouse: Editions Privat, 2000).
4. Elena Zubkova, *Russia After the War* (New York: M.E. Sharpe, 1998).
5. See, for example, the pieces by Cull and Shaw in this volume.
6. See Major and Mitter in the Introduction, p.12.
7. Scott Lucas, *Freedom's War: The US Crusade against the Soviet Union, 1945–56* (Manchester: Manchester University Press, 1999).
8. On the *malokartin'e* see Peter Kenez, *Cinema and Soviet Society* (London: I.B. Tauris, 2001).
9. Ibid., pp.194–8.
10. Tony Shaw, 'The Politics of Cold War Culture', *Journal of Cold War Studies* 3/3 (2001), p.74.
11. Also known as *That Hamilton Woman*, it starred Leigh and Olivier.
12. On the huge popularity of American cinema in the USSR in the 1920s, see especially Denise Youngblood, *Movies for the Masses: Popular Cinema and Soviet Society in the 1920s* (Cambridge: Cambridge University Press, 1992).
13. Richard Taylor, 'Ideology as Mass Entertainment: Boris Shumyatsky and Soviet Cinema in the 1930s', in R. Taylor and I. Christie (eds.), *Inside the Film Factory* (London: Routledge, 1994); R. Taylor, 'Red Stars, Positive Heroes and Personality Cults', in Richard Taylor and Derek Spring (eds.), *Stalinism and Soviet Cinema* (London: Routledge, 1993).
14. Kenez, *Cinema and Soviet Society*, p.120
15. Rossiiskii Gosudarstvennyi Arkhiv Literatury i Iskusstv (RGALI), 2456/1/773/1–77; Gosudarstvennyi Arkhiv Rossiiskoi Federatsii (GARF), 5283/21/19/2–3.
16. Rossiiskii Gosudarstvennyi Arkhiv Sotsial'no-Politicheskoi Istorii (RGASPI), 82/2/960/81–83; 17/125/292/93.
17. RGASPI, 17/125/214/4–20.
18. RGALI, 2456/1/1042/12.
19. RGALI, 2456/1/1224/154–55.
20. RGASPI, 17/125/291/84–94.
21. RGASPI, 17/125/292/31–32.
22. RGALI, 2456/1/946/18.
23. RGASPI, 17/125/372/19.
24. Youngblood, *Movies for the Masses*, pp.54–67
25. RGASPI, 17/125/372/49.
26. RGASPI, 17/125/372/201.
27. I. Stalin, *Sochineniia*, vol. xvi (Moscow: *Pisatel'*, 1997), pp.5–24.
28. V.O. Pechatnov, '"Strel'ba kholostymi": sovetskaia propaganda na Zapad v nachale kholodnoi voiny (1945–1947)', in A.O. Chubarian (ed.), *Stalin i kholodnaia voina* (Moscow: Institut vseobshchei istorii RAN, 1997), pp.173–4.
29. Jeffrey Brooks notes that neither Churchill's Fulton speech nor the Novikov telegram sparked an open anti-American campaign in *Pravda*, and that the press continued to promote the possibility of continued Allied cooperation into 1947: *Thank You Comrade Stalin: Soviet Public Culture from Revolution to Cold War* (Princeton, NJ: Princeton University Press, 2000), pp.207–8.
30. GARF, 5283/14/385/45; I.A. Pyr'ev, *Izbrannye proizvedeniia*, vol. i (Moscow, 1978), pp.343–5.
31. The significance of the *Khudsovet* is discussed in Laurent, *L'Oeil du Kremlin*, pp.128–33.
32. RGALI, 2456/1/1337/49.
33. RGALI, 2456/1/1337/45.
34. RGALI, 2456/1/1337/51; Tsentral'nyi arkhiv obshchestvennykh dvizenii Moskvy (TsAODM), 2361/1/16/10–19.
35. Rossisskii Gosudarstvennyi Arkhiv Noveishei Istorii (RGANI), 2/1/7/21. The Ministry was disbanded after Stalin's death, and cinema affairs were taken over by the Ministry of Culture.
36. RGASPI, 17/125/378/6.

37. A. Artizov and O. Naumov (eds.), *Vlast' i khudozhestvennaia intelligentsiia* (Moscow: Mezhdunarodnyi fond 'Demokratiia', 1999), pp.581–4.
38. RGALI, 2456/1/1337/29, 32.
39. RGALI, 2456/1/1240/10, 17. On Simonov's trip to the US, see Joshua Rubenstein, 'Ilya Ehrenburg – Between East and West', *Journal of Cold War Studies* 4/1 (2002), pp.44–65.
40. RGASPI, 17/125/378/81.
41. RGALI, 2456/1/1240/16.
42. RGASPI, 17/125/378/82.
43. RGALI, 2456/1/1240/30–31.
44. RGASPI, 17/125/378/59. Discussions about the need for a Russian national cinema first appear to have arisen at meetings of film-makers during 1943 and 1944.
45. On European attitudes to the US after the war see, for example, Richard Kuisel, *Seducing the French* (Berkeley, CA: University of California Press, 1993), and R. Pells, *Not Like Us* (New York: Basic Books, 1997).
46. L. May, *The Big Tomorrow* (Chicago: Chicago University Press, 2000), p.177.
47. RGASPI, 17/125/213/89.
48. RGALI, 2372/6/125/28.
49. RGASPI, 17/125/291/12–19.
50. RGALI, 2453/2/2/1–2.
51. V. Pudovkin, *Sobranie sochinenii*, vol. ii (Moscow: Iskusstvo, 1975), pp.87, 92.
52. RGALI, 2456/1/1034/35–7.
53. RGALI, 2456/1/1034/61–64, 75–6.
54. I. Lukovskii, *Admiral Nakhimov: Istoricheskaia drama v 4 deistviiakh* (Moscow, 1941).
55. RGALI, 2372/6/57.
56. I. Lukovskii, *Admiral Nakhimov: Istoricheskaia drama v 4 deistviiakh* (Moscow, 1944.
57. I. Lukovskii, *Admiral Nakhimov: Literaturnyi Stsenarii* (Moscow, 1944).
58. RGALI, 2453/5/1/8–9.
59 On this, see Eduard Mark, 'The War Scare of 1946 and its Consequences', *Diplomatic History* 21/3 (1997), pp.383–415; B. Kuniholm, *The Origins of the Cold War in the Near East* (Princeton, NJ: Princeton University Press, 1980).
60. G. Mar'iamov, *Kremlevskii tsenzor: Stalin smotrit kino* (Moscow: Kinotsentr, 1992).
61. RGASPI, 17/125/378/81.
62. RGASPI, 17/117/605/85–97.
63. RGASPI, 17/116/262/73–4; Artizov and Naumov, *Vlast' i khudozhestvennaia intelligentsiia*, pp.554–5.
64. Artizov and Naumov, *Vlast' i khudozhestvennaia intelligentsiia*, p.582.
65. RGALI, 2456/1/1234/16, 20–21.
66. RGALI, 2456/1/1236/11–16.
67. RGALI, 2453/5/12/4.
68. RGALI, 2456/1/1533/21.
69. *Kul'tura i zhizn'*, 31 Dec. 1946; *Vechernaia Moskva*, 2 Jan. 1947; *Sovestskoe iskusstvo*, 1 Jan. 1947; *Krasnaia zvezda*, 4 Jan. 1947.
70. RGASPI, 629/1/71/1–8, 18.
71. It would be interesting to know more about how the film was received abroad. Certainly at the Venice film festival in September 1947 it apparently only won a specially instituted prize – for the best mass scenes – thanks to pressure from the Soviet judge. But as the festival itself was a heavily politicized phenomenon of the Cold War, we obviously cannot read too much into this. RGALI, 2456/1/1537/217–28.
72. See, for example, Stephen Whitfield, *The Culture of the Cold War* (Baltimore, MD: Johns Hopkins University Press, 1991), ch. 6; May, *The Big Tomorrow*.

Future Perfect?
Communist Science Fiction
in the Cold War

PATRICK MAJOR

One popular cultural genre which has attracted growing attention in
Cold War studies – for America at least – has been science fiction
(SF).[1] After all, the conflict was conducted with increasingly
sophisticated technological means, notably the atomic bomb and later
the race into space, when reality appeared to be leap-frogging ahead
of the popular imagination. These developments conjured up both
hope and dread in the West, but this was also true east of the Iron
Curtain. With Sputnik's launch in 1957, the Soviet Union appeared
to have overtaken its arch Cold War rival in the technological stakes,
throwing off its inferiority complex towards the West. Space became
a focal point of identification for Soviet society, which created heroic
monuments to pioneers such as Tsiolkovsky and Gagarin, not least in
Star City, where statues in the socialist realist mode celebrated the
new celestial superman.[2] In due course the Cosmos Pavilion in
Moscow became the equivalent of the National Air and Space
Museum in Washington. Moreover, from the mid-1950s the
Communist Party was consciously extolling the 'scientific-
technological revolution' with the fervour of a pseudo-religion.[3]
Marxism-Leninism itself was supposedly a scientific doctrine,
explaining the dialectical inevitability of human progress towards a
classless society, allied to the natural sciences which took pride of
place on school curricula.[4] Yet, by the end of the Cold War the
Eastern bloc had become burdened with pollution and outdated
technology, when the present seemed to be making a mockery of the
once-vaunted future. The Chernobyl nuclear accident in 1986 came
to symbolize the human incapacity to control the very forces of
nature unleashed in the name of progress.

We can read science fiction both as a touchstone of the Soviet
Union's relationship with the Cold War 'other', since the genre was
perceived to be inherently Western, but also as a window on
communism's predictions about its own future. As one official
commentator put it: 'We, too, are in flight to a "social planet" where

no man has ever set foot before. There is much in what is said about communism that sounds miraculous to us, but the people of the future will treat these miracles as something quite ordinary and unremarkable.'[5] Science fiction is an ambivalent medium, however, capable of both utopian visions of a better future and dystopian warnings of catastrophe. In the former vein, much of 'hard', natural-science fiction has extolled the wonders of the universe and can easily become a fictionalized form of rationalist propaganda, whereby machines solve all man's problems. This was true in the modernizing West, but the pre-revolutionary utopian roots of Russian SF were also strong, in a country painfully conscious of its industrial backwardness, but where religion and folklore still encouraged Messianic thinking.[6] Like the process of industrialization itself, much of early Russian science fiction had been influenced by the West. In fact, ever since the eighteenth century, when the first Russian utopian statecraft novels had appeared, the impact of Western Enlightenment ideas was evident, for instance in Prince Mikhail Shcherbatov's *Voyage to the Land of Ophir* (1783), supporting the reforms of Catherine the Great. But utopian fiction was always to have a troubled relationship with the Russian censor, and during the French revolution such liberal tracts were banned. Prince Vladimir Odoevsky's 1840 story, *Year 4338*, despite its paternalistic leanings and prognostications about Russian technological world leadership, also remained unpublished. Later in the nineteenth century the genre became more associated with social millenarianism from the left. Nikolai Chernyshevsky's 1863 underground text, *What is to be Done?*, written in gaol and unpublished until 1905, depicted female emancipation and production collectives, preaching a utopian socialism à la Fourier and Owen.[7] During industrialization in the 1890s, however, Russian SF 'hardened up'. The *nauchnaia fantastika*, or scientific fantasy, emerged as a recognized genre, heavily influenced by Western authors such as Jules Verne and H. G. Wells. It was also at this time that the mathematician and amateur rocketeer Konstantin Tsiolkovsky, later hailed as the father of Soviet space flight, was producing popular texts on space travel, such as *On the Moon* (1887) or *Daydreams of Earth and Heaven* (1894).[8] For the later Soviet state, SF was to have a similar didactic function, popularizing science and reinforcing a belief in a positive future.

But for centuries 'soft', social-science fiction has also been a favourite vehicle for political satire, criticizing the present from the safe vantage point of the future. Western dystopian SF, from Wells on, regularly thought the unthinkable, addressing themes otherwise repressed in the collective psyche. The bomb has been central to many Western Cold War studies,[9] including David Seed's piece in the current volume, as well as the general theme of technology run amok. Already in the nineteenth century there had been instances of Russian dystopianism or anti-utopianism. Dostoevsky's *Dream of a Ridiculous Man* (1877) imagined flight to a parallel Earth-like paradise, but corrupted by its terrestrial visitor into acquiring its own civil society, slavery and war. Others at the turn of the century, such as Afanasev in his *Journey to Mars* (1901) or Fёdorov's *An Evening in the Year 2217* (1906), inveighed against a collective, conformist and automated future.[10] Such thinking was anathema to the later communist state, which always attempted to pigeon-hole dystopianism as a decadent Western import. Yet mysticism and transcendentalism were deeply embedded in the Russian genre, preaching humanism as much as socialism.[11] Part of my intention in the following article is to show that science fiction in the Eastern bloc increasingly came to diverge from official prescriptions and to engage in a semi-detached critique of the regime, but also of the Cold War itself, questioning assumptions about a better future. The towering figures of SF in the communist bloc, such as the Strugatsky brothers in the Soviet Union, or Stanislaw Lem in Poland, by no means toed a party line, and in certain instances bordered on dissidence.[12]

SF was one of the less regulated communist literary fields, offering exponents more leeway perhaps than mainstream authors. Officials tended to dismiss the genre, associating it with Western pulp fiction. But, according to one Soviet observer, '[w]ith the possible exception of poetry, SF stories exceeded all other literature in popularity; and in the unfolding ideological struggle, the genre had an importance second only to Samizdat's'.[13] And according to another, SF, including translations, 'achieved greater popularity in the USSR than in almost any other country in the world.'[14] Readership in the Eastern bloc at large was reportedly huge, with new editions of hundreds of thousands sold out within days of publication, commanding high black-market prices.[15] Especially in the 1960s, Soviet publishing houses such as Molodaia gvardiia (Young Guard) and Znanie (Knowledge) developed SF imprints to cater for the growing demand, as well as Mir, launching its 25-volume 'Library of Modern Science Fiction'. There was also a lively periodicals market, besides the venerable popular science journal, *Around the World*, when new magazines appeared in the early 1960s such as *Seeker* and *Fantastika*.

Elsewhere in the Eastern bloc, in Hungary for instance, the fanzine *Galaktika*, launched in 1972, achieved an international reputation.[16] The main readership was in a key group of communist society: young, urban male members of the technical intelligentsia and skilled workers, fostered by the system, but with a keen sense of belonging to a global scientific community.[17] Former German Democratic Republic (GDR) SF fanzines also reveal the levels of self-organization among *aficionados*, producing their own newsletters and closely in touch with developments on the other side of the Iron Curtain. Occasionally, as in the case of the Stanislaw Lem Club at the Technical University in Dresden, fans would fall foul of the authorities, accused of 'anti-Soviet' activity by mistrustful professors.[18] But besides the usual suspects of schoolboys and science students, it has been suggested that, because SF was not part of the 'official culture value system', it also attracted 'people opposing the officially established system, since it was a rather mild way to "tease" the authorities, and meet otherwise unavailable views'.[19] Science fiction, just as in the West, had a subversive potential.

Early communist SF tended to be of the utopian variety, which in itself created jurisdictional rivalries with the party itself. The classic *Urtext* of Bolshevik science fiction was Alexander Bogdanov's *Red Star* (1908), a Martian allegory written by a left-wing Bolshevik close to the underground leadership.[20] In the novel, Leonid, himself a Russian Bolshevik, is transported by a higher humanoid civilization in an atomic-powered spaceship to Mars, which, it transpires, is run on communist lines, including communal childcare, job-sharing, and a reverence for scientific truth. As one of his new Martian companions explains, 'Blood is being shed [down on Earth] for the sake of a better future. But in order to wage the struggle we must *know* that future. And it is for the sake of such knowledge that you are here.'[21] Mars thus provides a vicarious glimpse of a terrestrial future. Yet there were also key differences between Bogdanov's perfect world and what became 'developed socialism'. There were no politics, let alone a party, on the red planet. Moreover, the prominent role allocated to the technical intelligentsia by Bogdanov was criticized by some commentators as bourgeois recidivism. (In the 'prequel', *Engineer Menni* (1913), the technocrat became even more central to Bogdanov's depiction of the Martian workers' emancipation during the great irrigation schemes). And the author himself was soon to fall out with Lenin over his theories of 'empiriomonism' and his Machian critique of materialism.

Nevertheless, when the revolution came, Bogdanov went into numerous editions in the 1920s and was much read. Mainstream authors of the 'Cosmist school' also adopted science fiction as a revolutionary genre. The 'wonderful catastrophe' regularly ushered in the universal revolution. Alexei Tolstoy's classic *Aelita* (1922), another allegory set on Mars, this time portrayed a Martian workers' revolt against an Engineers' Council. In the poet Briusov's unpublished 1920s' play, *The Dictator*, galactic militarism was foiled by 'proletarian interplanetarism'. Yet it soon became apparent that SF was also a medium for critiquing the direction of the infant revolution. Evgenii Zamiatin's *We*, written in 1920, but only published in the United States four years later, featured a dystopian totalitarian society which treated its members as numbers, and was read by some as a critique of Soviet-style Taylorism under its Russian champion, Gastev. The poet and playwright Vladimir Mayakovsky's social satires in the later 1920s, *The Bedbug* and *The Bath*, featured devices such as a time machine which ditched unproductive members of society – in this case bureaucrats – *en route* to the future. Mikhail Bulgakov, too, made political statements in fantastic stories such as *The Fatal Eggs* (1927). All of these authors fell out with the consolidating regime. Mayakovsky committed suicide in 1930; Zamiatin was induced to emigrate in 1931 and Bulgakov died in 1940, unpublishable.

Besides mainstream authors dabbling in science fiction, there had, of course, been other professional writers, many themselves working scientists, but often of dubious literary merit. Imitations of Verne and Wells abounded. Alexander Beliaev perhaps typified this trend, specializing in adventure stories where technological gadgets drove the plot, and with a personal penchant for arctic exploration themes. Under the New Economic Policy, the pre-war publishing entrepreneur Soikin continued to produce a range of adventure stories, a large proportion of which were Western imports. In the mid-1920s a number of his magazines devoted to popular science appeared, including *Around the World* (*Vokrug sveta*), which was to continue through the Cold War. With the consolidation of the revolution from above, however, in around 1927, the centre of gravity of SF shifted towards the state, and from cosmic universalism to 'socialism on one planet'. Populist revolts by the disenfranchised masses gave way to stories which reinforced the central role of the state in guiding the country's industrialized future. This tendency was reflected in the campaigning from 1929–30 by the Russian

Association of Proletarian Writers against science fiction, continued in 1932 by the Union of Soviet Writers. Under the auspices of socialist realism, SF was denigrated for its symbolism and formalism. A 'theory of limits' stipulated the 'near target' (*blizkaia tsel*), and the 'theory of near anticipation' insisted on circumscribing the horizons to the foreseeable future. As hardline critics in the late 1940s still complained: 'Some authors suffer from cosmopolitanism; they are carried away by problems which are far from the urgent questions of modern life; they wander off into interplanetary space.' Or: 'Recently, at one of the meetings of the Union of Soviet Writers, L. Uspensky strove fiercely to prove the necessity of writing about things which will come to pass one hundred or even two hundred years from now. This, in our view, is not a fortuitous mistake.'[22]

Stalinist Science Fiction

Thus, from the early 1930s, under Stalin's influence, utopian Soviet SF gave way to a brand of straight adventure story revolving around technical hardware such as oil rigs, superplanes or solar energy, all clear extensions of existing technology. Furthermore, in 1930 Soikin was expropriated, a fate which was to befall other Eastern European publishing houses in the late 1940s. SF was demoted to the function of scientific popularizer, aimed mainly at adolescent boys, encouraging them to take up technical subjects at university. In fact, many such stories became disguised versions of the production novel, in which the collective waged a race against the plan deadline, and the scientist-hero triumphed, only now the workers wore spacesuits. In other countries too, such as the GDR, SF could hark back to traditions of the German 'engineer novel', in which the practical application of science prevailed within a knowledge hierarchy. The genre also became colonized by *krasnye detektivy*, or red detective stories, in which marvellous inventions were coveted by the agents of a foreign power (almost invariably a Western government), to be foiled by the combined efforts of Soviet scientists and their attendant authorities. This conspiratorial sub-genre persisted throughout Stalin's remaining lifetime. Specialists included Vladimir Nemtsov, with his Komsomol heroes Vadim Bagretsov and Timofei Babkin, or Alexander Kazantsev, in ripping yarns such as *The Arctic Bridge* (1946) or *The Northern Pier* (1952). These stories clearly reflected Soviet geopolitical concerns. In the war they were frequently targeted against the Germans, with prototype aircraft decimating the

Luftwaffe, for example, but during the Cold War the East had to use its intelligence superiority to redress the technological imbalance. In Valentin Ivanov's *The Energy Is under Our Dominion* (1949–50), NKVD agents foil a Western spies' plot to detonate a bomb on Soviet soil. In an East German story, a new wonder fuel is coveted by Anglo-American intelligence in the Sahara.[23] Of course, such story-lines betrayed much compensatory wishful thinking about the actual level of Soviet science. But the state's belief in the future perfect was almost boundless at this stage.

In the meantime, the more lurid tales of Western science fiction, which had always placed a greater premium on entertainment than improvement, were attacked as harbingers of militarism. During the period of the US atomic monopoly it was easy for Soviet critics to take the moral high ground. In March 1948, in an article entitled 'The World of Nightmare Fantasies', two Soviet critics attacked the American literary figure, Tommy Sonofagun, boy hero of a wartime pulp story, 'The Incredible Slingshot Bombs', who lays low his enemies with miniature atomic warheads, protesting: 'A hooligan with an atomic slingshot, isn't this the true symbol of modern imperialism?'[24] Instead, Soviet SF preached a more positive, humanistic attitude. Even the term 'science fiction' was for a long time eschewed in favour of 'scientific-utopian' literature. To be sure, commentators recognized some allies on the other side, such as Ray Bradbury, whose *Martian Chronicles* of 1950 had painted a more disturbing picture of the self-destructive nature of the bomb. But these 'awful warnings' were accused of cultural pessimism and defeatism. This juxtaposition was to continue for decades, long after the Soviet Union had acquired its own nuclear capability. One critic pointed in 1963 to 'the polarities in the Soviet and American fantasy writers' views of the future'. The 'remarkable activity in our fantasy literature in recent years was evoked by the powerful new advances in our country's science, with the successes in peaceful application of the atom and in space. On the post-war American science-fiction writer there fell the glare of the atomic explosion at Hiroshima'.[25] Even as late as the 1980s this official view had only slightly modified:

> Foreign (Western) science fiction focuses attention on the horrors of the future (the extinction of mankind in thermonuclear war, ecological disasters, monstrous mutations, the withering away of all spiritual life in the midst of material

affluence, and so on). This has a certain justification – humanity
needs to be warned ... But it is one thing to warn and another
to frighten, and here Western writers often go too far.[26]

Instead, Soviet SF writers placed their faith in 'the rational nature of
united humanity, that Reason which is capable of protecting our
planet from the dangers which threaten it'. According to Ekkehard
Redlin, long-running reader for the GDR's Neues Berlin publishing
house, 'warning literature, the utopian counterpart to critical realism,
has no place in socialist utopian literature'. It meant a 'critique of the
present which did not go beyond negation', in which the admonisher
remained an 'outsider', ideologically powerless to explain the deeper
meaning of the problem.[27]

The 'unspoken taboo'[28] on communist depictions of nuclear war
on Earth was also designed to protect faith in the defensive capacity
of the Warsaw Pact's 'peace camp'. Indeed, it was not until the mid-
1950s that Soviet civil defence planning openly discussed any form of
nuclear attack.[29] If fictional atomic strikes were ever shown, then it
was on other planets, and always unleashed by 'imperialist' alien
civilizations. Typical story-lines involved capitalist-militarists, holed
up on islands or asteroids, planning revenge attacks, but usually
incinerating themselves in the process. The GDR–Polish joint film
production of Lem's Astronauts, The Silent Star, released in 1960,
used this story-line, when an expedition to Venus discovers an extinct
civilization which had tried to launch a pre-emptive strike on Earth,
but paid the price with its own destruction. The surface of the planet
is a radioactive wasteland. When the expedition returns to Earth, the
implicit Venusians back home are the Americans: crew members
instinctively turn to their only US comrade to deliver the final pacifist
message that the Earth must learn its lesson. Leonov's story Mr
McKinley's Escape (Begstvo mistera Makkinli, 1961) also satirized
American shelter-building hysteria, and only included post-
Armageddon scenes as part of a dream sequence. Not until the 1970s
did the nuclear taboo loosen somewhat, but by the 1980s it was even
possible to read post-nuclear holocaust stories which did not
attribute blame, such as Adamovich's satirical The Last Pastorale
(Posledniaia pastoral', 1987), in which a Soviet submariner and a
Western woman shelter-survivor team up as the new Adam and Eve.[30]
By this point communist science fiction had been firmly harnessed to
the cause of peace, while authors learned to exploit this as room for
manoeuvre to pursue their own agendas.

In the interim, communist stories played up the peaceful applications of atomic power, seemingly immune to their impact on the environment. In line with the educational literature on this subject, socialist atomic energy was always used for humane purposes, with the iconographic emphasis on power stations and transport.[31] Nuclear trains, planes and submarines appeared with monotonous regularity. In an East German tale, Krupkat's *The Invisible Ones* (*Die Unsichtbaren*, 1958), we read a typical paean to progress, uncontaminated by notions of radiation or fall-out: 'What great changes we experienced in the atomic age! Atomic power transforms deserts into pleasant gardens. Atomic power drives the eternal ice from the arctic coasts. It relieves us from heavy manual labour, it becomes the pleasure-giving element in the hands of peaceful people.'[32] In another East German story the atom is used to vaporize the Moon in order to create a second sun and melt a polar ice-cap![33] Only in the 1970s and 1980s did environmental issues begin to creep into Eastern bloc SF stories, questioning the optimism and gigantomania of smoke-stack socialism, when mutations, pollution and climate change became permissible topics, as they had in the West back in the 1960s.

It might legitimately be asked at this point how much of the Western literature, of the sort which David Seed discusses elsewhere, could be read by Eastern audiences. In the early twentieth century, SF had been perceived as by definition 'Western'. Wells was widely available in Russia, and in 1920 he even visited the Soviet Union, meeting Lenin. But in the 1940s there was an effective embargo on Western texts, and only in the 1950s did magazines start publishing stories from the other side of the Iron Curtain again. By the mid-1960s, around 100 Western titles were in print, including books, and by the early 1980s more than 200 authors were available in 40 books and over a dozen anthologies.[34] Particular favourites, in declining order of popularity, were Ray Bradbury and Isaac Asimov, but also Robert Sheckley, Clifford Simak, Henry Kuttner and Kurt Vonnegut, whose *Slaughterhouse 5* was translated into Russian soon after its publication in 1969. Opinion polls revealed that, apart from a few home favourites such as the Strugatskys, foreign authors were often more popular than indigenous writers. Eastern stories were also far more likely to be set in a generic 'Western' setting than vice versa. Much of this opening up depended on the persistent efforts of editors and authors. Hungary's Peter Kuczka, editor of the Cosmos series, was a great 'Westernizer', and in the GDR, Neues Leben's younger editor, Olaf Spittel, was instrumental in new translations in the 1980s. In Poland in the 1970s, Lem waged a long and ultimately successful battle to have Philip K. Dick's *Ubik* published there.[35] In many ways Eastern readerships were far better informed than their Western counterparts, although exponents of the 'New Wave', such as America's Thomas Disch and Roger Zelazny, and Britain's J.G. Ballard and Brian Aldiss, were largely unpublished even in the 1980s, despite – or perhaps because of – their critical stance towards late industrial capitalism. This does not, of course, mean that their works did not percolate through the samizdat grapevine, but it remains for future research to establish how widespread such informal networks were.

Translation in the other direction was far more problematic. This was as much a matter of Western indifference as Eastern censorial control. A very few works were unilaterally published by Moscow's Foreign Languages Publishing House, but more by Western imprints. Occasional anthologies appeared from the 1960s, edited by liberal American SF voices such as Asimov, Merril and Sturgeon. The Strugatskys were published almost in their entirety in the mid-to-late 1970s, at the high point of *détente*, by Macmillan's 'Best of Soviet Science Fiction' series, as well as half a dozen or so other authors. In the 1980s this transatlantic openness dried up almost completely, so that the vast majority of these texts are now long out of print in the anglophone world, although their European readership was always more loyal, in the Federal Republic, but also in France. Lem succeeded better at staying in print throughout the Western world and may well be one of the most widely-read SF authors of all time.[36] But there were problems when, in a 1972 article, he critiqued the genre in general, and Western science fiction in particular, for prostituting its talents to a market dominated by editorial self-interest: 'Science fiction is a clinical case of a region occupied exclusively by trash, because in kitsch, the culturally and historically highest, most difficult, and most important objects are produced on the assembly line, in the most primitive forms, to be sold to the public at bargain prices.'[37] *Touché!* Lem, always the realist, later belittled the Western SF imagination's tendencies to project its psychological fears onto its 'evil' aliens, exposing its own inflated, paranoid view of itself: 'Yet the preconception that a power with armies of starships at its disposal could be dead set on taking over our property is as naïve as the assumption that one of the superpowers of earth would mobilize its armies in order to expropriate a grocery store.'[38] The only author to emerge unscathed was Philip K. Dick who, while enjoying the literary praise, did not appreciate his apparently Marxist affinities, and took it upon himself to report his contacts with Lem to the Federal Bureau of Investigation (FBI).[39] The latter's honorary membership in the Science Fiction Writers' Association also came into question, with a lobby pressing for his ouster, revolving around the rather petty issue of hard-currency royalties and failure to pay dues. The spirit of *détente* which united much East–West SF writing in the imagination thus foundered on the most mundane of issues!

Destalinizing the Future

Despite the purported void on the other side, it was not until 1957 that Soviet SF experienced its own Cold War renaissance, with the publication of Ivan Efremov's *Andromeda Nebula*.[40] There were two main reasons for this. In the wake of destalinization at the twentieth party congress in 1956 the socialist-realist strictures on fantastic literature had been relaxed. Now, 'warm wave' critics such as Uspensky were able to argue their case for a revival of utopian fiction against 'cold wave' hardliners. In 1958 an All-Russian Conference on Science Fiction and Adventure Stories was even held. Nevertheless, plots were not permitted to defy the known limits of science. Thus, time travel was banned and parallel universes discouraged. Early novels of the mid-to-late 1950s, including *Andromeda*, often contained helpful glossaries of scientific terms at the end. Long passages could be devoted to specialist explanations, with correspondingly little attention to characterization. The result was often two-dimensional, wooden heroes in the socialist-realist mould, prone to lecturing their readers.[41] Yet some of the technocratic utopias envisaged, where experts commanded administrators, were tacit criticisms of the bureaucratic *apparat* of the present and thus not entirely conformist. The pre-eminence of the scientist-hero has also to be read against the background of the growing and all-too real alienation of dissident scientists such as Pyotr Kapitsa or Andrei Sakharov from the Soviet military-industrial complex.[42]

Furthermore, 1957 was crucially the year of the launch of Sputnik, on 4 October, instantly giving the Soviets a well-publicized technological lead over the USA. Sergei Korolev, the Soviet design chief in charge of the launch, consciously linked the achievement to his mentor Tsiolkovsky. Writing in *Pravda* on the centenary of his birth, Korolev proudly stated: 'We are witnessing the realization of

Tsiolkovsky's remarkable predictions of rocket flights and the possibility of flying into interplanetary space – predictions made more than sixty years ago.'[43] The Soviet media had been steadily filling with popular science features on space travel.[44] Now science fact was in danger of overtaking science fiction. For Efremov the timing could hardly have been better:

> The first serial publication of Andromeda had not been completed when Soviet sputniks began their flights in orbit round the Earth. Confronted with this indisputable fact it was a pleasure to realise that the ideas on which the story had been based were correct ... At first I had thought that the gigantic transformations of our planet and life on it described in the story could not be effected in less than three thousand years. I based this calculation on world history, but did not take into consideration the rate of acceleration of technical progress and, more important still, the possibilities that communist society will offer mankind.[45]

Efremov thus foreshortened his original time-frame by a millennium. Nevertheless, *Andromeda* was still set 2000 years in the future and represented a milestone in the revival of the communist utopia. It embodied a number of typical features of communist 'space opera', a microcosm of communist society set on board a starship. Rather like *Red Star*, the intergalactic travellers inhabit a universe where moral self-control is the key, rather than an oppressive external system. There is no obvious Communist Party. Instead, the ship's historian plays the role of legitimizer in the presence of the scientists. Moreover, the future is not a place for indolence, but the continued application of labour to economic and scientific challenges. Science and art have achieved a neo-classical synthesis, within individuals who suffer no Marxian alienation. Indeed, much of the imagery is ancient Greek in origin. The Earth's continents are connected by the Spiral Way rail net; safe nuclear energy has been discovered, while thermonuclear stockpiles have been ejected from the Earth's atmosphere; even the Earth's weather systems have been tamed in Efremov's imagination, reminiscent – on a far grander scale – of Soviet schemes to reverse the flow of the Siberian rivers and irrigate the deserts of Central Asia. Although the vast distances between constellations have not been crossed, the intergalactic 'family' communicate with each other on telescreens in the Circle of Great Power. Higher life forms are recognized by virtue of their beauty. 'Even with the coming of communist society', muses Darr Veter, 'our civilization has remained fundamentally technical and only in the Era of Common Labour did we turn to the perfection of man himself and not only his machines, houses, food and amusements.'[46] Efremov also predicted the memorial iconography of the space age. Before the Astronautical Council building:

> stood a monument to the first people to enter outer space; the steep slope of a mountain reaching into clouds and whirlwinds was surmounted by an old-type spaceship, a fish-shaped rocket that pointed its sharp nose into still unattainable heights. Cast metal figures, supporting each other in a chain, were making a superhuman effort to climb upwards, spiralling their way around the base of the monument – these were the pilots of the rocket ships, the physicists, astronomers, biologists and writers with bold imaginations.[47]

Efremov also used space travel to underline basic differences between Soviet and American worldviews. The prompting for his 'Cor Serpentis' (1959),[48] was Murray Leinster's 'First Contact', first published in *Amazing Stories* in 1945. In the Americans' first encounter with alien lifeforms in deep space a Mexican standoff ensues, as each ship tries to second-guess the hostile intentions of the other, unable to back off for fear of being tracked back home. As one terrestrial crew member agonizes: 'The two races could be friends, but also they could be deadly enemies. Each, even if unwillingly, was a monstrous menace to the other. And the only safe thing to do with a menace is to destroy it.'[49] Although Leinster avoids this drastic solution, Efremov, on the other hand, could only imagine a peaceful encounter between equally civilized species of mankind. According to one of his crew: 'An intelligent being from another world that has reached outer space is equally perfect and universal – in other words, beautiful. There are no such things as intelligent monsters, human fungi or human octopuses.'[50] The crew even retrieve a copy of Leinster's story from the ship's data banks to poke fun at it, and when they do encounter their own first aliens (in a white ship unlike Leinster's black vessel), they indeed turn out to be humanoid and friendly. And the implication, as in *Red Star*, is that they are also progressive, since for the Terrans, 'Man acquired cosmic strength when he rose to the highest stage of communist society'.[51]

Such optimism was reinforced in 1961 by Gagarin's first manned orbit. In the ensuing months the world's first cosmonaut,

Khrushchev's golden boy, was sent on a gruelling world publicity tour.[52] Space travel soon became *de rigueur* in the communist SF world. It was under this impetus that many 'first-wave' post-war science fiction writers established themselves, in the heroic phase of the building of socialism, which later generations of East German authors, for instance, were prepared to mock even within the lifetime of the GDR.[53] A number of common themes emerged from such space adventures. At the most superficial level was the superpower rivalry with the United States. Readers learned of the inferiority of the capitalist system through the mishaps of its space crews. In Krupkat's *The Great Frontier* (*Die große Grenze*, 1960) a Soviet crew end up rescuing their American rivals from their helplessly stranded craft. Near-future scenarios accepted the continued existence of the Americans, including races to the Moon between socialist coalitions and capitalist conglomerates, who would not flinch from sabotage to win. In the longer term, however, it was assumed that the capitalists would have succumbed to the forces of history, by peaceful means, from which they were sometimes permitted to hole up in some far-flung corner of the galaxy as vestigial but spent forces. In the German context the tacit assumption of many novels was that reunification had also taken place at some point in the future, but again under socialist auspices. Space became symbolic of cooperative ventures, with the Soviet Union usually leading a coalition of communist and non-aligned states, sometimes under the leadership of a post-capitalist United Nations. The composition of spacecrews is thus indicative of the future world order. The captain is almost invariably Russian; the engineer or the pilot, evincing Teutonic know-how, may be German. There is also frequently a range of symbolic post-colonial crew members from Asia and Africa. In *The Silent Star*, for instance, a Japanese crew member displays her victim credentials by revealing that she lost her parents at Hiroshima; the language specialist is Chinese and the onboard scientist is Indian. And in the final scene the ground crew join hands, with the camera focusing on the chain of different skin pigments.[54] In del'Antonio's *Titanus* (1959) there is also a repentant American nuclear scientist aboard the multinational crew. Efremov went further in *Andromeda*, transcending nationality entirely. Referring to the Cold War as the 'Fission Age', nuclear catastrophe had been only narrowly averted. But,

> With inevitable persistence the new way of life [communism] had spread over the entire Earth and the many races and nations

were united into a single friendly and wise family. Thus began the next era, the era of World Unity, consisting of four ages – the Age of Alliance, the Age of Lingual Disunity, the Age of Power Development and the Age of the Common Tongue.[55]

But there were again limits to how far this science-fictional *détente* could go as the Cold War unfolded. Following real cooperative space ventures such as the Apollo–Soyuz link-up in July 1975, in one 1980 novel, Aitmatov imagined a joint US–Soviet space station, the *Parity*, which sends an expedition to make contact with a higher civilization. Although they bury their differences in space, and want to invite the aliens back to Earth, the authorities there maintain their traditional geopolitical self-interest and mutual suspicion, banning any close encounters, lest the terrestrial balance of power be disturbed.[56]

Marxism-Leninism and dialectical materialism also posed another series of constraints on the communist SF imagination. The laws of historical development had to prevail; human agency could not play an overdetermining role. Authors had to find plausible ways to sneak glimpses into the past or future without simply inventing time-machines or other 'unscientific' devices. In Krupkat's *When the Gods Died* (*Als die Götter starben*, 1963), it is lunar archaeologists who discover traces of a distant visitor civilization, but never meet them. Or else benign aliens represent the more advanced social relations of future communist systems, but they are always linked to humans as part of the same evolutionary scale. Hostile, blob-like alien invaders of the 'It-Came-from-Outer-Space' variety are almost unknown in Eastern bloc science fiction. As Krupkat explains:

> There should hardly be all too great differences between us and other space dwellers. That would contradict the laws of development which apply everywhere. Perhaps we shall discover life forms during space travel which are at a stage that we have left behind hundreds of thousands of years ago, perhaps also some whose development is millions of years ahead of ours. But in no case will they be the horrors of which you spoke. Those are merely the creations of human fantasy.[57]

As alluded to above, the socialist realism demanded even of utopian story-telling insisted that goals should be proximate rather than intangibly distant. Apart from Efremov, Soviet SF of the 1950s rarely ventured more than two centuries into the future. (In the West it could be thousands of years.) The future was supposed to be realizable. Thus, one humorous East German story by Manfred Bender of the late 1950s chose 1999 as its setting.[58] The GDR children's comic, *Mosaik*, clearly in the gravitational pull of Sputnik, took readers to the world of Neos, which bore striking similarities to an improved version of Leipzig, not too alien to readers.[59] Future scenarios often depicted a recognizable present, but one massively technologized, where citizens lived in fully automated houses. The communist future could be rosy beyond belief. In Krupkat's *Unsichtbaren* we thus read of a Berlin where:

> Magically, a new city had arisen on the banks of the Spree from the smoke-blackened ruins of the last world war. In bold architecture rose buildings with shimmering porcelain facades and glass walls, towering up ever higher towards the centre. At first sight not much was reminiscent of the old Berlin. Those who turned off the great new traffic arteries into the new capital, found amidst dreamlike parks many a place from the past: the Red Rathaus or the famous avenue 'Unter den Linden' with the Brandenburg Gate and other historical buildings.
>
> Colourful life swirled through the streets of the metropolis. Some Berliners had just finished their four-hour workday and they were now sitting comfortably under the multi-coloured awnings and umbrellas of the pavement cafés or park restaurants, promenaded along the avenues by the Spree, went shopping or visited the universities to hear the afternoon lectures. The people looked forward to the fine day and enjoyed it.
>
> Some early birds had headed north in their mini-planes for a quick sunbathe at the Baltic. It was only a twenty-minute flight to the Big Beach, Berlin's 'bathing strip'. There too, as in the capital, there were atomic climate conditioners which pleasantly prewarmed the still cool sea breeze before it was allowed to touch the skin of the Athenians of the Spree.[60]

Dissident Science Fiction

It is at this point that we can turn to the more self-critical aspects of Eastern SF. In the longer term, such futuristic visions of the perfect future can only have been hostages to fortune. There is anecdotal evidence that real space achievements were often measured against the failings of the communist system to deliver on Earth. Banal issues such as housing and foodstuffs continued to dominate people's everyday lives. In the real GDR frustrated citizens in one queue joked how 'there'll be butter again soon. Gagarin is already on his way to the Milky Way'.[61] And from 1965 it was clear to the Soviet leadership that Russia was falling seriously behind in the Moonshot race.[62] The Soviet media were subsequently under orders to downplay the programme. Rumours were also circulating of a nuclear accident at Kyshtym in 1957, which had indeed contaminated 20,000 square kilometres of the Urals.[63] When Lake Baikal was polluted with cellulose in 1969, a limited public discussion was tolerated until the early 1970s. The credibility of scientists themselves also suffered a blow, with the official dethronement of the controversial pseudo-biologist Lysenko in 1965, after the fall of Khrushchev, himself the great would-be leader-technocrat.[64]

It should not be surprising, therefore, if Eastern bloc science fiction writers developed more distance from the 'scientific-technological revolution'. Czech SF visions of the sixties were 'noticeably darker than those of the previous decade'.[65] Cestmir Vejdelek's *Return from Paradise* (*Navrat z raje*, 1961), often rated as the best post-war Czech SF story, was a tale of disillusionment, as the utopian planet Lucie transpires to be a dystopia ruled by a computer. Yet Gregor's *From Nowhere to Nowhere* (*Odnikud nikam*), and Straka's *The Second World Deluge* (*Druha potopa sveta*), both appearing in 1964 and dealing with radiation, struck similarly despondent notes. Others became more political. Jiri Marek's dystopia, *Blessed Ages* (*Blazeny vek*, 1967), satirized the recent Stalinist past in a city where citizens parade banners proclaiming: 'Citizens, stay in the Streets. Private Happiness is the Happiness of the Past!', or: 'We know that towards Real Freedom many people must be Compelled.' In East Germany, too, the most intelligent SF authors of the 1970s, Johanna and Günther Braun, débuted with a story which poked fun at the cybernetic utopianism of the computerized society, one which was in many ways more applicable to the West. But *The Great Wizard's Mistake* (*Der Irrtum des großen Zauberers*), published in 1972, a year after the accession of Erich Honecker as East German leader, had a particular home resonance with its plot of an ageing, manipulative magician bent on brainwashing society with modern technology, but unable to find a successor. Reading between the lines, the book was both a critique of the sorcerer, Ulbricht, but also of his untalented apprentice.

The acknowledged masters of this sharper, more critical 'social fantasy', as they called it, were the Soviet Union's Strugatsky brothers, Arkady and Boris, who began writing in the late 1950s, rather in the conventional adventure format. Yet their alien planets were usually only thinly disguised versions of Earth. Although their heroes initially remained committed idealists facing the dilemmas of intervention in the historical process, and thus resembled the communist functionary, the moral ambivalence of their cause increased.[66] As one critic put it: 'Towards the end of the "thaw", their novels become more and more reminiscent of an experimental firing ground littered with the spent shells of all possible liberal-humanistic utopias, exploded on the mines of history.'[67] The Strugatskys' *Hard to Be a God* (1964) was perhaps the most popular post-war Soviet SF novel ever. In it, a future Earth sends members of its Institute of Experimental History to other worlds, in order to prepare their Marxist development from feudalism. The Russian protagonist Anton agonizes about the ethics of interference, hence the novel's title. The Earth team are, however, under strict orders only to 'prepare the soil' for future development, but find themselves defeated by a human nature not yet ready for the noble demands of the socialist personality. Instead, the quixotic experiment degenerates into a form of proto-fascism and persecution of intellectuals, and the ethnographic team is evacuated at the climax. The one-way road through a Russian forest encountered at the beginning of the novel, littered with the debris of Operation Barbarossa, stands as a metaphor for the whole: 'the road was anisotropic – just as history is. *There is no way back.*'[68] Humanity has to be allowed to make its own mistakes. As the Strugatskys' *oeuvre* expanded, however, reaching over 20 books, the point of identification shifted ever further from the 'terraformers' to the objects of these experiments. In *The Inhabited Island* (1971), the Earth hero, Maxim, eventually joins the resistance, on an alien world run by a militaristic clique which uses mind control to keep its citizens docile. By the time of *The Youth from the Underworld* (1974), the narrative defection from the 'gods' to the lower depths was complete.[69]

Such critiques clearly required a careful line to be trodden. The usual device for explaining away the sideswipes at tyranny was overt reference to National Socialism. But there are many implicit connections in *Hard to Be a God* and *The Inhabited Island* with Stalinism, as bureaucracy and a secret police begin to take hold of society.[70] Some allegories therefore became early anti-totalitarian parables, in which a certain, carefully dosed destalinization was possible. When the Strugatskys went too far in criticizing the bureaucratizing tendencies of socialism, in *The Snail on the Slope* (1966–68), however, they encountered immediate difficulties in publishing their work except in obscure journals. Their next novel, *The Ugly Swans*, was put on ice by Molodaia gvardiia in 1968, circulating only as a samizdat text, until it was published in the West in 1972 (without the authors' permission). Set on Earth and involving a Stalinesque personality cult, a Legion of Freedom security service and 'woodpecker' informants, the hero Viktor Banev sides with the pariah 'slimies' (*mokretsy*), who are treated as mental patients. From 1969 there was a renewed clamp-down on Soviet SF works. In the 1970s Molodaia gvardiia suspended its SF series, and the 'Leningrad Collection' fell into abeyance, as did SF stories in the magazines *World of Adventure* and *Seeker*. 'Stalinist' authors such as Nemtsov and Kazantsev regained a certain editorial influence, while 'oppositional' SF authors such as Emtsev, Mirer, Iur'ev, Larionova, Al'tov, Savchenko, Snegov and Berdnyk abandoned writing altogether after failing to find an outlet for publication. Others, such as Parnov, allegedly sold out, becoming the acceptable face of Soviet SF at international conventions.[71] The Strugatskys remained *personae non gratae* until the breakthrough of their classic *Roadside Picnic* (1972), which gained them an international reputation, especially once filmed by Tarkovsky as *Stalker* (1979). But only in the late 1980s could even these stars publish other 'top drawer' works, such as *Crooked Destiny* (1989), a metafictional account of their tribulations with the censor.

Part of the historical contribution to Cold War literature will be to examine the pressures of the censor on the artistic creation of this literature. Currently the former GDR is most open to archival scrutiny. So far this has been done through inference and interviews by some authors with their colleagues.[72] Allegedly, only one work of GDR SF was directly censored and prevented from publication in the 1950s and 1960s. This remains to be seen in the light of the files. There were growing differences of opinion among publishing houses, between the Verlag Neues Berlin, which favoured treating utopian literature as contemporary literature, able to critique the present, and Verlag Neues Leben, which stuck to traditional views of the communist future. In Romania, too, one of the most fruitful SF environments in the earlier post-war decades, fantastic publishing, fell victim to Ceausescu's austerity programme. Between 1974 and 1982 no science-fantasy periodicals were published there.[73] Only in the late 1970s did a general *modus vivendi* come about between SF writers and the Soviet state, whereby fantasy stories were tolerated as long as they did not posit any fundamental, alternative political visions. Thus, by the 1980s SF was back in vogue, when even journals such as *Soviet Literature* were prepared to devote entire special editions to the genre.

Yet, it would be a mistake to think that all anti-Stalinist Eastern bloc SF was *de facto* pro-Western. The capitalist present was increasingly viewed as the dangerous dystopian future which true communism must avoid. To some, the developed socialism of the 1960s appeared to be pandering to the population's baser instincts and there was a perceived danger of convergence between the two systems in a form of mindless materialism. Stanislaw Lem, Poland's grand master of SF, was one of the first to voice these concerns. Using the device of Einsteinian relativity in *Return from the Stars* (1961), to bring back a cosmonaut 127 years after take-off, communism appears to have merged with capitalism in a strange hybrid, in which goods cost nothing and money has almost lost its value, but where the citizenry wander aimlessly through a miasma of advertising and pleasure-seeking. Natural instincts of sex and violence have been 'cured' chemically by the process of 'betrization'. But the pre-modern hero, Bregg, reacts against the 'prepared scale of values': 'if one did not adopt them, they attributed this – and in general, everything – to conservatism, subconscious resistance, ingrained habits, and so on. I had no intention of giving up such habits and resistance until I was convinced that what they were offering me was better ... I didn't want nursery school or rehabilitation.'[74] The Strugatskys' later novel, *The Final Circle of Paradise* (1965), was just as critical of the mind-numbing effects of the acquisitive consumer society. There, in the Land of the Fools, implicitly set somewhere in the West, a narcotized, post-Freudian system of self-gratification, but also stultification, is pilloried. As one gourmandizing academic tells the Russian protagonist: 'Carefree means happy – and we are so close to that ideal! Another few decades, or maybe just a few more years, and we shall attain the automated plenty, we will discard science as a healed man discards his crutches, and the whole of mankind will become one happy family of children.'[75]

Another powerful current within the Eastern SF canon was humorous science fiction, deploying tongue-in-cheek whimsy. This strikes me as symptomatic for a number of reasons. Firstly, humour enabled authors to poke fun at some of the megalomaniacal visions of the previous decades, and thereby gain some distance from them. But the ironic trope did not fundamentally critique science as such. It seemed to suit the authorities too. The grand earlier claims of science could be swept under the carpet with a smile rather than repudiated entirely. There was thus still a great divide between this form of wry wit and the extremely black humour of Western writers such as Philip K. Dick. The Strugatskys had experimented with humour in *Monday Begins on Saturday* (1965), written in the style of a folktale, set at the Research Institute of Sorcery and Magic, which is terminally bound up in red tape. The approach was a resounding success with readers. Authors elsewhere in the Eastern bloc, such as Czechoslovakia, drew on their strong surrealist inter-war roots. So much so that critics began to worry about 'overproduction of humorous and ironic SF' becoming a formulaic straitjacket.[76] The 'clown prince' of SF grotesque was undoubtedly Stanislaw Lem. His space protagonist, Pirx the Pilot, is in many ways a classic picaresque hero, negotiating everything which the universe throws at him, and surviving. Yet, in a case of West–East cultural cross-fertilization, Lem learned from Dick that buffoonery had its limits and that there was a place for seriousness in his own writing, at least in the form of a new sardonicism.[77]

Lem's ultimate greatness resulted from his ability to switch seamlessly from the absurd to the horrific. Part of this alienation from mainstream communist culture was an ontological one: critiques could hardly become more fundamental. The certainties of scientific knowledge were abandoned, although the quest was still always maintained. In his most famous work, *Solaris* (1961), there was no communing with the alien other. The plasmic ocean covering the world of Solaris remains inscrutable to the Earth research station investigating it: 'our scholarship, all the information accumulated in the libraries, amounted to a useless jumble of words, a sludge of statements and suppositions ... we had not progressed an inch in the 78 years since researches had begun.'[78] Lem thus displaces *Homo sapiens* from centre-stage in what one might term an act of cultural, rather than political, dissidence. The living ocean takes to ignoring its human visitors completely, just as the Strugatskys' alien visitors treat their trip to Earth as a 'roadside picnic'.[79] It is impossible to escape the theological connotations of these ideas. Indeed, the Russian authors increasingly turned to religious themes, dissatisfied with science as a panacea. As one commentator observed: 'The future is no longer an ideological or a technical affair, but a moral one, as the means have become more important than the goals. Civil or – since we are talking about SF – cosmic disobedience is offered as a new strategy on mankind's way into the future.'[80] The Strugatskys' last novels, such as *City of the Doomed* (1987), thus became more religious allegories than recognizable science fiction.

Although Lem's main contribution is undoubtedly to general cognitive theories of knowledge, towards the end of the Cold War he did show a concern for its geopolitical realities, often using oppositional superpower metaphors to make his deeper points about logic. In *Fiasco* (1986), an arms race on the planet Quinta is clearly a parody of the current Star Wars programme on Earth. Using game theory and literally disarming logic, the ship's onboard computer, DEUS, predicts the mutually self-defeating nature of technological escalation, as intelligent weapons gain ever-increasing autonomy from their creators, capable only of total destruction. In his next novel Lem's inveterate hero, Ijon Tichy, suffers a partial separation of the brain by a rogue laser robot on the Moon: 'The right hemisphere does tend to be more aggressive than the left', a psychiatrist comments, although the Earth has now become the potential victim of a third force of renegade microtechnology, threatening to rain down upon it.[81] The message of these allegories on the second Cold War is perhaps therefore that no one side can win, but that humanity, in the shape of the reader, can think its way out of the dilemma using its reason. But this was a reason with the more modest goal of the survivability, rather than perfectibility, of man.

In conclusion, I hope that it is clear that science fiction in the Eastern bloc offers a number of illuminating insights into the realities of the Cold War, which themselves often only became fully apparent when 'overdrawn' in fictional form. But it is also evident that communist SF should not be viewed simply as an extension of the state. Even in the seemingly more orthodox stories, the future scientocracy was often a coded critique of the contemporary party bureaucracy. At the same time, the extremes of state sponsorship or censorship shielded Eastern bloc authors from the formulaic lures of the Western market. The authors who have stood the test of time, unlike the hacks of the 1950s (who existed on both sides of the Iron Curtain), arguably displayed a greater sense of social conscience than their Western counterparts. And, although SF clearly fed off world events for its material, it was also involved in an internal debate within the genre, which often transcended the Iron Curtain, although the stylistic and intellectual traffic was always heavier from West to

East. The hard-boiled prose and exotic settings of the Strugatskys afforded the reader at least the illusion of a magic door to the outside. But SF under communism was capable of pointing ahead to 'third ways' which often transcended the binary logic of the Cold War, with which neither side would have felt entirely comfortable. Dissident science fiction in the communist bloc, because it took its science so seriously, preserved a cultural autonomy which came to reject not only communism as a failed utopia, but the Cold War as a mechanism with threatened the future *per se*.

NOTES

1. For the best recent overview: David Seed, *American Science Fiction and the Cold War: Literature and Film* (Edinburgh: Edinburgh University Press, 1999). See also H. Bruce Franklin, *Vietnam and Other American Fantasies* (Amherst: Massachusetts University Press, 2000), ch. 8.
2. Olesja Turkina, 'Das Innen und das Außen: Raumfahrtdenkmäler und Rekonstruktion des kulturellen Gedächtnisses in der postsowjetischen Gesellschaft', in Akademie der Künste (ed.), *Denkmale und kulturelles Gedächtnis nach dem Ende der Ost–West-Konfrontation* (Berlin: Jovis, 2000), pp.125–36.
3. Rosalind J. Marsh, *Soviet Fiction since Stalin: Science Politics and Literature* (London: Croom Helm, 1986), p.5.
4. Catriona Kelly, 'The Retreat from Dogmatism: Populism under Khrushchev and Brezhnev', in Catriona Kelly and David Shepherd (eds.), *Russian Cultural Studies: An Introduction* (Oxford: Oxford University Press, 1998), pp.256–7.
5. Yuri Ryurikov, 'Notes on Literature about the Future', *Soviet Literature* 4 (1960), p.129.
6. Darko Suvin, *Metamorphoses of Science Fiction: On the Poetics and History of a Literary Genre* (New Haven and London: Yale University Press, 1979), ch.11.
7. Frank H. Tucker, 'Soviet Science Fiction: Recent Development and Outlook', *Russian Review* 33 (1974), p.189. For an anthology: Leland Fetzer (ed.), *Pre-Revolutionary Russian Science Fiction: An Anthology (Seven Utopias and a Dream)*, (Ann Arbor, MI: Ardis, 1982).
8. Michael Holquist, 'Konstantin Tsiolkovsky: Science Fiction and Philosophy in the History of Soviet Space Exploration', in George E. Slusser and Eric S. Rabkin (eds.), *Intersections: Fantasy and Science Fiction* (Carbondale: Southern Illinois University Press, 1987), pp.74–86.
9. Paul Brians, *Nuclear Holocausts: Atomic War in Fiction, 1895–1984* (Kent State University Press, 1987); Spencer R. Weart, *Nuclear Fear: A History of Images* (Cambridge, MA: Harvard University Press, 1988); Martha A. Bartter, *The Way to Ground Zero: The Atomic Bomb in American Science Fiction* (New York: Greenwood, 1988).
10. Richard Stites, 'Fantasy and Revolution: Alexander Bogdanov and the Origins of Bolshevik Science Fiction', in Alexander Bogdanov, *Red Star: The First Bolshevik Utopia*, ed. Loren R. Graham and Richard Stites (Bloomington: Indiana University Press, [1908] 1984), p.5.
11. Orlando Figes, *Natasha's Dance: A Cultural History of Russia* (London: Allen Lane, 2002), pp.513–14.
12. My term 'communist science fiction' merely refers to SF written within the Eastern

bloc, not to the views of its authors.
13. Rafail Nudelman, 'Soviet Science Fiction and the Ideology of Soviet Society', *Science-Fiction Studies* 16 (1989), p.49.
14. Marsh, *Soviet Fiction*, p.138.
15. Ariadne Gromova, 'At the Frontier of the Present', in C.G. Bearne (ed.), *Vortex: New Soviet Science Fiction* (London: MacGibbon and Kee, 1970), p.10.
16. John Fekete, 'Science Fiction in Hungary', *Science-Fiction Studies* 16 (1989), pp.191–200: p.197.
17. Patrick L. McGuire, *Red Stars: Political Aspects of Soviet Science Fiction* (Ann Arbor, MI: UMI Research Press, 1985), pp.85–92.
18. Wolfgang Both *et al.*, *Berichte aus der Parallelwelt: Die Geschichte des Science Fiction-Fandoms in der DDR* (Passau: EDFC, 1998), p.47. A number of student members were expelled in 1973.
19. Sohar cited in Carl Tighe, 'Stanislaw Lem: Socio-Political Sci-Fi', *Modern Language Review* 84 (1999), pp.773–4.
20. Bogdanov, *Red Star*.
21. Ibid., p.47.
22. McGuire, *Red Stars*, p.16.
23. Heinz Vieweg, *Ultrasymet bleibt geheim* (Berlin: Verlag Neues Leben, 1956).
24. Bokhovitinov and Zakhartchenko, 'The World of Nightmare Fantasies', *Literaturnaya Gazyeta* (March 1948), in Brians, *Nuclear Holocausts*, p.8.
25. Larin in Tucker, 'Soviet Science Fiction', p.199.
26. Voiskunsky in *Soviet Literature* 1 (1982), p.170.
27. Angela and Karlheinz Steinmüller, *Literatur als Prognostik: Das Zukunftsbild der utopischen Literatur der DDR in den fünfziger Jahren* (Gelsenkirchen: Sekretariat für Zukunftsforschung, 1994), p.23.
28. Vladimir Gakov and Paul Brians, 'Nuclear War Themes in Soviet Science Fiction: An Annotated Bibliography', *Science-Fiction Studies* 16 (1989), p.68.
29. Leon Gouré, *Civil Defense in the Soviet Union* (Berkeley and Los Angeles: University of California Press, 1962), p.8.
30. *The Last Pastorale* translated in *Soviet Literature* (1987/88), pp.7–90. Significantly, the story was attacked by military figures in the Soviet media for being pacifist.
31. See, for instance, Karl Böhm and Rolf Dörge, *Gigant Atom* (Berlin: Verlag Neues Leben, 1957).
32. Günther Krupkat, *Die Unsichtbaren* (Berlin: Verlag Das Neue Berlin, 1958), p.12.
33. Heinz Vieweg, *Die zweite Sonne: Wissenschaftlich-phantastischer Roman* (Halle: Mitteldeutscher Verlag, 1958), p.219.
34. Tucker, 'Soviet Science Fiction', p.199; Mikhail Kovalchuk, 'English and American Science Fiction in Russian Translations', *Soviet Literature* 1 (1982), pp.162–8.
35. Lawrence Sutin, *Divine Invasions: A Life of Philip K. Dick* (London: Paladin, 1991), p.200.
36. For an overview: Richard E. Ziegfeld, *Stanislaw Lem* (New York: Ungar, 1985).
37. 'Science Fiction: A Hopeless Case – With Exceptions', reprinted in Stanislaw Lem, *Microworlds: Writings on Science Fiction and Fantasy* (San Diego, CA: Harvest, 1984), pp.45–105: p.69.
38. 'About the Strugatskys' *Roadside Picnic*', in ibid., pp.243–78: pp.246–7.
39. 'The Demons of Philip K. Dick', *The Guardian*, 23 June 2001. Dick, a paranoiac, mailed many of his stamped, addressed letters to the FBI via the dustbin, on the rationale that if he really were under surveillance, they would find their destination. Many did not, surviving only as carbon copies.
40. Ivan Efremov, *Andromeda: A Space-Age Tale*, trans. George Hanna ([1957]; Moscow: Foreign Languages Publishing House, 1959).
41. Much of Eastern-bloc SF was consciously aimed at children. See, for instance, Sabine Vollprecht, *Science-Fiction für Kinder in der DDR* (Stuttgart: Heinz, 1994).

42. David Holloway, *Stalin and the Bomb: The Soviet Union and Atomic Energy, 1939–1956* (New Haven and London: Yale University Press, 1994), pp.358–63.
43. Paul Dickson, *Sputnik: The Shock of the Century* (New York: Walker, 2001), p.104.
44. William E. Burrows, *This New Ocean: The Story of the First Space Age* (New York: Random House, 1998), p.176.
45. Efremov, *Andromeda*, jacket text.
46. Ibid., p.76.
47. Ibid., p.81.
48. 'Cor Serpentis' translated in *Soviet Literature* 5 (1968), pp.3–54.
49. Reprinted in Ben Bova (ed.), *Aliens* (London: Futura, 1977), pp.13–49: pp.26–7.
50. Efremov, *Andromeda*, p.25.
51. Ibid., p.31.
52. Jamie Doran and Piers Bizony, *Starman: The Truth behind the Legend of Yuri Gagarin* (London: Bloomsbury, 1998), pp.128–40.
53. Erik Simon and Olaf R. Spittel, *Die Science-Fiction der DDR: Autoren und Werke: Ein Lexikon* (East Berlin: Das Neue Berlin, 1988).
54. *Der schweigende Stern* (Maetzig, 1960).
55. Efremov, *Andromeda*, p.61.
56 Chingiz Aitmatov, *The Day Lasts More than a Hundred Years*, trans. John French (Bloomington, IN: Indiana University Press, [1980] 1983).
57. Günther Krupkat, *Als die Götter starben* (Berlin: Verlag Das Neue Berlin, 1963), p.76.
58 See Thomas Kramer, 'Die DDR der fünfziger Jahre im Comic MOSAIK: Einschienenbahn, Agenten, Chemieprogramm', in Alf Lüdtke and Peter Becker (eds.), *Akten, Eingaben, Schaufenster: Die DDR und ihre Texte* (Berlin: Akademie, 1997), pp.167–88.
59. Hannes Hegen, *Die Reise ins All* (Berlin: Verlag Junge Welt, [1959] reprint 1999).
60. Krupkat, *Die Unsichtbaren*, pp.117–18.
61. Sozialistische Einheitspartei Deutschlands-Zentralkomitee (Abt. Parteiorganisation), 'Information' Nr. 65, 26 May 1961, Stiftung Archiv der Parteien und Massenorganisationen der DDR im Bundesarchiv, DY 30/IV 2/5/295, fos.53–61.
62. James Harford, *Korolev: How One Man Masterminded the Soviet Drive to Beat America to the Moon* (New York: Wiley, 1997), pp.272 ff.
63. Paul R. Josephson, *Red Atom: Russia's Nuclear Power Program from Stalin to Today* (New York: Freeman, 1999), pp.279–80.
64. Paul R. Josephson, *New Atlantis Revisited: Akademogorodok, the Siberian City of Science* (Princeton, NJ: Princeton University Press, 1997), p.108.
65. Ivan Adamovic, 'Czech SF in the Last Forty Years', *Science-Fiction Studies* 17 (1990), p.52.
66 Stephen W. Potts, *The Second Marxian Invasion: The Fiction of the Strugatsky Brothers* (San Bernardino, CA: Borgo, 1991); Yvonne Howell, *Apocalyptic Realism: The Science Fiction of Arkady and Boris Strugatsky* (New York: Peter Lang, 1994).
67. Nudelman, 'Soviet Science Fiction', p.60.
68. Arkady and Boris Strugatsky, *Hard to be a God*, trans. Wendayne Ackerman (London: Eyre Methuen, [1964] 1975), p.218.
69. Halina Stephan, 'The Changing Protagonist in Soviet Science Fiction', in Henrik Birnbaum and Thomas Eekman (eds.), *Fiction and Drama in Eastern and Southeastern Europe* (Columbus: Slavica, 1980), pp.361–78.
70. Alice Stone Nakhimovsky, 'Soviet Anti-Utopias in the Works of Arkady and Boris Strugatsky', in Charles E. Gribble (ed.), *Alexander Lipson: In Memoriam* (Columbus: Slavica, 1994), pp.143–53.
71. Nudelman, 'Soviet Science Fiction', p.51.
72. Angela und Karlheinz Steinmüller, 'Die befohlene Zukunft: DDR-Science Fiction zwischen Wunschtraum und (Selbst-)Zensur', *Das Science Fiction Jahr 1994* (Munich, 1994).

73. Elaine Kleiner, 'Romanian "Science Fantasy" in the Cold War Era', *Science Fiction Studies* 19 (1992), p.64.
74. Stanislaw Lem, *Return from the Stars*, trans. Barbara Marszal and Frank Simpson (San Diego, CA: Harvest, [1961] 1980), p.50.
75. Arkady and Boris Strugatsky, *The Final Circle of Paradise*, trans. Leonid Renen (New York: DAW, [1965] 1976), p.54.
76. Adamovic, 'Czech SF', p.57.
77. Lem, *Microworlds*, pp.92–3.
78. Stanislaw Lem, *Solaris*, trans. Joanna Kilmartin and Steve Cox (London: Arrow, [1961] 1973), pp.22–3.
79. Arkady and Boris Strugatsky, *Roadside Picnic*, trans. Antonina W. Bouis (London: Gollancz, [1972] 2000).
80. Ben Hellman, 'Paradise Lost: The Literary Development of Arkadii and Boris Strugatskii', *Russian History* 11 (1984), pp.311–19: p.319.
81. Stanislaw Lem, *Peace on Earth*, trans. Elinor Ford (San Diego, CA: Harvest, [1987] 1994).

The Education of Dissent:
The Reception of the Voice of Free
Hungary, 1951–56

MARK PITTAWAY

In Budapest's Chinoin Pharmaceuticals Factory an extraordinary incident took place in August 1952. It was precipitated by a programme called the 'Black Book' on the Voice of Free Hungary, one of the American-backed 'free radios' that was broadcast into the country from Munich. The programme, which could best be described as black propaganda, broadcast information collected from escapees about party members and others sympathetic to the regime. The individuals targeted were presented as being part of a rogues' gallery of individuals, who supposedly acted in the interests of the regime against the people. One female Stakhanovite in the factory had learned through work-mates and relatives who listened to the station that she was mentioned on this programme, and had taken it to mean that 'she was described on a list as an exploiter of the workers'. As a result she had begun to hold back her production, and had stopped working as a Stakhanovite.[1] The ability of the Voice of Free Hungary to disturb the functioning of Stakhanovite labour competition on Budapest shop-floors was a mark of the extraordinary impact of an unusual broadcasting experiment. The station had begun broadcasting on 6 October 1951 as the Hungarian arm of the broadcasting operations of Radio Free Europe (RFE). RFE was a key plank of attempts by the United States to use the medium in an unprecedented programme of psychological warfare in Central and Eastern Europe during the early part of the Cold War.[2]

The historiography of the Voice of Free Hungary has centred on its controversial role during the 1956 Revolution. In the West the controversy began almost immediately after the Soviet intervention and the subsequent suppression of the revolution; a process completed by early 1957. Accusations centred on 'irresponsible' broadcasts to Hungary, supposed to have emanated from Munich, that incited violence in the country during late October. Others pointed to the mistaken suggestion that revolt in Hungary would be supported by Western military intervention, while other critics attacked the radio station's failure to back the reform communist Prime Minister, Imre Nagy.[3] Behind the Iron Curtain, in Hungary itself, the restored socialist regime blamed the broadcasts of Radio Free Europe for the events of 1956. For regime propagandists the assumed role of Radio Free Europe played a central role in the myth of 1956 as a 'counter-revolution' that formed an important pillar of the regime's legitimacy right down to 1989.[4]

While Kádárist accounts of Radio Free Europe's role can be dismissed as a gross distortion of the available evidence, the 'Western' accusations against the station are not so easily dismissable. Although recent scholarship has criticized the 'irresponsible' nature of some of the Voice of Free Hungary's broadcasting during the revolution, it has absolved the station of the damaging charge that it bore some of the moral responsibility for the events of October 1956.[5] In concentrating on the controversies that surround the station's output during the 1956 revolution, one absolutely crucial issue in assessing the role of the Voice of Free Hungary has been missed. All observers are united on the question of the influence of the Voice of Free Hungary on large numbers of radio listeners in Hungary both during the events of the revolution and the events that preceded it. During the early 1950s one Hungarian government official had remarked in a confidential report that 'the most dangerous effect of RFE's activities is that it results not in organized resistance, which is easily defeated and suppressed, but in atomized resistance, which is more difficult to control'.[6] Yet despite this recognition there has been no attempt to show how the broadcasts of the Voice of Free Hungary, and by extension other Western radio stations broadcasting to the country, managed to gain such a following.

Such an evaluation would have a relevance that goes beyond Hungary. In recent years, with the growth of interest in both the culture of the Cold War and in the techniques of psychological warfare employed by the United States in particular during the early 1950s, there has been considerable interest in the use of radio as a propaganda tool.[7] To date, work has focused on the politics of culture, through analyses of the policies of those controlling or seeking to control the relevant radio stations. Fewer analyses have sought to examine the content of broadcasting. Furthermore, despite its potential to reveal much about the development of popular political attitudes in the states that were targeted by radio stations there have been no studies of the actual reception of such radio stations.

This article, with its narrow focus on the social role of Western radio stations, and particularly the Voice of Free Hungary, within Hungarian society, does not pretend to fill this gap. It instead seeks to highlight some of the issues that a truly comparative social history of Western broadcasting aimed at societies behind the Iron Curtain should consider. It argues that in the Hungarian case the Voice of Free Hungary's success stems from its role in the social history of Hungarian broadcasting. When it began to broadcast in October 1951, it broadcast to a country in which there was a strong tradition of listening to foreign radio broadcasts, particularly the Voice of America. This trend had been intensified by the Stalinization of domestic radio programming that followed the imposition of socialist dictatorship in the country between 1947 and 1949. The beginning of the Voice of Free Hungary also coincided with the explosive growth of ownership of radio sets, which formed one of the few successful planks of the regime's policy in relation to the provision of consumer goods. The number of radio licence holders increased from 539,000 to 1,270,000 between 1951 and 1954. A representative statistical survey of household budgets and living conditions in the same year found that 66.1 per cent of 'working class' families owned a radio, and noted that 'the vast majority of urban families have a radio. In the villages the supply of electricity is the only thing in some places that prevents the use of radio'.[8] The Western radio stations, especially Radio Free Europe could be easily received on the People's Radio (*Néprádió*), the standard radio set owned by Hungarian households in this period; though in certain areas and at certain times – particularly where jamming was effective – technical help was needed to ensure good reception.[9] Ironically one of the few successes of the Stalinist regime's policy towards consumer goods created a mass audience for Western radio propaganda.

The Voice of Free Hungary, it is argued here, had an important role in shaping political attitudes, especially among the urban working class, towards the socialist regime. It built on the success of the Voice of America in particular in articulating and shaping pre-existing popular discontent with poor living standards and the lack of political freedom. This process, described here as 'the education of dissent', was probably the most important political role played by the Voice of Free Hungary during the early 1950s. The impact of Western radio's 'education of dissent' was clearly visible in the internal reports of the climate of opinion (*hangulatjelentés*) prepared by the internal security services, party and trade unions during the period by the middle of the 1950s. Certainly such sources should be treated with caution, given the fact that Stalinist propaganda frequently blamed Western radio stations for inciting popular opposition. Yet this does not mean that the incidents and the attitudes that underpin them can be easily dismissed as Stalinist fantasy. The reports clearly reveal the traces of pre-existing attitudes that were partially shaped and educated by Western radio broadcasts. It is particularly noteworthy that identical attitudes can be discerned in the statements of those who escaped before and after the revolution of 1956, collected by Western investigators (including those employed by the Research Department of the Hungarian section of Radio Free Europe).

The argument of this article is developed by first setting the Voice of Free Hungary within the broader context of the social history of Hungarian broadcasting, paying particular attention to the late 1940s and early 1950s. It then examines the policy of the Voice of Free Hungary itself and how it was able to articulate patterns of discontent in Hungarian society during the early 1950s. Following that, the effect of Western radio and the Voice of Free Hungary on patterns of public opinion in the country will be considered.

Broadcasting, Listening and Hungarian Society to 1951

It is impossible to write the history of the popular reception of the programming of the Voice of Free Hungary without situating it within the broader context of the social history of Hungarian broadcasting during the mid-twentieth century. This in itself is a difficult task simply because of the lack of real work done at all on the social history of broadcasting in the country. Much of the work that exists either consists of technological or institutional histories, which contain only fragmentary information on patterns of listening and issues of reception. Furthermore their frames of reference are almost entirely the national context, thus tending to ignore the vital issues of the role foreign broadcasters have played in reaching the Hungarian public.[10]

The history of domestic broadcasting in Hungary began in December 1925 with the first broadcast of the Budapest station of Hungarian radio to 16,927 registered listeners, who paid a regular licence fee to receive radio signals. The total number of licence fee payers increased dramatically throughout the inter-war years reaching a total of 383,505 by 1937. Radio throughout the inter-war years was overwhelmingly a preserve of the urban middle class; residents of Budapest, who at the time made up around 12 per cent of the population,[11] accounted for just over 35 per cent of all licence fee payers by 1937. One sociological survey of radio licence fee payers from 1933 revealed that only 4.8 per cent of listeners came from the rural population and 8.2 per cent from the ranks of industrial workers. Members of the 'intelligentsia', however, accounted for 52.6 per cent of listeners while independent businessmen and artisans made up another 24.1 per cent.[12] For much of the 1930s, radio was a favoured method of relaxation for large sections of the urban middle class, though the 'National Christian' regime then in power in Budapest sought to use radio as an instrument for shoring up its power among the population. This began a process by which the Hungarian state came to see radio as a tool of propaganda.[13]

During the Second World War, Hungarian radio functioned as a state radio, reflecting and representing the policies of the various governments that held power during the period.[14] By the early 1940s large sections of the Hungarian radio-owning public listened to foreign broadcasts, most notably those of the BBC Hungarian service. Around 40 per cent of radio listeners were believed to tune in to foreign broadcasts regularly in 1943. The BBC had a large share of this audience in the country at this time.[15] The Nazi occupation of the country on 19 March 1944 represented a turning point, in that in crucial respects Hungarian radio began to distribute the propaganda of the occupying forces.[16] Despite the official bans on listening to foreign stations, this practice continued; in August 1944 it was still estimated that the BBC 'had a large audience' in the country.[17] As Hungary turned into a theatre of military conflict with the arrival of the Red Army, this continued. There is much anecdotal evidence that as Soviet troops approached Budapest larger proportions of the population tuned into Kossuth Rádió, the service of the Hungarian Communist Party broadcast from Moscow.[18]

With the end of the Second World War, occupying forces in Hungary installed a 'popular front' coalition government which at first uneasily united the communist left and conservative right. While the events of 1945 led to something close to outright social revolution in the country, the Right were able to triumph in elections at the end of that year, capitalizing on discontent with the behaviour of the Red Army and a backlash among middle-class Hungarians. Hyperinflation in the first half of 1946, deep-seated class tensions, and bitter political struggle between Left and Right marked the period of rule by the 'popular front' coalition. Despite these tensions, the period of 'popular front' government between the end of the Second World War and the creation of socialist dictatorship between 1947 and 1949 saw real reform of many public institutions, including Hungarian national radio. Some three months after the 'liberation' of Budapest in April 1945 the new Budapest stations began their first 'experimental' transmissions, resuming regular programming on May Day 1945.[19] Although the listeners still remained overwhelmingly middle-class, much of the programming of the new radio reflected the hegemony enjoyed by the left-wing parties following the 'liberation'. It also reflected the 'democratic' ideology of post-war reconstruction that was prevalent in the country. Radio programming was markedly democratized, with the voices of the rural poor and industrial labour being given a marked prominence in much of the new programming.[20]

With the gradual recovery of the economy during the later part of the popular front era, the first real attempts were made to expand radio ownership beyond its urban, middle-class, Budapest-centred base. In early 1947 Hungarian radio launched the 'village radio' (falurádió) programme. A package was put together for rural dwellers that would allow them to buy both an inexpensive radio set and a licence together, in order to expand access. Its aim, proclaimed the periodical that was sent out to all licence fee payers, was to 'close the gap between town and country'. According to the director of the radio, quoted in a subsequent issue, its role was to 'quickly inform, educate and entertain the Hungarian village and the Hungarian peasantry'.[21] The way in which the management of Hungarian radio saw the radio as a tool to forge a new, egalitarian sense of Hungarian nationhood that accommodated traditionally subordinate groups such as industrial labour and the rural poor, looked forward to the policies of the socialist dictatorship. Its programming was a mix of the innovative and the traditional. Alongside programming aimed explicitly at workers and peasants there was a more traditional diet of light and folk music aimed at the still predominantly middle-class audience. The director of the drama division both pronounced on the need and conceded the failure of radio to 'escape from the social exclusiveness of much of our programming'.[22] In order to cater to the tastes of younger listeners, a considerable amount of air-time had been given over to jazz and other forms of contemporary dance music.[23]

Though there are no reliable figures of how many Hungarian listeners tuned into foreign broadcasts, the circumstantial evidence suggests that this tendency had not diminished with the end of the Second World War. In part this perhaps reflected perceptions among middle-class listeners that Hungarian radio formed a mouthpiece for the increasingly left-wing government and continuing uncertainty about the political situation in the country. Whatever the cause, official radio listings carried the frequencies of all Hungarian language broadcasts by foreign stations until 1948. In spring 1947 this consisted not only of limited programming carried by state radio stations in Belgrade, Bucharest and Vienna aimed at domestic Hungarian minorities, but also by the BBC, the Voice of America and Radio Moscow.[24] In addition the programme listings are also suggestive of some demand for radio programming in languages other than Hungarian, providing programme information for English language services from the BBC and the Czech language programming of Radio Prague.[25]

By the end of 1947 the era of popular front rule in the country was coming to an end with the onset of the Cold War. Over the next two years a single-party dictatorship came to power in the country. One of the key policies of the dictatorship was to increase radio ownership in absolute terms and also to increase the access of poorer social groups to radio ownership. By the end of 1947 the number of radio licence holders stood at approximately 385,000. A sociological survey that broke down licence fee payers by socio-economic group demonstrated that the middle-class preponderance among the listeners had been significantly eroded by May 1948. 30 per cent were described as members of the 'intelligentsia', 25 per cent as industrial workers, 2.5 per cent as miners, 22 per cent as belonging to 'other middle class groups', 7 per cent as the peasantry, with the remainder belonging to the category 'unspecified'.[26] In April 1949 the state began an explicit drive to expand radio ownership with the 'radio to the workers' (*Rádiót a dolgozóknak*) campaign. Its target was explicitly to expand radio ownership among the urban working class, with campaigns to popularize the notion of radio with a series of events in factories and communities across the country with live broadcasts at their centre. More practically the state cut the prices of radios and with a wave of publicity launched the *népszuper akció*, a straightforward promotional campaign designed to ensure that at least 20,000 people would be able to obtain radio sets cheaply.[27] By the end of 1949 the number of radio licence payers had risen to

539,000.[28] Campaigns of promotion continued into 1950 with attempts to install radios in schools, factories, workers' hostels and in other community buildings. Furthermore in May the ruling Hungarian Workers' Party initiated a campaign to 'recruit licence fee payers'. Party activists were organized in many communities and work-places to persuade people to purchase radios. Within the postal service, signing up new radio licence holders was identified as one of the targets that workers were to reach in their labour competitions. The campaign to expand radio ownership was one of the most visible signs of a distinctively Stalinist consumerism in 1950.[29] Those that signed up for new radios under the auspices of these campaigns during the first nine months of 1950 were not fully representative of the population. 40 per cent identified themselves as industrial workers, thus demonstrating the increasing popularity of the radio in industrial communities. The 'working peasantry' – the regime's term for all those living from agriculture except those identified as *kulaks* – continued to be under-represented, making up only 12.3 per cent of new subscribers. Though their under-representation was corrected by the mid-1950s, it was still marked in the early years of the decade.[30]

The late 1940s saw the programme content of domestic Hungarian radio change significantly, as the dictatorship sought to use radio as a propaganda instrument. Hungarian Radio's two Budapest stations were re-named Kossuth (evoking memories of wartime Hungarian Communist broadcasts from Moscow) and Petöfi (after the nineteenth-century revolutionary poet). By the early part of 1950 the programme content of the two radio stations had been thoroughly Stalinized. The amount of light music broadcast was cut back radically, while the jazz and dance music that had characterized programming in 1947 disappeared altogether with a series of programme changes completed at the end of October 1949.[31] The musical content of radio broadcasts consisted of folk music and work-place choruses. Clear weight was given to the explicit promotion of Russian culture. Air-time was given on a weekly basis to programmes supporting those learning the Russian language. Heavy emphasis was placed on general cultural and scientific education in programming, while the tradition of broadcasting aimed explicitly at the industrial working class and agricultural population continued. More traditional news items were supplemented with other programmes such as 'news from the production front', which ensured that radio programming reflected the productivist culture of the dictatorship.[32] A limited amount of the programming was not designed to be listened to by the individual or family within the home, but was broadcast to support group activities in the party seminar room or the work-place. Increasingly time was given over to programming aimed at the army, at those studying for party examinations, for party activists in factories and communities, as well as for those participating in labour competitions in industry.[33]

The expansion of radio ownership, particularly within the industrial working class, and the Stalinization of domestic radio programming occurred when certain 'American' cultural forms heavily discouraged by the new regime enjoyed popularity among Hungarian youth. The extent to which certain aspects of 'American' popular culture were able to permeate Hungarian society during the late 1940s, often as a consequence of earlier patterns of emigration, were revealed by social observers writing about poor rural communities.[34] The continued popularity of 'American' popular culture under the dictatorship continued to provide the basis for sub-cultures within working-class youth to emerge that were based on resistant identities. One worker in the early 1950s remembered that 'the young people who dressed in modern, Western style ... were called "imperialists", "agents of the West", etc. They liked dancing, especially American jazz music. There were many young people like this'.[35] Combined with the growth of censorship that the onset of dictatorship represented, this meant that the technically illegal practice of listening to foreign radio stations was widespread among those who had only recently gained access to a radio. This category included many working-class listeners, despite continual attempts to jam the signals by the Hungarian authorities. One worker who escaped the country in 1956 described his own listening habits in the early part of the decade:

> I only listened to the Hungarian news broadcasts on these radios. Usually from 8 p.m. to 10 p.m. I listened regularly to the 8.30 p.m. London news broadcasts and to the 9 p.m. VOA [Voice of America] program. Both of these programs were in Hungarian. What we heard over the radio, we usually discussed among friends if friends were reliable.
>
> I listened to our own radio, usually the whole family listened to the programme together. Sometimes we would have friends staying with us who also listened to the broadcasts. We were always careful not to tune the radio too loud ... Very often, I would be informed about the contents of foreign radio

broadcasts when I had been unable to listen. If there was some sensational news over the radio, we immediately told each other and asked each other's views.[36]

During the years of the early 1950s the state seems to have been unable to prevent individuals tuning into foreign broadcasts and does not seem to have made much effort to enforce rules against listening to them. One worker from the Budapest suburb of Ferencváros remembered that 'no special precautions were taken when the radios were tuned in. The neighbor kept his radio blaring even when the windows were open'.[37] This practice seems to have been exceptional; while the state seemed powerless to prevent people tuning into to Western radio within the confines of the home, such practices were effectively criminalized. Despite this, even in common spaces in communal hostels residents used radios to tune in to foreign broadcasts. According to one miner, resident in a workers' hostel in Tatabánya in the early 1950s, 'listening to western radio often formed a kind of initiation into the culture of the hostel'. Yet even here listeners took care to ensure that the authorities, either within the hostel or more broadly, would not learn about their listening habits.[38]

Attempts by the state to jam transmissions formed a more serious obstacle to those seeking to listen to foreign radio broadcasts in Hungarian than did the threat of arrest or other forms of retribution by the authorities. According to one working-class listener in the west of the country:

> Reception of these programmes depended upon what kind of radio a person had and where the jamming stations were situated. Sometimes the same program would be jammed on five wavelengths and of these, four would be jammed and one would receive excellent reception. In general the reception of the VOA broadcasts were excellent. BBC programmes' reception was fair, but only on short wave. It was very difficult to get Rome. With the exception of the Hungarian news broadcasts from Radio Moscow and from other radio stations behind the iron curtain, all foreign broadcasts in Hungarian were jammed.[39]

The recourse of the Hungarian regime to jamming foreign stations broadcasting to the country draws attention to the fact that, as radio ownership was increasing inside Hungary, Western powers and especially the United States used radio as an instrument of propaganda. The Voice of America seems to have been particularly effective during this period.[40] This may have, in part, been due to the disappearance of 'American' popular music from Hungarian radio as a result of the programming changes of 1949. It also reflected the deep political divisions inside the country as the institutions of socialist dictatorship were built and consolidated in the country. This political division created a demand for a source of news other than that approved by the party and state in Budapest. Reports prepared by the internal security services during 1949 demonstrate the clear nervousness of the regime about the effect of VOA propaganda on public opinion. VOA reporting was blamed for fuelling rumours of imminent war between the West and Hungary. According to many opponents of the new regime such a war would lead to the 'liberation' of the country.[41]

Reaching the Population: the Voice of Free Hungary in its Hungarian Context

The Hungarian state was permanently worried about the effect on the population of listening to foreign radio throughout the 1950s. The figure of the 'spreader of rumours', who disrupted either production or consumption after listening to Western radio broadcasts figured prominently in regime propaganda during the early 1950s and in early Stalinist culture more generally. One example of this was the 1952 comic drama entitled 'The State Department Store' (*Állami Áruház*), which was filmed in 1953. The drama pitted the honest workers of one Budapest department store, led by a managing director promoted from the shop-floor, against a band of individuals who bought up and hoarded goods. In both play and film the hoarders of goods responded to messages of incitement broadcast over the airwaves by the Voice of America.[42] By the time the film version was released it was in danger of becoming outdated even as propaganda. Increasingly the Voice of Free Hungary replaced the Voice of America as the foreign radio station whose broadcasts most worried the Hungarian authorities. Events in 1953 were to demonstrate why this was the case.

1953 was a dramatic turning point both in Hungary specifically and in Central and Eastern Europe more generally. The death of Stalin in March and later the events of June in the German Democratic Republic shook the bloc. Furthermore they were marked in Hungary in June and July by a change of both government and direction. After meetings between the Hungarian and Soviet party leaderships in Moscow in June, Imre Nagy became Prime Minister and announced the beginning of a 'New Course'. The Voice of Free Hungary was able to score a number of coups. As Hungarian Radio waited for an announcement from TASS, the Soviet news agency, to break the news of the death of Stalin in March 1953, the Voice of Free Hungary was the first to announce Stalin's death to the Hungarian population. Likewise its coverage of the events in Berlin in June provided the population with a counterpoint to the official view broadcast on Hungarian radio and printed in the press.[43]

In the climate of uncertainty that events both internationally and domestically had created, it became clear to the regime that Western radio stations and particularly the Voice of Free Hungary were shaping public opinion in the country. This was made apparent by incidents where the contents of reports from the Voice of Free Hungary provided material for anti-communist rumour-mongering amongst the population. In June 1953 Radio Free Europe reported that 28,000 workers in Csepel had gone on strike and that 600 had been interned by the ÁVH[44] in order to suppress the open expression of discontent. This was widely repeated by industrial workers: in the Zala oil fields, for example, it caused both excitement and consternation. The authorities were so concerned that they issued a strong denial through official media channels.[45] Opinions reported by the internal security services in the factories after the June events in Berlin heightened the sense of insecurity felt by the regime about the effects of the reporting of Western radio stations on public opinion. Whilst the events in the GDR did not lead to open mass protest in Hungary, they had an electrifying effect on the shop-floor. The notion that a population could express its discontent openly in a socialist state began, albeit slowly, to lift the lid on a well of discontent. Industrial workers in Budapest openly stated that 'the Hungarian party can learn from the German party that it is not correct to apply pressure all the time through the norms'. In one industrial suburb in the capital one party secretary reported that people were calling on the workers in Hungary to strike and follow the example of the GDR.[46]

The events of 1953 made the regime painfully aware of the impact of the Voice of Free Hungary domestically. It had begun to have an effect, however, as much as a year before, as the incident in the Chinoin Pharmaceuticals Factory in August 1952 described in the introduction to this article, attests. During campaigns to increase production norms in the factories in June 1952, some of the opposition expressed demonstrated the effect of Western radio and the propaganda of the Voice of Free Hungary in particular on public opinion. An example of this was when one worker in the city of Pécs linked the dispute over wages explicitly to the difference between the political systems on either side of the Iron Curtain. He argued that 'the American example' should be followed in order to guarantee Hungarian workers a better life.[47] Throughout 1952 in reports dealing with the climate of opinion compiled by the internal security services, party activists and social organizations, explicit references to stations such as the Voice of America disappeared to be replaced almost exclusively by references to the Voice of Free Hungary.

The Voice of Free Hungary began broadcasting to the country at a time of deep discontent with the socialist regime as it pressed on with a policy of forced industrialization. Industrial workers bore the brunt of policies to speed up production through labour competition, while they experienced raised production targets and falling wages from 1950 onwards.[48] The rural population suffered the effects of an ill-thought out collectivization drive, punitive taxation and widespread requisitioning of agricultural produce as the state sought to feed the cities. [49] Living standards fell dramatically during the early 1950s; according to trade union figures real wages were some 16.6 per cent lower in 1953 than in 1949, whilst the average income of households living from wages and salaries had fallen by 8 per cent over the same period. The consequences of declining living standards could be seen through the share of household budgets devoted to the consumption of certain categories of goods. Groceries accounted for 45.9 per cent of the budget of an average household in 1949, a figure that had risen to 58.8 per cent by 1953, whilst the share of expenditure on clothing had fallen from 18.2 per cent to 10.4 per cent. Furthermore the average household's consumption of meat, fat and milk was lower in 1953 than in 1938.[50] Popular discontent with the regime created the backdrop to the success of the Voice of Free Hungary in generating an atmosphere in which all sections of the population, including the traditionally left-wing industrial working class, were willing to listen to an anti-regime message.

From the beginning of broadcasting in late 1951, the Voice of Free Hungary placed particular emphasis on news, broadcasting news reports of ten minutes in length every hour. Its early programming consisted of propaganda programming aimed at target groups like the industrial working class and the peasantry; early programme titles included 'Views from the Life of the Western Worker' or 'The Small Farm in the West' that sought to contrast the lives of certain social groups with those on the other side of the Iron Curtain. The party membership was also targeted in an attempt to de-motivate ordinary party activists with the 'Call to the Communist Party'. There was also the 'Black Book', which created the incident in the Chinoin Pharmaceuticals Factory, that was broadcast briefly and then abandoned due to the early difficulties in securing reliable information on individuals. 'Reflektor', fronted by the journalist Imre Mikes who broadcast under the pseudonym Gallicus, provided anti-communist commentary on events inside Hungary. Others were fictionalized programmes such as that centred on the character of Bálint Bóda, who was supposed to have entered Hungary secretly to report on conditions in the country. [51]

To produce programming capable of targeting the working-class and peasant audiences that had just acquired radio sets and licences inside Hungary not only required good ideas but accurate information on the conditions and opinions of target groups. In Spring 1952, the staff of the Hungarian Department of Radio Free Europe sought contact with the refugee camp in Wels in Austria that received refugees that crossed the border from Hungary and into Austria. [52] Little is known about patterns of illegal emigration from Hungary between 1948 and 1956, except that it provided the Voice of Free Hungary with an invaluable pool of information that still forms one of the best collections of contemporary personal accounts of daily life in Hungary during the period. [53] Staff based in Linz and later in Vienna and Graz would interview escapees from Hungary; examining the transcripts of the interviews they would often ask for personal information on party officials and first of all, for considerable information on their work-place or community. They would then be asked about living conditions, working conditions and political opinions; interviewers seem mostly to have been interested in specific information about wages, the supply of goods in shops and conditions. Transcripts of interviews would be typed up in Hungarian and then they would be evaluated for accuracy. Evaluations would typically include some comment of the original interviewers; a typical comment placed on the transcript of one subject included the phrase 'a 19-year-old, intelligent factory hand who escaped in late November 1955. He reported his own experiences'. [54] Evaluation would often consist of attempting to cross-check facts on specific places or people referred to in the transcripts, often using an extensive library of clippings from the official Hungarian press. They would also point to interesting information and points that had clear propaganda value; in almost all cases the evaluators' focus on attempting to gain an accurate picture of patterns of daily life was striking. An example of this might be the comment of one evaluator on the transcript of an interview with a young woman who crossed the border in autumn 1954: 'the statements about the poor quality of preserved foodstuffs should be noted particularly. The regime makes a point of advertising preserved foods which should make life easier for those women who have little time for household duties. It appears from this report that this preserved food is simply uneatable.'[55] At the end of the evaluation process a new typescript would be prepared including the original Hungarian text, an English or German summary and the evaluator's comment. The typescript would be filed under a subject heading and an extensive collection of, largely, accurate information was created about living and working conditions in the country that could then be used in programming.

Popular discontent with the regime thus created the atmosphere in which the Voice of Free Hungary was able to succeed, providing it with an audience receptive to its propaganda. It also provided it with the small stream of escapees during the mid-1950s who provided much of the information that lay behind programmes aimed at particular social groups within Hungarian society. Programming such as 'Workers behind the Iron Curtain' drew attention to low living standards, restrictive labour legislation, poor working conditions and the lack of independent trade unions in the factories. These experiences were contrasted with what was reported in a programme like 'Workers in the West'.[56] In this way the broadcasts of the Voice of Free Hungary were to make use of information that came from the small number of escapees to support its propaganda, thus enabling it to play an active part in the education of the widespread pre-existing dissent that existed in Hungarian society during the mid-1950s in the run-up to the 1956 revolution.

An Education of Dissent?

A young miner from rural western Hungary remembered that in 1954: 'in general there was a great deal of discontent among the miners, they denounced the system, grumbled, because in spite of the difficult work their pay was low'. Such a climate in a Hungarian work-place was common from 1950 onwards and could be discerned as much from party or internal security service reports as from interviews with escapees collected by a Western radio station in an Austrian refugee camp. What was new in his account that would not have been found in a report on popular attitudes in the work-place three years earlier in 1951 was a willingness among working-class Hungarians positively to evaluate the situation of workers in the West in relation to their own. The same miner recounted one conversation with a work-mate who asked him where he came from. When he replied that he came from a village along Hungary's border with Austria the work-mate replied: 'If I was in your place I wouldn't stay here for a minute ... I'd go to the West where at least you are valued for as long as you can work, here you are just treated like a dog to whom they occasionally throw a bone so you don't starve.'[57]

It is difficult to say how far such a positive evaluation of the West during the mid-1950s was a direct result of the increasing popularity and influence of the Voice of Free Hungary in the country. Hungarians did have other means of evaluating the relative difference between living conditions at home and in the West. Traditional correspondence by letter with Western relatives continued, though this was closely-controlled and impacted on a relatively small number of people. There are very good reasons, however, for viewing such attitudes, at least in part, as the result of the interaction between extensive popular discontent with the regime and the broadcast output of the station. There is considerable, albeit anecdotal evidence of the considerable popularity of the Voice of Free Hungary within the country during the mid-1950s, some of which has already been cited within the body of this article. This is backed up by the various unrepresentative surveys that attempted, however unreliably, to estimate the size of the Voice of Free Hungary's audience inside the country. Between April and October 1952 the Information Department of Radio Free Europe conducted a survey of an unrepresentative sample of refugees from Hungary and those who had been granted official permission to leave. They found that of their sample, 69 per cent regularly tuned into the Voice of Free Hungary while 22 per cent listened occasionally. Some 48 per cent of the sample relied on the Voice of Free Hungary for information on world events as opposed to 19 per cent who relied on official Hungarian radio.[58] Though for obvious reasons the figures should be treated with considerable care, they nevertheless point to the popularity of the station in the country and a reputation for factual reporting – all gained within the first year of its operation.

Furthermore the traces of the political views promoted by the Voice of Free Hungary can be discerned in statements of popular attitudes towards events inside Hungary, whether these were recorded in official reports or interviews conducted after a successful escape from Hungary. In direct contrast to official propaganda that drew unfavourable comparisons between the living conditions of workers in Western and socialist countries, workers began to see the West in an increasingly positive light.[59] This had a direct effect on the nature and extent of worker opinions.

Programming like 'Reflektor', broadcast by the Voice of Free Hungary, explicitly linked anti-communism to working-class welfare throughout the mid-1950s. One programme broadcast on May Day 1956 was representative of much of this kind of propaganda:

> What would be the fate of an unfortunate progressive on this May Day, who either wrote or spoke out against piece rates, stating that they were damaging to the person ... Or for that matter someone who called for popular rule, with independent political parties, free elections, clean counting of votes and a sovereign national assembly?[60]

The link between working-class welfare and political democracy had been articulated by the Voice of Free Hungary throughout the mid-1950s. This link emerged in working-class opinion from 1953 onwards, in a way that seems to be direct testimony of its growing influence on public opinion in the country's factories and industrial communities. In the United Lighting and Electrics Factory, in the run-up to the 1953 parliamentary elections, workers were strongly opposed to the existence of only one list in the election stating that 'there will be voting, but no election'. These workers were hopeful that 'a bourgeois democracy will be created through a bourgeois revolution', thus contrasting the political system of the capitalist states with the repression on the socialist side of the Iron Curtain; an opinion that would never have been recorded two years earlier.[61] Propaganda that described the 'good life' that apparently existed in the United States by the mid-1950s also shaped workers' opinions and focused their anger about their low standard of living in socialist Hungary. In March 1954 one younger miner who was to escape to the West overheard a conversation among four or five older workmates who had been communists six years earlier. One miner stated that:

I don't understand why we work so much in Hungary and we work for nothing and with absolutely no outlook. We have to struggle and endanger our lives in the mines for just a small amount of daily bread. A worker can't give his family the comfort that a western worker enjoys, as they have to work much less than we do. In the United States they only have to work four hours and they earn enough to have their own property in their old age, their own car and house.[62]

The frequency with which such opinions appeared in reports from the mid-1950s onwards suggests that they were not entirely unrepresentative and that the Voice of Free Hungary in particular was relatively successful in educating pre-existing discontent with the socialist regime. This account therefore suggests that for a variety of reasons the propaganda of Western radio stations and particularly the Voice of Free Hungary was relatively successful in permeating Hungarian society. The account presented here has been less than comprehensive and can only be said to represent a first word on the subject of how the propaganda of Western radio stations was received. The relative success of the Voice of Free Hungary was based upon the way it was able to articulate pre-existing popular discontent in the country during the mid-1950s. This conclusion plainly does not answer the charge made that the station incited revolt in 1956, but it does explain the station's popularity and why its appeal to the population was credible during 1956. An answer to the question of whether the Voice of Free Hungary behaved irresponsibly during the events of 1956 is beyond the scope of this article.

NOTES

1. Magyar Országos Levéltár – Hungarian National Archive (hereafter MOL) M-Bp.-176f.2/184/4ö.e., p.213.
2. For a history of the Hungarian service of Radio Free Europe, see Gyula Borbándi, *Magyarok az Angol Kértben: A Szabad Európa Rádió Története* (Budapest: Európa Könyvkiadó, 1996); for general histories of Radio Free Europe, see Arch Puddington, *Broadcasting Freedom: The Cold War Triumph of Radio Free Europe and Radio Liberty* (Lexington: University Press of Kentucky, 2000); Robert T. Holt, *Radio Free Europe* (Minneapolis: University of Minnesota Press, 1958); Sig Mickelson, *America's Other Voice: The Story of Radio Free Europe and Radio Liberty* (New York: Praeger Publishers, 1983); K.R.M. Short (ed.), *Western Broadcasting over the Iron Curtain* (London: Croom Helm, 1986); for studies that place Radio Free Europe in the context of the broader 'cultural Cold War', see Frances Stonor Saunders, *Who Paid the Piper? The CIA and the Cultural Cold War* (Granta, London, 1999); Walter L. Hixson, *Parting the Curtain: Propaganda, Culture and the Cold War 1945–1961* (Basingstoke: Macmillan, 1997).
3. For the most recent evaluation of RFE's role in 1956, written from the perspective of the western controversy of the radio's role see Anne-Chantal Lepeuple, "'Radio Europe

Libre" et le Soulèvement Hongrois de 1956', *Revue d'histoire moderne et contemporaine* 47/1 (2000), pp.177–95; Puddington, *Broadcasting Freedom*, pp.89–114; Borbándi, *Magyarok az Angol Kértben*, especially ch.5.

4. For perhaps the most notorious statement of this view, see János Berecz, *Ellenforradalom tollal és fegyverrel 1956* (Budapest: Kossuth Könyvkiadó, 1986), especially pp.7–47.

5. See Lepeuple, '"Radio Europe Libre" et le Soulèvement Hongrois'; and Gyula Borbándi 'Magyarok felelössége a Szabad Európa Rádió 1956–os üsorpolitikájáért', in András B. Hegedüs *et al.* (eds.), *1956 Évkönyv 1966/1997* (Budapest: 1956–os Intézet, 1997), pp.281–3.

6. Quoted in Hixson, *Parting the Curtain*, p.63.

7. Hixson, *Parting the Curtain*; Stonor Saunders, *Who Paid the Piper?*; for the use of radio in the battle for hearts and minds in early Cold War Austria, see Reinhold Wagenleitner, *Coca-Colonization and the Cold War: The Cultural Mission of the United States in Austria after the Second World War* (Chapel Hill: University of North Carolina Press, 1994), pp.108–27.

8. *Statisztikai Szemle*, May 1955, p.466.

9. Personal interview with B. P-né, Dunaújváros, 9 Feb. 1995.

10. The two studies on which I have been heavily reliant are Tibor Frank (ed.), *Tanulmányok a Magyar Rádió Történetéböl 1925–1945* (Budapest: A Tömegkommunikációs Kutatóközpönt kiadása, 1975); and Béla Levai, *A rádió és a televízió krónikája 1945–1978* (Budapest: A Tömegkommunikációs Kutatóközpönt kiadása, 1980).

11. This was prior to the expansion of Budapest in 1950 to include the industrial suburbs that surrounded the capital.

12. Ferenc Glatz, 'Kultúrpolitika, hivatalos ideológia és Rádió (1927–1937)', in Frank (ed.), *Tanulmányok a Magyar Rádió Történetéböl*, pp.85–90.

13. Ibid., pp.49–77.

14. See Zoltán Szász 'A Magyar Rádió a második világháborúban (1939–1944)', in Frank (ed.), *Tanulmányok a Magyar Rádió Történetéböl*, pp.149–202.

15. Gabriel Milland, 'The BBC Hungarian Service and the Final Solution in Hungary', *Historical Journal of Film, Radio and Television* 18/3 (1998), p.355.

16. Zsuzsa Boros, 'A Magyar Rádió a német megszállás és a nyilás uralom idején (1944)', in Frank (ed.), *Tanulmányok a Magyar Rádió Történetéböl*, pp.203–42.

17. Milland, 'The BBC Hungarian Service', p.355.

18. Interview with Sz. J., Budapest, 9 April 1996.

19. István Vida, 'A demokratikus Magyar Rádió megteremtése és a Magyar Központi Híradó Rt megalakulása (1945)', in Frank (ed.), *Tanulmányok a Magyar Rádió Történetéböl*, pp.239–86.

20. For an idea of the kinds of programming included see Levai, *A rádió és a televízió krónikája*, pp.19–22.

21. *Magyar Rádió*, 28 Feb. 1947; *Magyar Rádió*, 16 May 1947.

22. *Magyar Rádió*, 1 Aug. 1947.

23. For a sample of the kind of programming involved see *Magyar Rádió*, 18 July 1947.

24. *Magyar Rádió*, 24 Oct. 1947.

25. *Magyar Rádió*, 5 Dec. 1947.

26. Levai, *A rádió és a televízió krónikája* (note 10), pp.53–60.

27. Ibid., pp.72–3.

28. *Statisztikai Szemle*, Dec. 1950, p.866.

29. Levai, *A rádió és a televízió krónikája*, pp.92–3.

30. *Statisztikai Szemle*, Dec. 1950, p.866.

31. Levai, *A rádió és a televízió krónikája*, p.82.

32. For a sample of radio programming in early 1950 see *Szabad Nép*, 5 Feb. 1950.

33. Levai, *A rádió és a televízió krónikája*, pp.82–9.

34. See István Markus, 'Egyszerü Feljegyzések 1947–böl', reprinted in his *Az Ismeretlen Föszereplö* (Budapest: Szépirodalmi Könyvkiadó, 1991), pp.109–10.

35. Columbia University Libraries, Bakhmetoff Archive, Hungarian Refugees Project Archive (hereafter CUL BAR CURPH) Box.1, Interview No. 2 – M, p.VI/3.

36. CUL BAR CURPH Box 2, Interview No. 8 – M, p.64.
37. CUL BAR CURPH Box 4, Interview No. 59 – M, p.XIX/1.
38. Mark Pittaway, 'Stalinism, Working-Class Housing and Individual Autonomy: The Encouragement of Private House Building in Hungary's Mining Areas, 1950–4', in Susan E. Reid and David Crowley (eds.), *Style and Socialism: Modernity and Material Culture in Post-War Eastern Europe* (Oxford: Berg Publishers, 2000), p.56.
39. CUL BAR CURPH Box.2, Interview No. 8 – M, p.64.
40. On the role of the VOA in Central and Eastern Europe more generally during this period, see Hixson, *Parting the Curtain*, ch. 4.
41. See the reports contained in Zala Megyei Levéltár – Zala County Archive (hereafter ZML) MSZMP ZMBA ir. 57f.1/71 ö.e.
42. For a review of the film made of the original play, see *Esti Budapest*, 4 Feb. 1953.
43. For the role of the Voice of Free Hungary in 1953, see Borbándi, *Magyarok az Angol Kértben*, pp.129–31.
44. *Az Államvédelmi Hatóság* (Authority for the Defence of State), the Hungarian political police from 1949 until the 1956 Revolution.
45. ZML MSZMP ZMBA ir.57f.1/80ö.e., p.55; for the denial see BBC *Summary of World Broadcasts*, 29 June 1953, p.25.
46. MOL M-Bp.-95f.2/215ö.e., pp.54–5.
47. Politikatörténeti és Szakszervezeti Levéltár – Archive of Political History and Trade Unions (hereafter PtSzL) SZKL SZOT Közgazdaság/13d./1952; *Feljegyzés a normarendezéssel kapcsolatos problémákról 1952. május 31*, pp.1–2
48. For industrial policy in the country and its impact on industrial workers during the early 1950s, see Mark Pittaway, 'The Social Limits of State Control: Time, the Industrial Wage Relation and Social Identity in Stalinist Hungary, 1948–1953', *Journal of Historical Sociology* 12/3 (1999), pp.271–301; Mark Pittaway, 'The Reproduction of Hierarchy: Skill, Working-Class Culture and the State in Early Socialist Hungary', *Journal of Modern History* 74/4 (2002).
49. Mark Pittaway, 'Retreat from Collective Protest: Household, Gender, Work and Popular Opposition in Stalinist Hungary', in Jan Kok (ed.), *Rebellious Families. Household Strategies and Collective Action in the Nineteenth and Twentieth Century* (Oxford: Berghahn, 2002), especially pp.218–20; István Rév, 'The Advantages of Being Atomized: How Hungarian Peasants Coped with Collectivization', *Dissent* 44 (1987), pp.335–50.
50. PtSzL SZKL SZOT Szociálpolitika/13d./1953; *Adatok és példák a Szakszervezetek Országos Tanácsa III. Teljes Ülésének beszámolóhoz*, pp.1–5.
51. Borbándi, *Magyarok az Angol Kértben*, pp.54–6; Irén Simándi, *A Magyar gazdaság a Szabad Európa Reflektorában (1951–1956)*, mss., Budapest, 1998.
52. Borbándi, *Magyarok az Angol Kértben*, p.93.
53. The collection of interviews and transcripts has been available freely to researchers since 1996. It is housed, along with the research records (though not the management information which has gone to the Hoover Institution and is expected to become available to researchers in late 2003), of the national departments of RFE in the Open Society Archives in the Central European University in Budapest.
54. Open Society Archives (hereafter OSA) RFE Magyar Gy.6/Item No. 11555/55, cover page.
55. OSA RFE Magyar Gy.6/Item No. 10820/54, p.1.
56. Borbándi, *Magyarok az Angol Kértben*, p.138.
57. OSA RFE Magyar Gy.6/Item No. 8083/54, p.12.
58. Borbándi, *Magyarok az Angol Kértben*, p.148.
59. For an example of this kind of official propaganda, see *Népi Demokráciánk Eredményei* (Budapest: Magyar Dolgozók Pártja Központi Vezetősége Agitációs- és Propaganda Osztály, 1955), pp.19–23.
60. Quoted in Imre Mikes (Gallicus), *Reflektor* (Munich: Újváry 'GRIFF' Verlag, 1977), p.88.
61. MOL M-Bp.-95f.2/77ö.e., pp.10–12.
62. OSA RFE Magyar Gy.6/Item No. 8083, pp.12–13.

The Debate Over Nuclear Refuge

DAVID SEED

Recent readings of Cold War culture have characterized the period from 1945 to 1965 as showing a marked reduction of the number of narratives sustaining that culture. For Thomas H. Schaub, the hopes of political renewal before the Second World War gave way to what he terms the 'liberal narrative' of sceptical realism where a habit of mind replaces political belief.[1] Similarly Tom Engelhardt has argued that 'between 1945 and 1975, victory culture ended in America'.[2] By this he means the grand narrative of national triumph over an evident and often subhuman enemy went into an extended crisis during the Cold War where it became increasingly difficult to identify even the general category of 'enemy-ness'. The confusion expressed by a character in Pat Frank's novel *Alas, Babylon* (1959), is symptomatic. Although the enemy in the nuclear exchange is unambiguously the Soviet Union, he cannot learn any outcome: 'What I would like to know', he complains, 'is who won the war? Nobody ever tells you. This war I don't understand at all. It isn't like World War One or Two or any other wars I've ever heard of. Sometimes I think the Russians must've won.'[3]

One of the most sophisticated models for such narrative commentary has been projected by Alan Nadel in his 1995 study *Containment Culture,* where he extrapolates the notion of containment from US foreign policy into American culture as a whole:

> Containment was the name of a privileged American narrative during the cold war. Although technically referring to U.S. foreign policy from 1948 until at least the mid-1960s, it also describes American life in numerous venues and under sundry rubrics during that period: to the extent that corporate production and biological reproduction, military deployment and industrial technology, televised hearings and filmed teleplays, the cult of domesticity and the fetishising of domestic security, the arms race and atoms for peace all contributed to the containment of communism, the disparate acts performed in the names of these practices joined the legible agenda of American history as aspects of containment culture.[4]

Although Nadel describes containment as a narrative, it really features in his analysis as a grand strategy inflecting the narratives he discusses in different conservative directions. Typically his argument moves by analogies, so that, for example, Holden Caulfield's obsessive hunting out of 'phonies' in *The Catcher in the Rye* involves him in bearing a flawed testimony similar to that used in the hearings into supposed Communists during the McCarthy period. Nadel discusses examples of containing potentially uncontrollable forces, the most dramatic of which was the bomb. One of his earliest texts is John Hersey's *Hiroshima* which, he argues, contains the event of the bombing through the generic strategies Hersey uses for representation.[5]

In his survey of the impact of the atomic bomb on American culture, Paul Boyer argues that by the late 1940s civil defence had become a charged political and social issue.[6] Part of the debate included the possible re-planning of city layouts with arterial highways to allow for mass evacuation.[7] In 1948 the first Civil Defence planning office was set up and that same year *New Yorker* correspondent Daniel Lang reported on the Munitions Board survey of caves and abandoned mines which might be used for storage. A high-ranking officer told Lang: 'People have got to be educated. They've got to become underground-conscious'; and he continued, that industry should also start considering the construction of underground factories.[8] Finally in 1950 President Truman established the Federal Civil Defense Authority (FCDA). According to a recent history by Andrew Grossman, the FCDA operations helped to promote the 'core myth of early Cold War emergency planning: not only was strategic nuclear war manageable from a civil defence perspective, but it was also no different from a conventional war that the United States could and would "win".'[9] As Patrick Major shows in his essay, 'Future Perfect?' here, one striking difference between US and Eastern bloc science fiction lay in the willingness of American authors to depict the horrors and futility of nuclear war, whereas in the communist countries this subject was virtually banned so as not to compromise official ideology on the pacifist policies of their governments.

During these years science fiction stories and novels began appearing which, in their various ways, took issue with this government-promoted minimization of the effects of nuclear war. Whereas the official line broadly stressed limitations of scale and the survivability of such a war, this fiction articulated in narrative form fears of genetic mutation and civic collapse. The debate about nuclear war rapidly turned into a series of speculations about which areas of normal social life would be the first to collapse. Indeed, by 1952 nuclear themes had become so widespread in science fiction that H.L. Gold, the editor of *Galaxy* magazine, complained that 'over 90 per cent of stories still nag away at atomic, hydrogen and bacteriological war, the post-atomic world, reversion to barbarism, mutant children killed because they have only ten toes and fingers instead of twelve'.[10] The debate over nuclear safety was joined by a number of SF (science fiction) novelists like Martin Caidin and Philip Wylie who were active in civil defence organizations.[11] This essay will compare the contributions to the civil defence debate made by non-fictional and fictional accounts of the fall-out following atomic detonations to see how different media present perspectives on this controversy.

The continuing debate over the consequences of nuclear explosions was entered by David Bradley in 1948 whose *No Place to Hide* was written in opposition to bland government reassurances that there was no need for the public to worry about fall-out. Bradley served as a medical monitor at the Operation Crossroads tests which took place in Eniwetok Atoll in 1946. His account was written for the general reader, carefully avoided all but the minimum of scientific explanation, and followed the sequence of a diary narrative from his privileged position as eye-witness. His conclusions were stark and uncompromising. First Bradley insists categorically: 'There is no real defence against atomic weapons.' From this premise he continues: 'There are no satisfactory countermeasures and methods of decontamination.' Extrapolating this point into the situation of nuclear attack, he virtually denies the possibility of civil defence or even treatment for the injured: 'There are no satisfactory medical or sanitary safeguards for the people of atomized areas.' Cold comfort indeed for Bradley's readers who lived in the major cities of the USA, although he stresses that Operation Crossroads should not be conceived in national terms: 'It is a test conducted by many different people, and a world of men, women, and their children will participate in its results.'[12]

Bradley stresses that these are biological, not political, conclusions and throughout *No Place to Hide* he constantly draws the reader's attention to the natural aspects of the South Pacific. As Paul Boyer has pointed out, the site of the atomic tests is described as a paradise violated by modern militarism.[13] The atoll is referred to variously as a Shangri-La, a land of lotus-eaters, and a Garden of Eden. The splendour of the tropical sunsets, the astonishing wealth of deep-sea life, and the aerial beauty of the atoll all take Bradley's breath away, and he waxes lyrical (and nostalgic) over the harmony of Bikini:

> Not so long ago Bikini must have been a beautiful island. It still has areas of palm and pandanus and breadfruit where all is peace and sunshine and the whispering of the trades. The hot sand, littered with shells and bits of crimson coral, the grass and dense undergrowth, the sparkle of the lagoon, and the booming of the surf on the reef give one the impression of complete timelessness.[14]

Although Bradley articulates ecological concern in his account, he does not recognize how the very encoding of the Pacific islands as a paradise reflects their appropriation by Western culture. The aerial views he enjoys are not available to the islanders who make up a suppressed presence in his narrative. Conspicuous by their absence after US deportation, they represent a displaced colonial 'other' which continues to be exploited by the military-industrial powers. Even when recognizing this latest phase of colonization, Bradley tends to focus mainly on the territory not the islanders in question.

   This emphasis does not arise from indifference by Bradley towards the islanders, however. Rather, it is an aspect of his use of place within the broader purpose of his book: namely, to bring home to an unconcerned American readership the dangers of nuclear fall-out. His denial of refuge anticipates by several years Nevil Shute's 1957 novel *On the Beach* and its 1959 film adaptation, which caused so much concern to Eisenhower's administration that its grim depiction of ever-extending fallout was discussed by his cabinet. Historically the Pacific islands have been used as refuge from the pressures of modern life by Westerners like Gauguin and Stevenson. In the description of Bikini given above, Bradley tacitly recognizes that the pristine harmony of the place has already receded into the past. The Cherry Lagoon represents the effects of this change in its doubleness. On one side remain unspoilt rocks; on the other, 'all the crud and corruption of civilization' lies spread out along the beach, a line of rusting debris. Similarly, on Kwajalein island the military installations from the last war are already rusting into disuse and turning into the ruins which J.G. Ballard was to use in his 1964 story, 'The Terminal Beach'. The Pacific atolls, are in short, a hybrid place bearing the traces both of their past and of recent Western interventions in their landscape. Their very names sound remote and exotic but Bradley

uses the atomic tests to close up any sense of distance. Thus, 'Bikini
is San Francisco Bay.' Towards the end of his book Bradley moves
from the Pacific tests which, however benign he tries to make them,
constitute in his terms a kind of assault if only on the order of
Nature, to nuclear attack on America by analogy.

What of the tests themselves? They are described as a controlled
experiment which fails, although the extent of this failure only
becomes evident late in the book. The first test, an air blast, has been
awaited with anxiety by all the crews concerned, only to be an anti-
climax. There is no widespread destruction, although Bradley seizes
the opportunity to meditate on the bomb's use of a 'primordial force'
in Nature. The second test, an underwater one, has a different impact
as spectacle. First there comes the flash, and then water spout which
levels off at a certain height:

> where it [the flash] had been now stood a white chimney of
> water reaching up and up. Then a huge hemispheric mushroom
> of vapor appeared like a parachute suddenly opening. It rapidly
> filled out in all directions until it struck the level of the first
> layer of clouds, about 1800 feet. Here, as though striking a layer
> of plate glass, this shock wave … spread out by leaps and
> bounds beneath the clouds.[15]

Here Bradley draws on what had already become the standard
mushroom metaphor of the atomic blast and creates an effect which
has now become known as the nuclear sublime. A number of
commentators have pointed out the ambiguous spectacle conveyed in
early descriptions of such a blast, sometimes encoding the image as a
male orgasm.[16] Bradley avoids the crude excitement over the triumph
of a male-gendered technology and, as soon as the radioactive rain
cloud forms, he moralizes it as an 'evil curse' hanging over the test
fleet.

In fact the most powerful sections of No Place to Hide prove to be
the least spectacular and concern the spread of radiation after this
second blast. Bradley uses his many visual details to set up by contrast
the peculiar threat posed by radiation which can only be detected by
special instruments. The traditional traces of war – the smashed
superstructures of battleships, abandoned material, and so on – bear
no relation to the new danger. The sailors discover that scrubbing the
decks, for instance, merely allows the radiation to penetrate deeper.
The boats look the same but are so dangerously changed that the
original plan of sailing the target fleet back to America has to be

abandoned. And then there is the damage to the environment. Tests reveal that radiation has contaminated fish and might well spread from species to species in a totally unpredictable fashion, as was later confirmed in part by the notorious case of the Japanese fishing boat, the *Lucky Dragon*.[17] The naval crews described in these tests function like a public which Bradley is trying to instruct. Their incomprehension reflects the need for what is virtually a paradigm shift in their model of reality where a potentially fatal source of danger is so difficult to conceive of. Bradley closes his book with the unmeasured ecological consequences of Operation Crossroads spreading out into the Pacific and here the significance of his title emerges. It is an adaptation of the spiritual 'There's no hidin' place', which denies the possibility of escaping God's scrutiny. Bradley's analogy implies that radiation is a kind of nemesis hanging over humanity which can be neither contained nor resisted.

Bradley's was not the only popular account of radiation to come out of Operation Crossroads. Richard Gerstell also served as a monitor at the same tests and, encouraged by Secretary of Defence James Forrestal, in 1950 he published *How to Survive an Atomic Bomb*. Gerstell was attempting to perform an exercise in reassurance through the genre of the self-help manual framed as an extended dialogue between himself and an anxious citizen. Despite his refrain of 'keep your head', Gerstell constantly produces unconscious black comedy in trying to play down the nuclear threat and reduce it to a series of essentially practical problems of housekeeping.[18] When his hypothetical citizen asks, 'But is there much chance of our getting bombed?' the answer is rather less than reassuring: 'Not much chance. Not on purpose, anyway.'[19] Gerstell's description of how a family should respond to nuclear attack only confirms his lack of realism: 'In case of air-raid warning, Dad will go around and cover all the windows. Mum will turn off the pilot-light in the stove and the light under the gas heater and refrigerator. Brother will run out and shut the garage doors, and collect what little drinking-water is needed for storage. Sister will find Bumpy, the pup, and take him down to the cellar.'[20] In its military precision, this account totally overlooks the chaos that would be created by nuclear attack. This was later depicted in Philip Wylie's *Tomorrow!* (1954), which showed outbreaks of looting; and in Martin Caidin's *The Long Night* (1956), which dramatized the panic to escape a fire-storm.[21] Both novels were written by authors actively involved in civil defence organizations. Apart from the psychological factor, Gerstell constantly reveals contradictions or omissions in his account. Everyone should be prepared, but the warning of attack might only give them a few seconds to act. The family unit should stick together, but children will probably have to be evacuated. And, though each household should try to be self-sufficient, their survival kit should not include a Geiger counter because they will not know how to use it. Finally, unlike Bradley, Gerstell hardly addresses the ecological questions at all beyond simply denying that wildlife would be doomed.

Gerstell's manual and the coda to Bradley are both examples of an emerging post-war genre of hypothetical narrative where writers try to imagine a nuclear attack by transposing aspects of the Hiroshima and Nagasaki bombings and the Pacific tests on to the American scene. The Cornell physicist Philip Morrison produced one of the earliest of these narratives in his contribution to *One World Or None* (1946), where he imagined the effect of a single atomic bomb dropping on Manhattan. Ignoring the spectacle of the blast itself, Morrison uses an ideally clear visual point of view which renders the human casualties with graphic precision:

> The district near the centre of the explosion was incredible. From the river west to Seventh Avenue, and from south of Union Square to the middle thirties, the streets were filled with the dead and the dying. The old men sitting on the park benches in the square never knew what happened. They were chiefly charred black on the side toward the bomb. Everywhere in this whole district were men with burning clothing, women with terrible red and blackened burns, and dead children caught while hurrying home to lunch.[22]

The first general images locate the central blast area for the reader. Then, as Morrison moves on to the casualties, he gives instances of fatalities among the most vulnerable civilians – the elderly and children.

Morrison implies – and it is a general theme of *One World Or None* – that there is no viable protection against nuclear attack. The only true defence is the political one of co-existence, hence the title. Either we learn to live together, or we will have no future. This was not the same message put out by John Lear's two articles 'Hiroshima, U.S.A.', which appeared in *Collier's* magazine for 5 August 1950. Once again an atomic bomb drops on Manhattan. Lear made his transposition explicit and drew on John Hersey's *Hiroshima* to give a series of vivid local images like the disappearance of a man standing at ground zero who is transformed into the 'radiant heat etching of a man in the act of wiping his brow', or a Bronx housewife who 'went to the kitchen window to see what caused the light; on the way, the windowpane came to meet her, in thousands of slashing bits. Noticing that she was bleeding, she fainted.' Transforming a national landmark into a metaphor of America's strength, Lear makes the ruin of the Empire State Building a symbolic comment on the state of the whole country: the building 'stared down at the shambles through paneless windows, like a fighting colossus with his eyes blacked and all his teeth knocked out'.[23] Lear had a problem of scale, however, which reflected an uncertainty in his purpose. On the one hand, he wanted to bring home the horrors of nuclear attack and a graphic colour illustration – a speciality of *Collier's* – of Manhattan in flames shows the scale of destruction. The second part of Lear's article was devoted to civil defence measures. This time the illustrations showed British Civil Defence (CD) crews working in simulated settings of bomb damage which closely resembled scenes from the Second World War. Taking the British practice as an example, Lear railed against those in America who opposed taking any defensive measures. But his was a broken-backed argument because he had already dramatized the impossibility of prevention.

From the late 1940s onwards a sub-genre of nuclear war fiction began to emerge which focused on the symbolic location of an atomic shelter and which repeatedly interrogated the problem of survivability. Household, neighbourhood and local community became synecdoches for the nation as a whole and offer variations on the theme of the garrison state developed during the early Cold War period in the United States. One of the first fictional narratives to incorporate this emerging preoccupation with fall-out shelters was William Tenn's 'Generation of Noah', which he wrote in 1949 but could not get published until 1951 because editors rejected it as being 'too fantastic'. Here a sadistic father drills his six-year-old son to run to the family shelter within the three minutes of their warning time. During one of these practices the son trips, is delayed, and as a punishment has to recite his future fate: 'Then, when the bombs fell, I'd – I'd have no place to hide. I'd burn like the head of a match. An' – an' the only thing left of me would be a dark spot on the ground shaped like my shadow.'[24] It is not clear whether Tenn drew on Bradley's book for his story, but certainly the son's 'lines' have incorporated the iconography of Hiroshima. The father is an early survivalist who obsessively fits out his shelter with generators, Geiger counters, and other supplies against nuclear attack. When the long-dreaded 'judgement day' finally comes, the son is five seconds late entering the shelter but the father has been so traumatized by the real thing that he gathers the whole family together to swear an oath that they will never again punish any human being. Within the opposition the story sets up between the mother's gentleness and care on the one hand, and the father's 'scientific' method of bringing up his children on the other, it is the latter which collapses under actual nuclear attack. The collapse of the father symbolizes a failure of authority and nerve and Tenn's title sets up an implicit analogy between nuclear war and an irresistible force of Nature like a deluge, a point I shall return to later.

It has been argued by Andrew Grossman that for political reasons civil defence measures of the early fifties targeted the growing population of the suburbs and also gave a position of central importance to women as 'essentially genderless human resources', partly to stress their role managing the home to maximize survival.[25] These issues were fed into the first novel by the science fiction author Judith Merril, *Shadow on the Hearth* (1950), for which she consulted David Bradley, John Hersey's *Hiroshima*, the Smyth report, and magazines like *Collier's*, *Time*, and *Popular Science*. This preparatory reading reflected Merril's conviction that science fiction was far from fantasy. In an interview of 1971 she declared: 'I believe quite firmly that today the science fiction writer is the only writer who is completely relating to his environment. The essence of good science fiction is that it must relate to all knowledge available to the author at that time.'[26] Acting on this principle, Merril wanted to check details with Bradley on radiation: diagnosis time, kinds of nuclear blast, and the timing of symptoms. As evidence of her capacity to do a 'reasonably good job' on this subject, she enclosed a copy of her 1948 story, 'That Only a Mother', which she had written in opposition to the denial by the US Army of Occupation that infanticides were occurring around Hiroshima and Nagasaki.[27] Published in 1948, the story describes the fears during pregnancy of Maggie, whose husband is away working at Oak Ridge nuclear enrichment plant. Maggie's fears that her baby may be malformed from radiation transmitted by her husband are brushed aside by the various experts who surround her with reassurances and prescriptions. Merril's title reflects the way in which the male experts infantilize Maggie by not taking her fears seriously, wrongly in this particular context since children embody the future. The dialogue between fear and reassurance has been internalized by Maggie herself who repeatedly censors her thoughts by refusing to articulate the dreaded possibilities confronting her. The story powerfully dramatizes the social imbalance between the medical 'authorities' and a female patient, and the psychological reluctance to accept the results of radioactive contamination. The story demonstrates a reluctance to admit consequences which are realized when Maggie's child is born limbless.[28] The discussion of mutations within the story is contextualized by references to Hiroshima and Nagasaki.

While working on her novel, Merril wrote to David Bradley in February 1949. Apart from documenting Merril's scrupulous preparation for her novel, the letter to Bradley sheds important light on her general purpose and method. It was to be 'aimed at the women's magazines', because 'women LOVE to read about diseases ... and also about dangers to their children, homes, and family'. While she respected *No Place to Hide*, she described it as a 'man's book', continuing: 'Few women have read it or will, because the technique you used for relief from strain, the tropical isle stuff, fishing, etc., is men's reading exclusively.'[29]

The novel which Merril produced, *Shadow on the Hearth*, draws on sources like Hersey, Bradley, Morrison and others in a selective and original way. Firstly, Merril situates the action in a household in the New York suburb of Westchester when the city is attacked by several atomic bombs falling in the bay near Manhattan. These form part of a general attack on the whole country; at least one device has hit the Capitol in Washington. This information is given as a news announcement before the novel's title page, then the perception of the blasts is registered by Gladys Mitchell, the protagonist, who merely sees a strange flash of light followed by a dark cloud. Merril has no interest in trying to capture the spectacle of the blasts, only in exploring their consequences for a typical suburban household. In that respect she anticipates a policy which government publications were anxious to promote during the 1950s, namely that 'the family is the mainstring of civil defence'.[30] Morrison's article (unnamed but unmistakable) has lodged in Gladys's memory, feeding her fears of what has almost certainly happened to her husband whose work- place is in the city. Hersey's method of semi-documentary realism is applied in the countless details of home life which give authenticity to Merril's narrative. Even her choice of title reflects an awareness of nuclear imagery.[31] One of the most famous photographs from Hiroshima showed the shadowy outline of a man imprinted on the entrance steps to a bank, clearly repeated in the American context by John Lear and by Ray Bradbury whose 1950 story, 'There Will Come Soft Rains', shows an outline of human figures imprinted on the side of their house by nuclear blast.[32] Apart from their traditional connotations of threat, shadows in the nuclear context hint at the grim irony of a technological device destroying humans so completely that it only leaves a two-dimensional trace.

Merril makes no attempt to identify or demonize the attackers, although no reader of 1950 could fail to draw the inference that the bombs had been launched by the Soviet Union. In contrast with earlier science fiction accounts of alien attack, the most famous being H.G. Wells' *War of the Worlds, Shadow on the Hearth* literally domesticates the theme of attack. Merril herself was a former Trotskyite and in 1950 a member of the United World Federalists.[33] Although she saw her book as a 'very political novel', its politics emerge from the management of public information about the results of attack. She approached the issue as a medical problem, highlighting 'diagnosis', 'treatment', 'timing of symptoms', and 'detectability' in her working notes for the novel. The attack itself is seen as an anonymous physical force to which the citizens must respond as best they can, and, not surprisingly, she gives doctors privileged status in her narrative.[34]

Although popular writing on the nuclear threat tended to privilege the family, Merril uses the household in a symbolic as well as realist way. To get a sense of how this operates we need to consider a news announcement made over the radio by the governor of New York who declares: 'There will be no more attacks. A screen of radar shields every inch of our borders, from below sea level to the far reaches of the stratosphere. Nothing can get through. We are living inside a great dome of safety, our whole nation protected by the great network of warning devices.'[35] In *One World Or None* Louis Ridenour had declared radar obsolete and Merril retains this perception as an irony in the order of her events. The announcement comes after multiple attacks have demonstrated the failure of this early warning system. The governor uses the figure of a protective dome created by military technology over the American nation, but Merril's novel actually dramatizes the penetration of a series of symbolic interiors by the atomic bombs and their resultant fall-out. If we consider the house as a key site of family life, the daily routine of that life has been radically damaged by the presumed death of Gladys's husband. If we think of it next as a physical protective space, the house offers refuge to a scientist who proves to be very helpful to the family. Here the house is differentiated from the nation which has black-listed him.[36] Similarly, when looters attack the house, their successful repulse contrasts with the nation's apparent helplessness before nuclear attack. In short, circumstances force a radical change on the function of the house and, as we shall see, on Gladys's life style.

Within the novel, official ideology is based on a series of concentric spaces: radar puts a 'roof' over the nation, the nation over the state, the state over the household, the household over its members. Merril's novel belies this protective layering at virtually every point. Officials and official information are subjected to a constant ironic scrutiny. Soon after the attack two figures in anti-radiation suits arrive at Gladys's door: a doctor and a neighbour, now acting as local wardens. The moment they lift their visors they cease to be (in the eyes of Gladys's younger daughter), men from Mars. Echoing an identical moment with a tractor driver in *The Grapes of Wrath*, Merril makes a similar point about estrangement: 'the simple act of revealing their faces changed them from fictional monsters to human beings'.[37] As in Steinbeck's novel, revelation of features situates the figures within a set of relationships. Not only does the warden supply Gladys with verbose mimeographed instruction sheets; he also patronizes her constantly and offers himself as comforting substitute for Gladys's missing husband. Here an important principle emerges in Merril's narrative. No information is introduced without that information or its supplier being questioned. A fugitive physicist, for example, tells Gladys of the dangerously misleading suggestion her other visitors were promoting, that urine analyses could be performed instantly in the latter's truck. How to respond to the crisis is shown to be a shared predicament where opposing points of view have to be debated or tested.

The most moving point in the novel comes when she realizes that her youngest daughter has suffered radiation poisoning from a contaminated toy which threatens her life. Thus nation, house and body prove equally vulnerable to radiation. Out of this situation of common need, the house ceases to be a private dwelling occupied only by the Mitchells and turns into a communal space offering shelter to neighbours. David Dowling has glossed this aspect of the novel negatively: 'the novel proceeds like a situation comedy, with the living room as the set and many entrances, exits, and visits from neighbours and officials'.[38] This description fails to take into account the crucial fact that staying in the house is a necessity imposed by life-threatening circumstances. The simulation of family and social life continues against a background of new dangers and urgencies where domestic spaces change correspondingly. It is absurd to refer to 'visits', without recognizing the total change in outside life which Merril depicts. Counterpointed against Gladys's activities inside her house, Merril inserts nightmarish sections dealing with an unnamed man's experiences at the hands of the emergency services. Within the topography of the novel, outside signifies darkness, chaos and threat. Furthermore, the superficial resemblance between Merril's narrative and a situation comedy reinforces its purpose in making nuclear attack familiar to the reader.

As these transformations are taking place, Gladys's role and self-image are changing. The most immediate consequence of the attack is that she becomes estranged from the 'script' of domestic life which recedes into an 'old worn-out film'; a shopping list contains words 'from another world'. Later in the novel, when the police bring the family maid for questioning, the situation reminds Gladys of a 'grade-B gangster movie'. Thus, at many points Gladys registers the strange resemblances which intermittently characterize her experiences. One fundamental change which takes place is a revision of her role within the household. Gerstell's conservative and traditional allocation of roles assumes an unlikely stability in the family situation which Merril addresses head on. One symbolic event which shows the change taking place occurs when Gladys herself decides to fix a gas leak, donning her husband's work shirt. At a later point she thinks back speculatively about the events on the day of the attack and reflects 'If Jon were here ...' but then catches herself up: 'That was silly too. All the ifs were silly. Jon wasn't there. The other time, the other war, it was different.'[39] Gladys engages in an extended dialogue throughout the novel with her own thoughts and with the voices she hears around her. In this way she quietly interrogates her own situation, gradually becoming a more articulate critic of the emergency procedures being implemented. As she takes charge of her household she becomes increasingly restive of 'experts'. When the scientist and a doctor discuss her daughter's illness, she silently complains: 'Why did they have to talk in code?' And she defies the authorities by not taking her daughter to hospital as recommended. This debate over how to deal with the current situation of crisis takes place during the countless practical tasks in the house which give the novel its realism. *Shadow on the Hearth* received an exceptionally

positive review in the *New York Times* which compared the novel to
Huxley and Orwell, and which praised Merril for her
characterization. The reviewer continued: 'Indeed there's so much
about the standard operating procedure of housework in the story
that it is frequently impossible to believe that a war is really on.'[40]
Conversely, in the novel it is equally impossible to forget that
domestic life has become transformed by the national crisis.

Merril's originality in *Shadow on the Hearth* lay in her attempt to
imagine a female viewpoint on nuclear attack as it impacted on family
life and the life of a neighbourhood. The novel is framed by radio
announcements of the beginning of the attack and the end of the
subsequent war. In other words there is an official narrative of
unprovoked attack (implicitly modelled on Pearl Harbor), followed
by war and national triumph. The official announcement closes off
this narrative with the national anthem, but Merril's narrative refuses
this closure.[41] Her editors at Doubleday imposed a change on the
novel's ending which contradicted the whole drive of her narrative,
namely to have Gladys's husband return home and thereby re-
establish the fractured family unit. It was not until 1966 in the reprint
of the novel that Merril could restore her original text which is
significantly more open-ended. Despite the ending of hostilities,
Gladys reflects: 'Isn't anything safe? Not the rain or the house? Not
even a little blue horse?' This is spoken in the privacy of her thoughts.
Characteristically, the last line of the novel is a rejoinder in an
unfinished dialogue: 'But the war's *over*,' she said.'[42] The novel leaves
the reader an open question about the irreversible loss of security
experienced by Gladys and, by implication, countless other citizens.

Throughout her career Merril remained preoccupied by the nuclear
threat. She refused to share her fellow novelist Robert Heinlein's faith
in nuclear shelters. Partly because he was then living near the
underground NORAD (North American Aerospace Defense
Command) complex at Colorado Springs, Heinlein had built a shelter
for his family in 1961 'as an act of faith, as an example to others'.[43]
Merril did not follow suit and later in the 1960s renounced US
citizenship in protest over the Vietnam War. From 1967 to 1981 she
was an active member of the Canadian citizens' group Hiroshima-
Nagasaki Relived and during an interview of 1986, she recorded her
disagreement with Heinlein and Poul Anderson on nuclear attack: 'if
you talk about holocaust, you come down to the fact that from what
we now know, there is no aftermath'.[44]

Merril's novel was adapted for television and, under the title
Atomic Attack, shown on the ABC Motorola TV Playhouse in 1954.[45]

A voice-over introduces the action as follows: 'The play you are about to see deals with an imaginary H-bomb attack on New York City and with the measures that Civil Defence would take, in such an event, for the rescue and protection of the population in and around the city. It is the prayer of every one of us that such imaginings shall remain forever fictions.'[46] This introduction was probably designed to avoid the panic created by Orson Welles' dramatization of *The War of the Worlds*, but it inevitably has the effect of reassuring the viewer that the action is a kind of make-believe. In contrast, Merril's novel uses the methods of realism to impress the reader with the likely possibility of nuclear attack. A second difference lies in the play's tendency to make its points explicitly whereas *Shadow on the Hearth* constantly positions the reader to draw out the implications of previously routine acts like eating and playing. Thus, the play establishes the typicality of the family from the start in showing the hubbub of a breakfast scene. When one of the girls complains: 'Oh why can't we be like other families, a nice normal group of people?' the mother replies: 'We are ... normal as oat-meal and apple pie.'

The scenic construction of *Shadow on the Hearth* made its adaptation relatively straight-forward, though at the cost of losing much of the novel's psychological dimension.[47] Close-ups of the mother suggest her thoughtfulness dealing with the attitudes of other characters who each personify different ways of reacting to the current crisis. For example, the science teacher admits to her that he recoiled from physics when he realized that science was being directed into weapons of mass destruction. The mother, unnamed and therefore more determined by her family role, is contrasted with a hysterical neighbour in a dialogue between practical action and despair. As a new ethic of mutual help emerges, the mother makes this explicit: 'I know this much now, that we'll oftentimes do things for others that we'd never dream of doing for ourselves.' Such commentary on each episode makes the play more didactic than *Shadow on the Hearth*. The other major difference between novel and play is in the latter's use of radio announcements. The novel contains occasional news flashes, primarily to give characters hints of external but primarily domestic information. The play, by contrast, punctuates the action with announcements about the American response to the (still unnamed) enemy's assault. Where Merril kept revealing ironic gaps between official statements and the situation of Gladys's household, the play suggests an uncritical parallel between the national military campaign and the experience of the characters.

Success in one coincides with success in the other. The end result is that the play risks arriving at a crude notion of triumph. When the radio announcer states that: 'the enemy's will and ability to fight have now virtually been broken', the daughter Ginny asks: 'Are we winning?' The mother's reply, the last line in the play, shows unambiguous confidence: 'Not yet, darling, but we're going to.' The novel gradually questions characters' presumption of security. The play identifies the external enemy with the internal danger of despair and shows a congruence between national and personal goals which will be resolved at an imminent point of victory.

In 1958 Merril told Philip Wylie that her novel was appearing on civil defence reading lists and that *Atomic Attack* was being shown in civil defence and Atomic Energy Commission programmes.[48] This would have struck a chord with Wylie who, from 1945 through to the late 1950s, when he realized the destructive potential of the H-bomb, had been a tireless campaigner for civil defence projects at the federal and local levels. In 1950 he proposed the 'Miami plan' for local civil defence organizations and in his 1951 article, 'A Better Way to Beat the Bomb', proposed that each city should train its own civil defence personnel who should be prepared to move to neighbouring cities if need be. However, Wylie expressed most concern at the 'failure so far of the average citizen to assimilate what has been told, to infer what that means, and to deduce what might happen and what he *could* be ready to do that he *could* arrange rapidly and *could* pay for'.[49] Wylie's repeated target in his writings, fictional and non-fictional, was the morale of city-dwellers under nuclear attack. Among the Wylie papers at Princeton is the script of a film on this subject – to be called *The Bomb* – which was enthusiastically supported by General Vandenberg among others.

In the event the film was never made and Wylie chose the medium of fiction to warn the American public against its apathy. His 1954 novel *Tomorrow!* describes the bombing of twinned mid-western cities modelled on Minneapolis and St Paul. Wylie dedicated the work to the staff of the Federal Civil Defense Authority, one member of which reviewed the novel and recommended its promotion among civil defence officials.[50] The novel assembles different perspectives on civil defence ranging from indifference to downright hostility: one city leader is convinced civil defence drills are 'Communist-inspired'. The enlightened central figure, a clear surrogate for Wylie himself, is a city news editor who publishes an attack on the collective denial felt by the public. Contextualizing the situation within the history of end-of-the-world apocalyptic fears, the editor insists that these fears have led the public to adopt positions of ridicule towards civil defence:

> a condition is set up in which a vast majority of the citizens, unable to acknowledge with their minds the dread that eats at their blind hearts, loses all contact with reality. The sensible steps are not taken. The useful slogans are outlawed. The proper attitudes are deemed improper. Appropriate responses to the universal peril dwindle, diminish and at last disappear.[51]

Reality is about to assert itself in the form of a nuclear attack, so the editor's words come too late and he is atomized, the unheeded Jeremiah of the city. Although Wylie designed the novel as a warning, partly by counting down his chapters to 'X-day', the day of attack, the novel gets its most powerful effects from negative images of mass panic, appalling injuries, and the sheer bewilderment of the citizens. Indeed, ultimately, as he himself later acknowledged, Wylie lacked confidence in his own narrative and used the *deus ex machina* of a cobalt-coated super-bomb with which the USA wipes out Leningrad, coating the rest of the Soviet Union in radioactive dust. The details of neglected, indeed useless, civil defence measures mingle in with the general spectacle of social collapse which must have worried Wylie so much that he feared the partial restoration of civil order would not be enough to allay the fears triggered in the reader. When he exchanged letters with Eugene Rabinowitz, the editor of the *Bulletin of the Atomic Scientists*, the latter complained that the ending 'would satisfy the American smugness about being ultimately the inevitable victor'.[52] In effect Wylie changed narratives at the end of *Tomorrow!*, attempting to revive a kind of triumphalism he had been arguing elsewhere was out of date. Only a few years later he shifted his position again, deciding that the sheer destructive potential of the H-bomb made civil defence impossible.

Wylie's conviction that civil defence measures would be effective if only the public were properly educated was not shared by other writers of this period. Two novels from the 1950s, for example, demonstrate a cultural difference between the USA and Britain over the use of the subway as a potential place of refuge. Where underground stations in London served as improvised shelters during the Second World War, the New York subway in the next two novels becomes the site for a release of violent impulses which play themselves out in lurid twilit settings suggestive of a collective unconscious finding expression. Andrew Grossman has shown that

Project East River, an elaborate civil defence project centred on New York in the early 1950s, included recognition that mob action might well be one result of nuclear attack, a result serious enough for the authorities to consider how to isolate and disable the ringleaders.[53] Harold Rein's *Few Were Left* (1955), describes the sheer incomprehension of the few survivors who crawl through the tunnels looking for means of survival. As they head up-town, they encounter a larger group run on military lines by the self-styled 'Co-ordinator'. At this point the novel shifts towards political parable as a character tries to compete with the Co-ordinator over whether the surviving remnant should live in slavery or freedom. When his attempted rebellion against tyranny fails, the novel ends with the point-of-view character being stoned to death.

Rein shows this tyranny to be a gradual result of the chaotic post-war circumstances of New York. Richard Foster's *The Rest Must Die* (1959), however, foregrounds the issue of law and order as soon as the bombs drop. Foster describes the same terrain as Rein – the darkened tunnels, the stalled trains, the near impossibility of access to the surface – but this time dramatizes the speed with which civilized restraint collapses. The cover of the novel proclaimed: 'The law of the jungle was supreme'; and the narrative describes a mounting surge of violent hostility between the survivors, some of whom attempt rape while others commit suicide in despair. The tunnels become divided up into gangland areas where armed struggles take place:

> The battle with the people who were living on the Long Island tracks was in its second day, but no one had any doubts but that it would soon be over. Cut off from regular food and water supplies they could not last long. Five times they had rushed Gimbels basement and five times had been beaten back. Each time, the number of dead was appalling, especially on the part of those from the Long Island tracks. Not many were killed from Gimbels because they had all the advantage of position and more guns.[54]

The combat is presented as a form of rivalry over looting which implicates all survivors and dramatically reverses the civil defence imperative of co-operation. Earlier spokesmen like Richard Gerstell presented a utopian vision of family members (and, by implication, members of the national family), working harmoniously together, whereas Foster draws on the naturalistic tradition of social

Darwinism to depict a kind of spontaneous and fragmented civil war which breaks out.

The novelist James Blish, who served in the Civil Air Patrol during the 1950s, engaged in his fiction with issues of nuclear civil defence throughout that decade. He too attacked what he saw as a deceptive fashion in shelters. His 1953 story, 'First Strike', describes an America where such shelters have become routine, but the narrator reflects: 'Just how much "shelter" they would have provided in the event of an actual atomic raid was not even an open question. Like all summer shelters, it was really a flimsy affair.' The shelter's very existence reflects ironically on the passivity of the public, exactly the kind of passivity which Judith Merril's protagonist questions: 'During the Cold War of 1950–1962 ... most Americans allowed themselves to be pushed about by the civil defence authorities without the slightest emotional conviction that anything might happen to *them*.'[55] The figure of a protective shield which US radar establishes too late in *Shadow on the Hearth* becomes a literal container in 'The Box' (1949), where Blish describes the erection of a huge grey membrane over New York.[56] This 'barrier', 'screen', or 'box' has gone up so suddenly that it causes mass panic in the city. Through tortuous irony Blish presents the dome as a defensive construct being secretly planned by the US military and at the same time being shadowed by an unnamed enemy which is secretly responsible for the dome appearing over New York. In a sequence of reversals, the device is revealed to be fatal because it prevents air from penetrating the membrane, slowly suffocating the city; and secondly the 'experiment' on New York proves to be a covert form of attack by a devious enemy bent on trying out this technology on its opponent.

Blish further wove his scepticism about nuclear shelters into his 1958 novel, *A Case of Conscience*. During his revisions to the original short story he encountered James W. Deer's article on the 'shelter race' in a 1957 number of the *Bulletin of the Atomic Scientists,* which presented a depressingly fatalistic image of the cycle of arms production and defence measures: 'The play has begun, and we are the actors. The end is implicit from the nature of the beginning. Within the framework of fusion bombs, guided missiles, and shelters, there is nothing we can do but go ahead and play out our part in the preordained ritual.'[57] Deer locks human action into a script over which the agents have no control. From a future-retrospective vantage point frequently used in science fiction, Blish adapts the notion of the shelter race into an extended crisis which drives human society underground:

Defensive though the shelter race seemed on the surface, it had
taken on all the characteristics of a classical arms race – for the
nation that lagged behind invited instant attack. Nevertheless,
there had been a difference. The shelter race had been
undertaken under the dawning realization that the threat of
nuclear war was not only imminent but transcendent; it could
happen at any instant, but its failure to break out at any given
time meant that it had to be lived with for at least a century, and
perhaps five centuries.[58]

Where Deer posits a nuclear narrative so truncated and obvious that
the end is clear from the beginning, Blish extends his fictive history
over centuries and presents the shelters as a multiple form of
imprisonment. The underground world has become a form of Hell
and the shelter economy an entrapping commercial imperative which
virtually excludes change. This is Blish's version of the military-
industrial complex and it is a measure of his gloom about the Cold
War arms race (which by the time of his narrative has extended into
a world-wide situation), that the underground society can only be
mediated to the reader through an enlightened visitor from another
planet. The novel exploits the by now familiar iconography of
nuclear defence narratives in its very title where, as David Ketterer
has argued, 'case' signifies container rather than instance: 'The
various containers of one kind or another and the images of
containment which permeate the novel all serve to illustrate its
central ambiguities. To what extent do containers (including
conscience, if it is one) protect and screen the contained from the
external truth of reality?'[59] Once again, a defensive measure proves in
Blish to have entirely negative consequences in inducing mass
neurosis among the novel's underground society.

    The end of the 1950s was signalled by the publication of two
novels which presented the most negative accounts of nuclear war.
Walter M. Miller's *A Canticle for Leibowitz* (published in three
sections during the 1950s and collected in 1959), showed nuclear
war to be an unavoidable destructive phase of historical cycles which
were doomed to repeat themselves. And Mordecai Roshwald's *Level
7* (also 1959), described the garrison state mentality as futile and
dangerously abstracted from reality. Here the protagonist is an
operative in a deep-level nuclear bunker responsible for pressing the
button to launch nuclear bombs. A nuclear exchange does take place,
ironically resulting from technological errors in the system, and the
novel ends unusually with the narrator dying from radioactive

seepage which belies the supposed safety of the bunker. A professor of sociology, Roshwald presents a powerfully critical image of the mentality of an operative insulated by electronic screens and monitors from the fatal consequences of his actions. In this grim narrative he realizes the true enormity of what he has done only shortly before his death.

By the 1960s fictional treatments of nuclear defence had reduced in number and had also veered towards absurdism and satire as if the subject was no longer accessible to 'straight' description. A number of factors played their part in this change. First, there had been a gradual loss of public confidence in the efficacy of fall-out shelters despite President Kennedy's campaign to promote them.[60] Second, a 'crisis fatigue' may have set in after a decade of increasingly out-moded civil defence practices – an over-emphasis which was reflected in the subjects of science fiction in the 1950s. Then there were the political developments in the Cold War, especially a relaxation of tension following the death of Stalin. Lastly, the rise of black humour in the USA was historically related to a growing credibility gap between official statements and actuality which was to come to a head during the Vietnam War.

Black humour challenges the very premises of Cold War debate. Gina Berriault's *The Descent* (1961), the novel and film *Dr. Strangelove* (1963), and Leonard C. Lewin's *Report from Iron Mountain* (1967), all question the rationality of nuclear confrontation between the superpowers.[61] Berriault satirizes the fashion for shelters as a collective self-deception; *Dr. Strangelove* lampoons the arms race as a distortion of the sex drive; and Lewin inverts the relation of peacetime to war by presenting the latter as a new norm. The debate over civil defence even entered the *Twilight Zone* TV series when an episode called 'The Shelter' was screened in 1961. Here a false alert triggers such extreme panic among the neighbours of a doctor who has built a fall-out shelter that they turn on each other with an unbridled hostility that could easily lead to murder. In his 1962 guide *How to Survive the H-Bomb – And Why*, journalist and novelist Pat Frank turned away from the optimistic descriptions of communal self-help of its 1959 predecessor, *Alas, Babylon*, but the new book still contained unwitting comic details that undermined his general case for expecting the worst. Although he was attacking a public fatalism, his opening lines would hardly have inspired confidence: 'If you live in North America there is only one certain way to survive a nuclear war: Move to Tasmania.'[62] On the one hand, Frank tries to plead the cause of communal or group fall-out shelters, the cost of which could be tax-deductible; on the other, he repeatedly denies that there are any effective 'arks' that would protect citizens, even admitting that his earlier novel *Alas, Babylon* had seriously under-estimated the extent of fall-out.

Philip Wylie decisively turned his back on his own earlier campaigning for civil defence awareness in his 1963 novel *Triumph*, which dramatizes the futility of even the most lavishly equipped nuclear shelter if war came to the USA. The shelter described in that novel is ludicrously elaborate, ludicrous because only possible for multi-millionaires and ludicrous also because it proves useless before the massive destruction wrought by the super-bombs each side exchanges. Wylie thematizes this perception through one of his characters who reflects, as the bombs fall, on the illusions promoted by nuclear holocaust fiction:

> There were also lots of prophetic books and movies about total war in the atomic age, and all of them were practically as mistaken as plain people and politicians and the Pentagon planners. In all of them that I recall, except for one, we Americans took dreadful punishment and then rose from the ground like those Greek-legend soldiers – Jason's men – and defeated the Soviets and set the world free.[63]

The accounts summarized here, which could be exemplified by novels like Pat Frank's *Alas, Babylon* (1959), are attacked for clinging on to the fake triumphalism which Wylie himself smuggled into *Tomorrow!* In the 1963 novel this grand narrative is explicitly separated from the probable actuality of nuclear war and summarized in a character's notebook which is destroyed along with the writer herself. The narrative of righteous national triumph thus becomes reduced to an entry in a document which is never read by any other character, within a possible future where any readership will have ceased to exist; and that reflects the austere irony of Wylie's title and the measure of his final pessimism about nuclear defence.

From the very beginning then, scepticism has informed American fictional accounts of refuge from nuclear war. The physicist Freeman Dyson has argued that the fall-out shelter programme could never have succeeded because it was perceived to be blatantly inadequate, socially divisive, and promoting an unacceptable image of the USA attacking one population while keeping its own safe. Apart from, economic and political considerations, he finds the ultimate impossibility of the programme in its contradiction of a national ideology of 'freedom under the open sky', where the very idea of underground would be anathema.[64] Historian Paul Boyer has further suggested that interest in civil defence lapsed after the stopping of atmospheric nuclear tests.[65]

Government civil defence pamphlets and the writings of figures like Pat Frank and Robert Heinlein, all appeal to the national traditions of the handyman and of self-help in suggesting ways to build a family shelter. Heinlein's 1964 novel *Farnham's Freehold*, describes the fortunes of a nationally emblematic family during a nuclear attack. The father has fitted out an impeccable shelter where, as if the point was not obvious, the safe combination is the date of US Independence Day. After being shot forward in time to a future dictatorship of America, the family manages to return to the novel's present where the narrative concludes with an enduring image from earlier American history: the frontier trading post. Through this family, Heinlein suggests that the very fate of the nation depends upon citizens like Farnham clinging on to values of preparedness, technological know-how, and so on. Despite its blatant anachronism, descriptions of self-help preparations for nuclear attack re-surfaced during the debate over Reagan's Strategic Defence Initiative. One of the key figures here was Dean Ing whose *Pulling Through* of 1983 combined within the same volume a narrative of nuclear war with extensive advice on how to build and stock a fall-out shelter. By the 1980s, this kind of appeal to handyman skills had come to seem increasingly ludicrous and the science fiction novelist Frederik Pohl pointed out Ing's unconsciously negative lesson: 'If you read Dean Ing's brilliant novel you will see how, with only moderately optimistic assumptions, perhaps as many as one-third of the American people can survive a nuclear war and enter into an existence of twelve-hour, seven-day drudgery, with few amenities and an excellent chance of grisly disease.'[66] Praise for a survivalist novel ironically questions the very value of that survival.

Historically, US science fiction has tended to celebrate the potential of new forms of technology – hence the recurrence of the inventor as a character in these narratives – but in the novels just described nuclear attack is the main, and of course negative, expression of technological achievement. On the whole, these writers describe scenarios where attack is anonymized and de-politicized as an abstract force triggering essentially domestic situations of crisis and conflict. This is not to say that the narratives are apolitical, only that their politics focuses on issues like survival, the efficiency of the emergency services, and the control of information. Essentially they present versions of scepticism or pessimism about survival which suggest a deep unease about the possession of nuclear weapons throughout the Cold War period.

NOTES

1. Thomas H. Schaub, *American Fiction in the Cold War* (Madison: University of Wisconsin Press, 1991), p.5.
2. Tom Engelhardt, *The End of Victory Culture: Cold War America and the Disillusioning of a Generation* (London: HarperCollins, 1995), p.10.
3. Pat Frank, *Alas, Babylon* (New York: Bantam, 1976), p.192.
4. Alan Nadel, *Containment Culture: American Narratives, Postmodernism, and the Atomic Age* (Durham, NC: Duke University Press, 1995), pp.2–3.
5. Ibid., pp.53–67. It is sometimes unclear whether Nadel is accusing Hersey of a kind of cultural appropriation of this event by converting the victims into textual sources, or whether *any* account of Hiroshima risks distortion, in which case presumably the safest response would be silence.
6. Paul Boyer, *By the Bomb's Early Light: American Thought and Culture at the Dawn of the Atomic Age* (Chapel Hill: University of North Carolina Press, 1994), pp.175–7, 326, etc.
7. Ibid., p.321. Urban re-planning was discussed in Ralph Lapp's *Must We Hide?* (1949).
8. Daniel Lang, *Early Tales of the Atomic Age* (Garden City, NY: Doubleday, 1948), p.113. Mine shafts for use as nuclear shelters made a ludicrous re-appearance at the end of *Dr. Strangelove* and underground automated factories featured in Frederik Pohl's 1959 post-holocaust story, *The Waging of the Peace*, where automated production methods have become the new enemy.
9. Andrew D. Grossman, *Neither Dead Nor Red: Civil Defence and American Political Development during the Early Cold War* (New York and London: Routledge, 2001), p.42.
10. Quoted in Edward James, *Science Fiction in the Twentieth Century* (Oxford and New York: Oxford University Press, 1994), p.89.
11. I have discussed Wylie and Caidin's relevant fiction in David Seed, *American Science Fiction and the Cold War* (Edinburgh: Edinburgh University Press, 1999), pp.19–22.
12. David Bradley, *No Place To Hide* (Boston: Little, Brown, 1948), pp.165, p.16.
13. Boyer, *By the Bomb's Early Light*, p.92.
14. Bradley, *No Place To Hide*, pp.106–7.
15. Ibid., pp.92–3.
16. Among the many examples, see Ira Chernus, *Dr. Strangegod: On the Symbolic Meaning of Nuclear Weapons* (Columbia, SC: University of South Carolina Press, 1986) and Carol Cohn, 'Sex and Death in the Rational World of the Defense Intellectuals', *Signs: Journal of Women in Culture and Society* 12/4 (1987), pp.687–718.
17. The case was described in Ralph E. Lapp's *The Voyage of the Lucky Dragon* (Harmondsworth: Penguin, [1957] 1958).
18. In that respect Gerstell anticipates the Federal Civil Defence Authority's 'Grandma's Pantry' campaign later in the 1950s which was promoted through images of old-fashioned kitchens and slogans like 'With a well-stocked pantry you can be just as self-sufficient as Grandma was' (quoted and discussed in Elaine Tyler May, *Homeward Bound: American Families in the Cold War Era* (New York: Basic Books, 1988), pp.91–2).
19. Richard Gerstell, *How to Survive an Atomic Bomb* (Washington DC: Combat Forces

Press, 1950), p.105.
20. Ibid., pp.121–2.
21. Caidin at that time was working with the New York State Civil Defence Commission.
22 Philip Morrison, 'If the Bomb Gets Out of Hand', in Dexter Masters and Katharine Way (eds.), *One World Or None* (New York: McGraw-Hill, 1946), p.3.
23. John Lear, 'Hiroshima, USA: Can anything be done about it?', *Collier's*, 5 Aug. 1950, pp.11, 15.
24. William Tenn, *The Wooden Star* (New York: Ballantine, 1968), p.14.
25. Grossman, *Neither Dead Nor Red*, pp.77–8, 102–3. Grossman rejects Elaine Tyler May's view (*Homeward Bound,* 1988) of a 'hegemonic paternalism' in the FCDA as being based on insufficient data.
26. Dorothy Dearborn, 'She'd Give Up Everything For A Trip To The Moon', *Evening Times-Globe* (Saint John, New Brunswick), 10 April 1971, p.7.
27. Judith Merril and Emily Pohl-Weary, *Better to Have Loved: The Life of Judith Merril* (Toronto: Between the Lines, 2002), p.89. The story was rejected by *Collier's* because it caused 'revulsion' in the readers.
28. 'That Only a Mother' (*Astounding*, June 1948), was collected in Merril's *Out of Bounds* (New York; Pyramid, 1960). For valuable critical commentary on this story, see Elizabeth Cummins, 'Short Fiction by Judith Merril', *Extrapolation* 33/3 (1992), pp.202–14.
29. Letter by Judith Merril, 19 Feb. 1949; Merril Collection, National Archives of Canada, Ottawa.
30. *Six Steps to Survival* (1957), a government pamphlet on civil defence, available in the 'Virtual Atomic Museum' at www.rdrop.com/~jsexton/cd/six/.
31. In fact this appropriateness was probably coincidental because the title was chosen by Merril's publishers in preference for her own more explicit references to nuclear war (Merril and Pohl-Weary, *Better to Have Loved*, p.99).
32. This story, collected in *The Martian Chronicles* (1950), draws an explicit analogy between the outlines of the family members and photographic negatives, as if they are memento images of the family long after the family itself has been destroyed.
33. According to Peter Tate, Merril was a member of the United World Federalists and also a supporter of Gary Davis's World Citizen Movement ('The Fantastic World of Judith Merril', *Western Mail*, 14 Oct. 1966, p.7.
34. For commentary on the increasing prominence of doctors in the debate over fall-out from the mid-1950s into the following decade, see Paul Boyer, *Fallout* (Columbus: Ohio State University Press, 1998), pp.81–6.
35. Judith Merril, *Shadow on the Hearth* (London: Roberts and Vintner, 1966), p.21.
36. Here Merril reflects the 'mania for finding spies everywhere': Paul Brians, *Nuclear Holocausts: Atomic War in Fiction, 1895–1984* (Kent, OH: Kent State University Press, 1987), p.17. Brians' survey is an invaluable guide to this body of fiction.
37. Merril, *The Shadow on the Hearth*, p.39.
38. David Dowling, *Fictions of Nuclear Disaster* (Basingstoke: Macmillan, 1987), p.59.
39. Merril, *Shadow on the Hearth*, pp.131–2.
40. Charles Poore, 'Books of the Times', *New York Times*, 5 June 1950, p.29.
41. In that sense it is not helpful to lump Merril's novel in with other narratives under the heading of 'The "Civil Defence" Plot', as Martha A. Bartter does: *The Way to Ground Zero: The Atomic Bomb in American Science Fiction* (Westport: Greenwood Press, 1988), pp.122–3.
42. Merril, *Shadow on the Hearth*, p.192.
43. Robert Heinlein, letter to Merril, 7 November 1962; Merril Collection, Ottawa.
44. English-language transcript of interview with Elisabeth Vonarburg and Luc Pomereau in *Solaris 69* (1986), p.2; Merril Collection, Ottawa.
45. The TV play script was written by David Davidson and the production directed by Ralph Nelson.
46. This and subsequent passages transcribed from video recording of *Atomic Attack*.
47. Merril registered misgivings about this simplification when she saw the film and later

recalled: 'For the first time I became aware of the major differences in the media', Merril and Pohl-Weary, *Better to Have Loved*, p.100.
48. Letter of 19 Aug. 1958; Merril Collection.
49. Philip Wylie, 'A Better Way to Beat the Bomb', *The Atlantic Monthly* (Feb. 1951), p.42.
50. Val Peterson, 'They Said It Would Never Happen ...' *The New York Times Book Review*, 17 Jan. 1954, pp.4–5. Wylie had written to Truman to stress the importance of people remaining in the cities while under nuclear attack and sent an advance copy of *Tomorrow!* to Eisenhower.
51. Philip Wylie, *Tomorrow!* (New York: Rinehart, 1954), pp.124–5.
52. Letter from Eugene Rabinowitz to Philip Wylie, 18 Jan. 1954; Wylie papers, Princeton University.
53. Grossman, *Neither Dead nor Red*, p.62.
54. Richard Foster, *The Rest Must Die* (New York: Fawcett, 1959), p.150.
55. James Blish, *So Close To Home* (New York: Ballantine Books, 1961), p.63.
56. 'The Box' was also collected in ibid.
57. James W. Deer, 'The Unavoidable Shelter Race', *Bulletin of the Atomic Scientists* 13/2 (Feb. 1957), pp.66–7.
58. James Blish, *A Case of Conscience* (Harmondsworth: Penguin, 1963), p.96. In his 1956 story 'To Pay the Piper' (collected in *Galactic Cluster*, 1959), Blish dealt further with the neurosis-inducing conditions of living in underground shelters in the aftermath of a nuclear and biological war.
59. David Ketterer, 'Covering *A Case of Conscience*', *Science-Fiction Studies* 9 (1982), p.208. Ketterer notes Blish's use of the Deer article at p.199.
60. Kennedy's shelter campaign is discussed in Spencer R. Weart, *Nuclear Fear: A History of Images* (Cambridge, MA: Harvard University Press, 1988), pp.253–8.
61. For a discussion of these and similar works, see Chapter 11 of my *American Science Fiction and the Cold War*. In Gina Berriault's novel preachers promote the cause of shelters by giving them an epic grandeur ('the greatest migration in the history of mankind is to be the migration underground into the shelters'), and by convincing their audience that descent really constituted a spiritual ascent (*The Descent*, London: Arthur Barker, 1961, pp.110–11).
62. Pat Frank, *How to Survive the H-Bomb – And Why* (Philadelphia: J.B. Lippincott, 1962), p.9. Similarly, his nomination of Los Angeles as the city least likely to survive would have offered little comfort to his readers in that city.
63. Philip Wylie, *Triumph* (Garden City, NY: Doubleday, 1963), p.96. Paul Brians suggests that the exception mentioned was *On the Beach* (*Nuclear Holocausts*, p.347).
64. Freeman Dyson, *Weapons and Hope* (New York: Harper & Row, 1984), pp.88–9, p.92.
65. Boyer, *Fallout*, pp.110–22. Among other reasons for the reduction of concern after 1963, Boyer cites the remoteness and abstraction of nuclear reality, the tranquillizing effect of the 'peaceful atom' programme, and the emergence of the New Left in the USA.
66. Endorsement in Dean Ing, *Pulling Through* (New York: Ace, 1983), p.i.

'Some Writers are More Equal than Others': George Orwell, the State and Cold War Privilege

TONY SHAW

George Orwell's reputation for intellectual integrity and political independence came under the microscope in 1996 when declassified documents proved that shortly before his death in January 1950, the author had had secret dealings with the British Foreign Office's new anti-communist propaganda outfit, the Information Research Department (IRD). The records showed that not only had Orwell expressed his 'enthusiastic approval' of the IRD's techniques and aims, he had also furnished the secret organization with a list of 'crypto-communists' and 'fellow-travellers' in the arts, Fleet Street and Parliament whom it ought not to trust.[1] These revelations sparked a public row among politicians, journalists and academics about Orwell's revered honesty and his relationship to the Cold War. The veteran Labour Member of Parliament Tony Benn was shocked and disgusted to learn that Orwell had 'given in' to official blandishments, the Marxist historian Christopher Hill called Orwell 'two-faced', while the left-wing journalist Paul Foot labelled him a 'McCarthyite' informer. Others, including the former editor of *The Observer*, David Astor, and the political scientist (and Orwell biographer), Bernard Crick, staunchly defended Orwell's actions on the grounds that he was protecting democratic socialism against the very real threat posed by Stalinism.[2] Since 1996, a host of historians, political scientists and literary scholars have added to the debate about Orwell's IRD connections. While some like Frances Stonor Saunders have criticized Orwell for having confused the role of the intellectual with that of the policeman, the majority – like Peter Davison and Timothy Garton Ash – have put their weight behind Crick and Astor. Another of Orwell's supporters, the eminent Soviet historian, Robert Conquest, managed to muddy the waters of the debate by proudly admitting to having been on the IRD's payroll during the Cold War.[3]

The above war of words forms part of the struggle over Orwell's works and reputation *after* the Cold War. What this article focuses on instead is the struggle to 'claim' Orwell's name (legend, even) *during* the Cold War. As Orwell scholar John Rodden reminds us, literary reputations are made, not born, and variously built, fashioned, manufactured, suppressed and distorted. George Orwell's image and legacy was contested feverishly in the decades following his death from tuberculosis at 46 years of age in 1950. More specifically, a myriad of politicians, intellectuals and commentators argued about what Orwell's stance on the Cold War would have been had he lived to see the conflict reach its maturity. While some did this out of intellectual curiosity, many others did so in order to strengthen their own position in the Cold War.[4] This article seeks to cast a fresh perspective on this discourse by scrutinizing the indirect role that official Western propagandists played in it, and by examining the part these officials had in raising Orwell's profile to the dizzy heights that it achieved during the Cold War. The study focuses above all on why, how, and with what effects the British and American governments used Orwell's two best known novels, *Animal Farm* (1945) and *Nineteen Eighty-Four* (1949), as part of their anti-Soviet and anti-communist propaganda campaigns. My analysis is divided into three parts. The first section outlines why Orwell and his works were so valuable to Western propagandists. The second section examines the part that British and American propaganda officials played in disseminating *Animal Farm* and *Nineteen Eighty-Four* world-wide in print form. The final section looks at how the novels were transferred to cinema and television screens and at the political changes the books underwent in the process. The article concentrates throughout on the period from the mid-1940s to the mid-1950s. This was the formative stage of the Cold War and the period during which Orwell's legendary status was established. I hope this study adds to our understanding of how politics and literary culture interacted during the Cold War, and how popular Cold War images could be formed with clandestine assistance from government.

George Orwell – Public Asset Number One

Having spent a good deal of his writing career alerting people to the systematic misuse of language in modern politics,[5] and having penned scripts for the Indian section of the British Broadcasting Corporation's (BBC's) Eastern Service during the Second World War,[6] George Orwell would surely not have been surprised to see his work being posthumously exploited by governments during the Cold

War's battle for hearts and minds. Indeed, as we shall see, Orwell himself was quick to turn *Animal Farm* to the West's advantage in the late 1940s. But what was it about Orwell the man, and *Animal Farm* and *Nineteen Eighty-Four* in particular, that official Western propagandists found so appealing, so much so that they were willing to spend hundreds of thousands of dollars promoting them? There would appear to be at least four main reasons for this.

The first and most obvious reason was that Orwell was a man of the Left. Through books like *The Road to Wigan Pier* (1936), his eye-witness account of the ravages of unemployment, his near death when fighting for the republicans in the Spanish Civil War, his vocal opposition to the British Empire, together with his patriotic calls for the socialist transformation of Britain during the Second World War (best exemplified in the bestselling *The Lion and the Unicorn*, 1941), Orwell was to many people a socialist paragon. Because he had never actually been in the Communist Party, Orwell lacked the 'inside knowledge' that former party members like his friend and fellow author, Arthur Koestler, could bring to their denunciations of Soviet communism during the Cold War. Yet, to official propagandists in Britain and the United States, Orwell's distance from the Communist Party rendered him less of a tainted 'fanatic', and one whose long-standing social democratic ideals might help win over the doubters on the liberal or non-communist Left to the West's cause. In sum, Orwell's radical, left-wing reputation would ensure wider currency, stronger credibility and greater efficacy in the officials' ideological battle against the Soviet Union.

The second reason revolved around Orwell's reputation for being an outsider. To this day (despite the body-blow of the 1996 revelations), Orwell's image remains that of a troublemaker, an activist, novelist and essayist who refused to succumb to political or social orthodoxy. A perfect example of this was *Animal Farm* itself, which many publishers passed over in 1944 and 1945 – with the help of a warning from the Ministry of Information – partly due to its allegorical depiction of 'Uncle Joe' Stalin's brutality.[7] Orwell's independence of mind formed the basis of his reputation for political and artistic integrity; this might help to explain why his warnings about the dangers of writers being turned into captive animals in *Nineteen Eighty-Four* and elsewhere struck such a chord with many of his readers.[8] Orwell was a supporter of Attlee's ruling Labour Party in the late 1940s but this never stopped him criticizing government policies he found objectionable. In one of his last essays he spelt out his desire for 'a Socialist United States of Europe' independent of Russia and America, which many took as a broadside against Foreign Secretary Ernest Bevin's apparent pro-Americanism.[9] Such views appealed to those inside and outside the Labour Party in the late 1940s who wanted British social democracy to act as a 'Third Force' in international relations, between American capitalism and Soviet communism. While these criticisms made for uncomfortable reading among IRD officials, the advantage was that they confirmed Orwell's autonomy.[10]

The third reason relates to *Animal Farm* and *Nineteen Eighty-Four* themselves. For a start, both books were short, direct and written in Orwell's characteristically clear style, making them accessible to almost everyone, including, in *Animal Farm*'s case, children. This made them easily translatable and suitable for radio and cinema adaptation. At the same time, the novels were multi-layered, and psychologically and politically complex, and thus could be a challenge to the literary-minded. This is why most critics adored the books, and why both novels suffered ideological misreadings.[11] Orwell in fact aimed to project two principal themes in *Animal Farm*: first, to 'expose the Soviet myth', and, by extension, to condemn tyranny universally; and secondly, and more positively, to show that the Stalinists had betrayed the Bolsheviks' original intentions and thereby to express his faith in the ultimate achievability of socialism.[12] In essence, *Nineteen Eighty-Four* was a natural extension of these themes and was intended as a warning against the threat of totalitarianism, whether from the Left or the Right.[13] However, given that *Animal Farm* was so incisive a fable on the history of Soviet communism, and that *Nineteen Eighty-Four* had not only been written during the early years of the Cold War (it was published in June 1949, just after the collapse of the Berlin Blockade) but also that the 'comrades' and show trials depicted in the book obviously drew so heavily on Stalin's Russia, it was relatively simple for the British and American governments to deploy the two novels as straightforward anti-Soviet propaganda. Moreover, the fact that the books did not mention communism directly, and that they were novels rather than essays or pamphlets, made them appear less like propaganda (as most people understood the word), thus rendering them potentially more persuasive.

Finally, Orwell's death in 1950 cleared the way for officials and others to appropriate his name and work without fear of contradiction from the man himself. Orwell was extremely protective of *Animal Farm* and *Nineteen Eighty-Four,* both before and after their publication. He vehemently opposed the latter being 'mucked about with' by publishers, and consistently corrected misinterpretations of key aspects of the novels. He was particularly distressed by the use to which right-wing Cold Warriors put his writings in his later years.[14] After January 1950 this policing role was primarily left to his widow, Sonia Blair, but her insistence on the right to vet adaptations of *Animal Farm* and *Nineteen Eighty-Four* frequently fell on deaf ears. Orwell's 'tragic' early death, robbing the literary world of someone who had been cut off in his prime, also undoubtedly helped foster his legendary status, and consequently boosted the sales and authority of his works. Soon labelled by some intellectuals and politicians a 'prophet' or 'saint',[15] Orwell for Western propagandists became a malleable, prized asset whose powerful rhetoric and vision would be 'clarified' and then spread as deeply and as widely as possible.

War of the Words: Pressing Orwell into Western Service

Orwell became famous in Britain when *Animal Farm* was published by Secker and Warburg in August 1945. In what John Rodden has described as 'probably the single most significant event for expanding Orwell's reputation in his lifetime', the fable was then selected as a September 1946 Book-of-the-Month Club choice in the United States. During 1946–49 the book sold 460,000 copies through the Club and soon became an American bestseller. *Nineteen Eighty-Four* was published in Britain and the United States simultaneously in June 1949, and, thanks partly to the boost provided by another choice of the Book-of-the-Month Club, sold over 400,000 copies in its first year alone. *Nineteen Eighty-Four* confirmed Orwell's place in the modern literary pantheon. If *Animal Farm* had occasioned comparisons of him as political author with Voltaire and Jonathan Swift, *Nineteen Eighty-Four* prompted leading European and American intellectuals to rate Orwell alongside Fyodor Dostoevsky, H. G. Wells and Aldous Huxley in the anti-utopian tradition.[16] Both novels were immediately seen as defining texts on either the emerging or freezing East–West divide, from differing and competing angles.[17]

In the late 1940s and early 1950s, the British and American governments conducted an intensive campaign to widen the political impact of *Animal Farm* and *Nineteen Eighty-Four*, first mainly in Central and Eastern Europe, later in the developing world. They were sometimes assisted by Orwell himself. In January 1947 the British Central Office of Information wrote to Fredric Warburg, Orwell's publisher and friend, asking for his comments on a proposal for the publication of *Animal Farm* 'in a cheap English edition in Hungary', but nothing came of this.[18] However, in March a Ukrainian edition appeared, complete with a preface written by Orwell spelling out what the book meant to say.[19] In Germany, where the Ukrainian translation had been published, the novel was eagerly sought by anti-communist publishers, probably with the support of *Amerikadienst*, the translation bureau and news service of the US High Commission. In mid-1947 Orwell lent his support to these activities. His agent, Leonard Moore, corresponded with Russian anti-Stalinists in the Soviet zone about how copies of *Animal Farm* could be smuggled into the East. Orwell even expressed his willingness to subsidise its distribution, telling Moore that it was the right time for such a project since, 'the US is altering its policy, and doing more anti-Russian propaganda'. Orwell was also a sponsor of the Books in Germany programme organised by the British Foreign Office.[20]

The Foreign Office's maximization of *Animal Farm* and *Nineteen Eighty-Four* was handled primarily by the Information Research Department. Established in early 1948, the IRD was the first major initiative in Western propaganda, antedating by several months similar ventures in 'psychological warfare' by the US government.[21] Books were central to the department's efforts to produce and disseminate unattributable (or 'grey') anti-communist propaganda in Britain and overseas. In early 1949 – around the time that Orwell gave his list of 'crypto-communists' to the IRD's Celia Kirwan, Arthur Koestler's sister-in-law – IRD stepped up its publishing activities significantly. It approached several independent publishers, including Oxford University Press and Penguin, with proposals for anti-communist books, suggesting they be based on IRD briefing papers which had already been distributed to selected journalists. Allen Lane at Penguin was particularly responsive, believing there was 'a need for a book for the English public dealing with communism in an objective and serious way'. Related or not, Penguin later produced many editions of one such IRD paper, *The Theory and Practice of Communism*, written by Foreign Office Sovietologist Robert Carew Hunt. In 1951 and 1954 Penguin also published their first editions of *Animal Farm* and *Nineteen Eighty-Four* respectively, both of which were reissued almost annually thereafter.[22] IRD also circulated books and journals to posts abroad. For example, *Tribune*, the Labour weekly for which Orwell had acted as literary editor in the early 1940s, was widely distributed on the grounds that 'it combines the resolute exposure of communism and its methods with the consistent championship of those objectives which left-wing sympathizers normally support'.[23] At the same time, IRD tried to find a publishing house with known left-wing affiliations to 'front' a series of books that would 'appeal to organized labour' and 'project "social democracy" as a successful rival to communism'. Orwell himself suggested Victor Gollancz to Celia Kirwan, but neither a deal with this company nor with Odhams, publishers of the Labour Party's newspaper, *The Daily Herald*, came to fruition.[24] Eventually, the IRD set up its own, ostensibly independent, publishing company, Ampersand, in 1950.[25]

During the late 1940s and early 1950s the IRD successfully commissioned a number of prominent authors to write articles or pamphlets, including the London School of Economics's Harold Laski (who compared British and Soviet trade unionism), Labour MP Richard Crossman (who re-assessed the Nazi–Soviet Pact of 1939), and the former leader of the German Communist Party, Ruth Fischer, who looked at how the Soviets controlled communist parties outside their borders.[26] It also negotiated the foreign rights to books which offered dramatic exposés of communism, such as Douglas Hyde's *I Believed* (1951), or others which testified to the failure of the Marxist utopia, such as the highly influential collection of essays by former intellectual supporters of the Communist Party, *The God That Failed*, edited by Richard Crossman and published in 1950.[27] By 1955 the department could modestly boast that it was selecting and distributing approximately 24 anti-communist commercially published books per year.[28]

Amidst this wordy crusade Orwell's work consistently took pride of place. In April 1949 plans were set in train for the distribution of suitable translations of *Animal Farm* in large parts of the Middle East, where British interests were paramount. Ernest Main of the British Embassy in Cairo, which was concerned about the susceptibility of Saudi Arabian oil workers to communist propaganda, told the head of IRD, Ralph Murray, of his colleagues' enthusiasm for an Arabic-language edition to be distributed in Cairo: 'The idea is particularly good for Arabic in view of the fact that both pigs and dogs are unclean animals to Moslems.' The IRD agreed to fund the project and arranged copyright clearance: 'the more the merrier', commented the department's Adam Watson.[29] Murray was naturally extremely keen to make *Animal Farm* available in the Soviet Union. In June 1949 Orwell received a request for advice on investors needed to raise 2000 Deutschmarks for the production of a Russian-language version of *Animal Farm*: 'we ask you please not to think that this letter has been sent to you with any base mercenary motives, but exclusively in the interests of the cause of combatting Bolshevism, which cause your book serves so brilliantly'. The request came from V. Puachev of *Possev*, a weekly Russian-language social and political review with offices in London and Frankfurt, run by a group of Russian refugees which distributed anti-Soviet propaganda amongst the Red Army occupation forces in Germany and Austria. Orwell had already given the group permission to publish, free of charge, a Russian translation in serialized form, but it lacked the resources to publish and distribute a large print-run of the book. Orwell sent Puachev's letter to the IRD, who then passed it on to the Foreign Office, whose translator vouched strongly for the émigré group's credentials: 'we do of course know the Possev people do a good job'. In November 1949 Celia Kirwan informed the Voice of America director, Charles Thayer, of the imminent publication of a Russian translation of *Animal Farm*, 'undertaken by an impoverished but respectable group of Russian refugees in West Germany'. The book, *Skotskii Khutor*, duly appeared in 1950.[30]

As the Kirwan-Thayer correspondence suggests, the frostier East–West relations grew the more the IRD promoted Orwell's works in tandem with its sister agencies in the United States. This made sense given the latter's greater financial resources. Starting with a Korean edition of *Animal Farm* in 1948, the US State Department sponsored the translation and distribution of Orwell's books in more than thirty languages. From 1953 onwards it joined hands with the United States Information Agency (USIA), whose distribution network was vast. By the late 1950s the USIA operated libraries in 162 cities in all major countries in the world, with the exception of those with Communist Party-dominated regimes which steadfastly refused offers of facilities.[31] In November 1950 the Foreign Office and the United States Information and Educational Exchange (USIE) arranged to produce jointly an illustrated Arabic version of *Animal Farm*. Aimed at the lower end of the reading market in the Middle East, the book was set at a price to compete with the 'cheapest thrillers' (£8 Egyptian), and was published under the cover of a Cairo company, Al Maaref Publishing House.[32] At roughly the same point, the IRD purchased the right to circulate a strip cartoon of *Animal*

Farm via local newspapers in large parts of Latin America, the Far East, Europe, the Middle East, India, Ceylon and Pakistan. This 'brilliant satire on the Communist regime in the USSR', noted Ralph Murray, was 'a most effective propaganda weapon, because of its skilful combination of simplicity, subtlety and humour'. Officials kept a loving eye on the production of the cartoon strip, discussing characterization of the animals with the animators and continually stressing the anti-communist elements of the story. Distribution proved very successful, though the Belgrade embassy refused it on political grounds and Tel Aviv because pigs were deemed unsuitable.[33]

By April 1951 the IRD's thoughts had turned to making a film strip of this cartoon for schools overseas, complete with an accompanying narration.[34] In the same month, as part of a State Department memorandum titled 'Participation of Books in Department's Fight Against Communism', US Secretary of State Dean Acheson authorised payment for the translation rights to *Nineteen Eighty-Four*. The memo stated that *Animal Farm* and *Nineteen Eighty-Four* 'have been of great value to the Department in its psychological offensive against Communism', justifying official overt and covert help with translations.[35] In June 1951, Acheson ordered the US embassy in London 'to assist foreign publishers' in bringing out further translations of *Animal Farm*: 'Offer $100 PORT[uguese] book and serial rights; $50 VIET[namese] book rights. Publication RIO and Saigon. Use contingency funds, Reply soonest.'[36] By the end of 1951, both the State Department and IRD were reporting the imminent availability of Chinese copies of *Animal Farm*, including a special pictorial version.[37]

Ten years after the end of the Second World War the sales of, comments on, and spin-offs from *Animal Farm* and *Nineteen Eighty-Four* had made George Orwell one of the best-known authors in the English language. Words or phrases culled from the two novels – 'four legs good, two legs bad', 'unperson', 'doublespeak' – had begun to be assimilated into the Western political lexicon and imagination. To a great extent the Orwell 'legend' was confined to the Anglophone world. But commercial interests had made his works available – if only in libraries – across many regions of the globe, assisted partly by British and American official propagandists shouldering the cost of rights, translations, distribution and, in some cases, adaptation and production. By 1955 the IRD was able to report that it had bought the rights to *Nineteen Eighty-Four* in Burmese, Chinese, Danish, Dutch, French, German, Finnish, Hebrew, Italian, Japanese,

Indonesian, Latvian, Norwegian, Polish, Portuguese, Spanish and Swedish.[38] Reflecting its determination to render Orwell more entertaining and accessible in the colonies, the department had also bought the right to circulate the cartoon strip of *Animal Farm* in Cyprus, Tanganyika, Kenya, Uganda, Northern and Southern Rhodesia, Nyasaland, Sierra Leone, Gold Coast, Nigeria, Trinidad, Jamaica, Fiji, British Guiana and British Honduras.[39] No other books had been singled out for such treatment either by London or Washington.

There is no way of knowing how many people in these and other countries actually read *Animal Farm* and *Nineteen Eighty-Four*, still less whether they interpreted the books in the way the British and American officials hoped they would, and then thought and acted accordingly. That said, it just might be more than a coincidence that it was in Western Germany, where in the early years of the Cold War Western policy-makers most feared a communist take-over, and where Orwell's works seem to have been exploited as anti-Soviet propaganda weapons more than anywhere else, that Orwell's standing far exceeded that in any other non-Anglophone country. One important factor in bringing this about was the championing of Orwell by the highly influential monthly *Der Monat*. Its editor was the American Melvin Lasky, a leading member of the Central Intelligence Agency (CIA)-funded Congress for Cultural Freedom (CCF), an intellectual and artistic movement set up in Paris in 1950 that led a liberal offensive predominantly against communists and fellow-travellers during the Cold War.[40] As for Eastern Europe, in which at least some ambitious Western propagandists hoped *Animal Farm* and *Nineteen Eighty-Four* might have a destabilizing effect, Orwell was officially labelled, as *Pravda*'s 1950 review of *Nineteen Eighty-Four* put it, 'an enemy of the people'.[41] Accordingly, none of his books were officially published in the Soviet Union or in any other East European nation aligned with Moscow throughout the Cold War. Librarians followed instructions to keep his books off their shelves, and *Nineteen Eighty-Four* received an official import ban in the Soviet Union until 1988.[42] Despite these restrictions translated, samizdat versions of Orwell's works were passed around behind the 'Iron Curtain', especially among dissident Soviet and Eastern European intellectuals. In his classic of totalitarian literature, *The Captive Mind*, published after his flight to France in 1953, Lithuania's Czeslaw Milosz observed that intellectuals were 'amazed' that a writer who had never lived in Russia should have so keen a perception into its life. Some Western intellectuals have consistently argued that *Nineteen Eighty-Four*, secretly circulated among writers of the Petofi Club in Budapest, was a catalyst of the 1956 Hungarian uprising. *Animal Farm* came into many people's hands courtesy of balloon operations run by the Free Europe Press, the publication arm of the National Committee for Free Europe. Set up in 1949, this body was a central component of the US 'state-private' network during the Cold War of the 1950s.[43] Finally, lest we overlook the effects that *Animal Farm* and *Nineteen Eighty-Four* had in Britain and the United States, it should be noted that by the late 1950s the novels were prescribed reading on school curricula in both countries, and in many of Britain's remaining colonies. How and why this occurred is a complex issue, but the fact that many teachers taught *Animal Farm* as a horrifying 'animallegory' of Soviet despotism and played up the Soviet parallels in *Nineteen Eighty-Four* is surely of some significance, both for the Cold War of the late 1950s and beyond.[44]

Seeing is Believing: Filming Orwell

Animal Farm and *Nineteen Eighty-Four* were adapted for the radio on several occasions in Orwell's lifetime, and many times afterwards. The BBC's cultural channel, the Third Programme, broadcast Orwell's own scripted version of *Animal Farm* in 1947 (repeating it in 1952), and *Nineteen Eighty-Four* in 1950. In April 1947 Orwell gave permission for a Dutch version of *Animal Farm* to be broadcast, and the Voice of America broadcast *Animal Farm* and *Nineteen Eighty-Four* in Eastern Europe in 1947 and 1949 respectively.[45] However, these adaptations, which seem to have been faithful to the books, were intended for and largely restricted to the literary-minded. What really lifted Orwell's profile during and beyond the first decade of the Cold War were the four adaptations of *Animal Farm* and *Nineteen Eighty-Four* that appeared on television and at the cinema between 1953 and 1956. This cluster of American and British film and television treatments was, according to John Rodden, the biggest single factor in establishing Orwell as both 'The Prophet', a man whose work had grave political implications for the future, and a 'public' writer, one whose name and work were known by far more people than merely those who had read his books.[46] Each of these film and television productions had strong Cold War connotations. Two of them were intimately connected with official Cold War propagandists. 'Screening' Orwell therefore took on more than one meaning, as we shall see via an analysis of each of the treatments in turn.

In September 1953, National Broadcasting Company's (NBC's) Studio One broadcast the first screen adaptation of *Nineteen Eighty-Four*. NBC was the largest and most powerful of the four main television networks in the United States, and lent vigorous support both to Senator Joseph McCarthy's subversion allegations and Washington's tough approach towards communism overseas in the 1950s. So close was the relationship between NBC executives and government that programmes such as *Battle Report – Washington*, a news series covering the Korean War, were produced in the White House.[47] *1984*, as the one-hour television play was titled, starred Eddie Albert as Winston Smith, Norma Crane as Julia, and Lorne Greene as O'Brien. It was watched in 8.7 million homes, a 53 per cent share of the market, making it the highest-rated Studio One programme that year. It received numerous plaudits from critics. 'I cannot recall seeing any other television drama so imaginatively and effectively presented', opined *The New Yorker*.[48] The play was a relatively straight adaptation of the novel but, perhaps inevitably given recent Cold War events – Stalin's death in March, the Soviets' crushing of the East Berlin uprising in June, and the Korean War armistice in July – and McCarthy's ubiquity, it was nevertheless interpreted by most commentators as an anti-communist warning. Some media organs jumped at the opportunity to drive this point home to the public, especially Henry Luce's magazines *Life* and *Time*. An arch-conservative and anti-socialist, Luce wielded his publications empire as a powerful anti-Soviet instrument in the Cold War. His contacts in officialdom were legion, and included the post-war vice-president of *Time*, C.D. Jackson, who had been appointed Special Assistant for psychological operations by Eisenhower in early 1953.[49]

BBC Television's adaptation of *Nineteen Eighty-Four*, broadcast on 12 December 1954, was the most ambitious and expensive television drama in Britain to date: one hour 51 minutes long, with 22 sets, 28 actors, and an established television star in Peter Cushing (who played Winston Smith).[50] This play was, in some respects, *too* faithful to the book. Viewers and critics in their droves found its evocation of Orwell's picture of Winston's daily existence in Oceania – grim, suffocating, fearful and pointless – shocking, and complained that the production was 'pornographic' and 'sadistic' in its depictions of adultery and violence. One viewer, housewife Beryl Mirfin, reportedly collapsed and died of a heart attack after the play's torture scenes.[51] When, much to the consternation of many, the play was shown again on 16 December, it attracted the largest audience to date in British television history.[52] A month-long debate followed in Parliament and the mass media about Orwell, the novel, broadcasting censorship, and the links between television violence and criminal behaviour.[53] During this the *The New York Times* called the play, perhaps accurately, 'the subject of the sharpest controversy in the annals of British television'. Some proof of this was the series of death threats received by the film's producer, Rudolph Cartier, for whom the BBC hired bodyguards.[54]

Since its inception, the IRD had forged close links with the BBC's overseas and domestic services, enabling the Foreign Office both to offer the corporation regular guidance about programming and to disseminate some of its most valuable anti-communist material.[55] BBC-IRD ties were strengthened further by a number of BBC senior executives having other prominent Cold War roles. For example, Harman Grisewood, the controller of the BBC's Third Programme during this period, was in the early 1950s also chairman of the British Society for Cultural Freedom, an IRD-backed offshoot of the Paris-based CCF.[56] Documents relating to BBC Television's *1984* reveal no evidence of BBC-IRD collaboration on this project. Neither the producer, Cartier, nor the adapter, Nigel Kneale, had explicit Cold War motives for being involved with it. Cartier intended the film to act as a warning against totalitarianism in all its forms (fascism, communism, and McCarthyism), whereas the apolitical Kneale wanted to recreate on screen what he saw as Orwell's 'brilliant ... setting down of a nightmare – our own age gone mad, gone bad ... [in which] Science is the slave of power, for power's sake'.[57] This did not stop newspapers on the Right adopting the play as a welcome anti-Soviet salvo. Lord Rothermere's *Daily Mail*, for instance, praised it for exposing 'the beastliness of Communism – something which we must fight with all our strength of mind and will', while Lord Beaverbrook's *Daily Express* began serializing a severely abridged version of *Nineteen Eighty-Four*, all of which prompted one Labour MP to accuse the Conservatives of 'stealing' Orwell.[58] There is little doubt that responses like these and the sensationalism surrounding the play brought Orwell's work to the attention of thousands of people who up to this point had either never read *Nineteen Eighty-Four* or even heard of him. As *The Times* put it on 15 December: 'The term "Big Brother", which the day before yesterday meant nothing to 99 per cent of the population, has become a household phrase.' After the telecast, *Nineteen Eighty-Four* was catapulted into what the book industry has since called 'supersellerdom'.[59]

However, letters to the BBC indicate that the play (and Orwell's book) had been interpreted in a variety of ways by ordinary viewers, many entirely divorced from contemporary politics; some, for instance, just expressed 'horror' at such 'pessimistic' material being aired on the Sabbath.[60] At the same time, it is noteworthy just how many commentators across the political spectrum referred to the BBC's 'coverage' rather than 'production' of Orwell's book, as if it were a real event that the cameras were at. This not only lent *Nineteen Eighty-Four* greater reverence but also encouraged people to see the book not as fiction but as a 'true' account of the nature of totalitarianism generally and of life behind the 'Iron Curtain' specifically. Significantly, it was soon after the BBC play that Isaac Deutscher famously called *Nineteen Eighty-Four* 'a sort of ideological superweapon in the cold war', with dominant Western readings of the book eliding Orwell's attack on capitalism.[61]

December 1954 also saw the release in New York and London of the first cinematic version of *Animal Farm*. This Anglo-American production warrants detailed analysis due to its political distortion of Orwell's book and its enduring use as an educational tool. In March 1951 Sonia Blair sold the animation film rights of *Animal Farm* to the American producer, Louis de Rochement. Acting as the conduit and providing the bulk of the finance for this deal (roughly £90,000), was a former Hollywood agent, Carleton Alsop, who worked for the Office of Policy Co-ordination.[62] This was a body created in 1948 by the US National Security Council to conduct unattributable anti-Soviet psychological operations and which was housed within the CIA for administrative support.[63] For the project de Rochement hired the self-styled father of British animation, John Halas, who, together with his wife Joy Batchelor, ran Europe's largest animation company, in London. This had the advantage of being cheaper than recruiting Disney or Fleischer, Hollywood's established animators, and, by hiding its American (not to mention CIA) origins, gave the finished product greater international propaganda potential.[64]

In constructing what was to be the first feature-length animation film to be made in Britain aimed at the general public and the first animated cartoon of a 'serious' work of art, Halas and Batchelor expected to work in their usual autonomous fashion. Yet advice on the script came continually from several interested parties. De Rochement, who in 1952 produced with the Federal Bureau of

Investigation's (FBI's) help the red-baiting melodrama *Walk East on Beacon*, insisted on Napoleon's authoritarian demeanour being accentuated and that changes be made to his key-note end speech.[65] Fredric Warburg, treasurer of the British Society for Cultural Freedom, and a man who had misinterpreted *Nineteen Eighty-Four* as marking his close friend's break with socialism, regularly visited the film studio.[66] And, in January 1952 a draft script was assessed by the US Psychological Strategy Board (PSB), an organization that between 1951 and 1953 acted as the nerve centre for US Cold War strategic psychological operations. One of the PSB's propaganda lines during this period was to accuse the Soviet regime of having perverted Marxism, and promoting a wider reception of *Animal Farm* corresponded nicely with this.[67] The PSB's film experts criticised the draft script for having a 'confusing' theme and 'no great clarity of message'. For the film to have its fullest impact - and contribute to the PSB's three-fold 'consolidate, impregnate and liberate' strategy – ease of understanding was considered essential. PSB officials argued, therefore, that it was far better to simplify, even at the cost of modifying Orwell's meaning, rather than confuse the audience with an overly precious adherence to the book's text.[68]

The differences between the film version of *Animal Farm* and Orwell's book indicate strongly that this behind-the-scenes advice bore fruit. A film that appears at first sight to follow Orwell's narrative very closely in fact contains three sets of significant alterations. First, in the book there is no doubting Orwell's depiction of Napoleon (Stalin) as a despicable tyrant, nor that de Rochement's desire to magnify his authoritarian nature made commercial sense. Yet the book states that during the seminal Battle of the Windmill (the Second World War) 'all the animals, except Napoleon, flung themselves flat on their bellies and hid their faces'.[69] This represented Orwell's attempt to be fair to Stalin who remained in Moscow after the launching of 'Operation Barbarossa', directing affairs from the rear. In the film, however, Napoleon is singled out as the only animal (apart from Squealer) that does not fight, other than cowardly issuing a few orders from the safety of the farmhouse in response to direct attacks on him. Similarly, the book attributes Napoleon's trading with humans partly to the economic needs of the Soviet Union in the 1920s and 1930s, whereas in the film Napoleon's motives are reduced to pure greed (in the shape of jam for himself and the other pigs). Second, the film also virtually does away with the book's human characters and its references to the iniquities of capitalism and limitations of liberty. Far less is made in the film of why the animals rebel in the first place; the 'tyranny of human beings' in Orwell's opening chapter is reduced on screen to Jones' drunken cruelty. The role that the humans play throughout the book in trying to stamp out the rebellion via black propaganda and the flogging of animals for singing the revolutionary anthem is cut. Two of Orwell's central characters, Pilkington and Frederick (the British and German governing classes), are virtually elided. Other than Jones himself, the humans are reduced in the film to an indeterminate pub rabble. In doing so, the film plays down the significance that the book attached to capitalist in-fighting, and Orwell's condemnation of Britain and Germany's strategy of isolating the USSR prior to the Second World War.

This line of interpretation is given a further twist in the final scene, which amounts to a wholesale inversion of Orwell's ending. The book concludes on a bleak note, with the now clothed pigs drinking, brawling and gambling with their human farmer neighbours, and agreeing they have a common interest in keeping the lower animals and lower classes subservient. The 'creatures outside', reads the last sentence, 'looked from pig to man, and from man to pig, and from pig to man again; but already it was impossible to say which was which'.[70] Here, Orwell was suggesting that there was no difference between old tyrannies and new, between capitalist exploiters and communist ones. Moreover, the raucous farmhouse party is meant to satirize the cynical power politics of the first wartime meeting between Churchill, Stalin and Roosevelt at Teheran in November 1943, and to predict their inevitable future conflict based on self-interest. This is why Pilkington and Napoleon draw the ace of spades together at the end of their card game. By participating in this future struggle, warned Orwell, the masses would once again be serving their oppressors' ends.[71] The film changes this dénouement in two ways. First, the audience is not allowed to feel that the capitalist farmers and communist pigs are on the same debased level. The farmers are excluded from the scene altogether. Consequently, the watching creatures see only pigs enjoying the fruits of exploitation – a sight which impels them to stage a successful counter-revolution by storming the farmhouse, led by the inveterate cynic, Benjamin. The result is not only an uplifting ending that made commercial sense (as John Halas later argued), but also one which shows that an apparently invincible force can be beaten. It tied in nicely with the strand of US policy in the mid-1950s that encouraged those living under the communist yoke in Eastern Europe to 'liberate' themselves.[72]

Animal Farm was eagerly promoted by the American Committee for Cultural Freedom (ACCF), the US offshoot of the CCF. Media contacts spread word of 'one of the most important anti-communist documents of our time'; discount rates were offered to students and labour unions; and strenuous efforts (ultimately forlorn), were made to persuade Metro-Goldwyn-Mayer (MGM) to act as the film's distributors.[73] The IRD also made strenuous efforts to distribute it among 'the slightly educated' in the colonies and in other parts of the developing world, such as Indochina.[74] The film proved to be far from a box-office success, however. 'It was a serious cartoon and the distributors didn't know what to do with it,' said a spokesman for the Motion Picture Association of America in New York.[75] That said, if the critical response to the movie is anything to go by, the film's paymasters must have been pleased by its reception politically. While notable reviewers on both sides of the Atlantic actually accused the filmmakers of engaging in leftist subversion of Orwell's message and of having deliberately redirected the fable's satire away from the Bolshevik Revolution,[76] the majority recommended it as a faithful interpretation of Orwell's anti-communism. In labelling it 'a merciless commentary on the Slave State' and 'the child's guide to the Communist fallacy' respectively, Britain's *Catholic Herald* and *Daily Mail* indicated how keenly conservative newspapers exploited such 'respectable' opportunities for anti-Soviet propaganda, and how that propaganda might have been enhanced by animation's instant accessibility and apparent ideological innocence.[77] As things turned out, the film seems not to have penetrated Eastern Europe where, CIA distribution efforts notwithstanding, it was banned.[78] The film was easily translatable, however, and versions soon appeared in several languages, including Japanese, Swedish, German, Italian, French and Finnish. Beyond the 1950s, the movie was widely used as a pedagogical tool for British and American schoolchildren reading Orwell, thus helping to provide a new generation with a tendentious grounding in the origins of the Cold War.[79]

Finally, like Halas and Batchelor's *Animal Farm*, the 1956 cinematic version of *Nineteen Eighty-Four* was also an Anglo-American production. It, too, originated within the US government and it also, as might be expected, altered Orwell's message. There is good reason to believe that US propaganda officials had been looking to transfer *Nineteen Eighty-Four* to the big screen and thereby make it more 'comprehensible' to a wider public for some years; after all, the book was required reading for CIA and PSB officials in the early 1950s, a measure of its perceived power as an anti-communist propaganda tract.[80] The film rights for *Nineteen Eighty-Four* were acquired from Orwell's estate in 1953 by the former president of RKO, Peter Rathvon. Rathvon enjoyed a close relationship with the US government in the 1950s, financing films for the Motion Picture Service, a semi-official organization linked to the USIA which assigned some of Hollywood's top director-producers to films that best projected American values at home and overseas.[81] In 1955, production of *1984* began at Associated British's Elstree Studios outside London, with Michael Anderson as director. A subsidy of $100,000 was provided secretly by the USIA on the understanding that it had control of the script.[82] Distribution was to be handled by Columbia, a company which had produced a raft of anti-Soviet movies in the late 1940s and early 1950s, and whose president, Harry Cohn, was counted among C. D. Jackson's best 'friends' in Hollywood.[83] Help also came from the ACCF, whose executive director, playwright Sol Stein, gave Rathvon advice on the publicity for the film and its screenplay. In particular, Stein argued that for the film to do justice to the book and make audiences aware of the immediate dangers posed by communism, it ought to take the form of a docu-drama in which everything looked as contemporary as possible. For instance, rather than wearing sashes as in the book, Stein suggested the members of the Anti-Sex League have armbands. Most importantly, the book's ending had to be changed. As Stein put it, rather than leaving the audience in 'total despair', with Winston Smith capitulating to Big Brother, it was essential at least to hint 'that human nature can not be changed by totalitarianism ... so that the viewer, like the person behind the Iron Curtain, will be left with some small measure of hope'. This could be done, Stein proposed, by emphasizing the enduring love between Winston and his fellow rebel, Julia.[84]

Virtually all of Stein's suggestions appear in the final print of *1984*. Right from the very start of the film, when the narrator places events in 'the immediate future' and shocking pictures follow of atomic explosions, Orwell's world seems to be just around the corner. Hints of 'reality' are all around: Oceania's Thought Police tote machine guns rather than lasers, and Eurasian prisoners are paraded through an easily recognizable Trafalgar Square. Added to this, the film obfuscates Orwell's critique of international politics, namely the expedient nature of great power alliances (like that in the Second World War) and his warning of a world divided into three super-states locked in never-ending combat (a Cold War), in which the masses are fed on a diet of propaganda and coercion. In the film, Oceania's war with Eurasia is attributed wholly to the designs of Big Brother, not the workings of the international system. Moreover, Eurasia remains an enemy throughout rather than, as happens towards the end of the book, suddenly being announced as an ally. Thus, Orwell's reference to the bankrupt nature of the Grand Alliance during the Second World War, which was intended to force people to question their leaders' motives, is excised. Furthermore, while, as in the book, Big Brother is never identified in the film, the unmistakable indications are that Oceania's ruling party is modelled on the Soviet regime, with Nazi flourishes. Thus, whereas some of Orwell's nomenclature such as 'comrades' stays in the film, other key points are taken out; Oceania's currency, for example, is changed from dollars, denoting American imperialism, to sterling. None of the explicit comparisons between 'Ingsoc' and the communists, which O'Brien makes in the book while brainwashing Winston, find their way onto the screen. Consequently, the important point that Russian communism is in fact inferior to 'Ingsoc' in terms of its ability to break its opponents' will and its ultimate quest for equality rather than power is omitted. Finally, the film concludes (at least in the British version), like Halas and Batchelor's *Animal Farm*, on an upbeat, bittersweet, counter-revolutionary note. Winston and Julia (Jan Sterling) overcome their brainwashing at the Ministry of Love and die, clutching each other, in a hail of Thought Police bullets as Winston shouts 'Down with Big Brother!'[85]

Despite these changes, *1984* came nowhere near to being what the USIA's chairman had envisaged as 'the most devastating anti-Communist film of all time'.[86] The movie certainly attracted the interest of the critics, some of whom thought the ending was 'more true to life', and others who called it 'our own kind of doublethink'. Peter Rathvon felt compelled to respond to the latter charges, arguing, in newspeakian-terms, that the ending was 'more logical', and one which Orwell himself 'would have written' if he had not been dying during the novel's composition.[87] However, the movie emphatically 'bombed' at the box office.[88] Part of the explanation for this would seem to lie in the poor performances by the lead players, especially Edmund O'Brien as Winston and Michael Redgrave as O'Connor (O'Brien in the book).[89] But what undid the film probably

more than anything else was its attempt to straddle several genres –
horror, romance, science fiction, thriller – with the result that many
viewers were left confused. This can be attributed to commercial
considerations and Columbia's need to maximize its profits by
appealing to as wide an audience as possible.[90] The money spent by
the US government on what ultimately looked a cheap and shabby
production therefore cannot have been worth it. Indeed, the project
might have served as a painful lesson in the difficulties of
constructing effective propaganda when commercial and ideological
interests are not in unison. The final word on the film was left to
Sonia Blair. Having publicly castigated it at the time as a desecration
of her husband's intentions, she decided to withdraw it (together
with all of the other 1950s adaptations of *Nineteen Eighty-Four*)
when the rights expired in the mid-1970s, 20 years after their
original release date. The adaptations thenceforth became, as *The
Times* put it, 'unfilms'.[91]

Conclusion and Epilogue

George Orwell attracted a remarkably heterogeneous following
during the Cold War. Those who adopted and adapted his name and
work spanned the whole political spectrum: Communist,
Conservative, Anarchist, Trotskyite. This article has focused on the
role played by state propagandists in the Orwell 'claiming game'. It
has shown that officials were capable of using Orwell skilfully and
clumsily, for the most part promoting his works, on other occasions
distorting them. In the main, Washington and London concentrated
on presenting Orwell as a new Man of the Right, one of the 'God
That Failed' school of apologists. Accordingly, *Animal Farm* and
Nineteen Eighty-Four were promoted as 'evidence' of the heinous
crimes committed by the leaders of the Soviet Union and of the
genuine threat posed to democracy (rarely capitalism) by
communism. For its part, Moscow heavily censored Orwell, and
attacked him as a crude Western lackey who hated communism and
Nineteen Eighty-Four specifically as a 'monstrous' piece of capitalist
'misanthropy'. Like their Western counterparts, Soviet propagandists
also acted more imaginatively at times, moulding Orwell for their
own purposes. J. Edgar Hoover's Federal Bureau of Investigation was
not a little piqued in 1959, for instance, when it learned that a Soviet-
backed East Berlin Russian-language newspaper was satirising the Big
Brother-like activities of the FBI in the United States. Hoover's

mechanization of surveillance, according to the article, made a reality of Orwell's vision of Americans' private lives being viewed by means of secretly placed television screens.[92] Of course, Orwell was far from being the only author to have his work plundered by official Cold War propagandists. Arthur Koestler's *Darkness at Noon* (1941), Victor Kravchenko's *I Chose Freedom* (1947), and Alexander Solzhenitsyn's *One Day in the Life of Ivan Denisovich* (1962), are just three examples of literature which also acquired privileged status in the West with at least some help from Western governments.[93] However, none of these writers could rival Orwell in the book selling stakes. By the time of the collapse of the Berlin Wall in 1989, *Animal Farm* and *Nineteen Eighty-Four* had sold almost 40 million copies in more than 60 languages, more than any other pair of books by a serious *or* popular post-war author. Such colossal figures help to explain why some commentators class Orwell as the most influential political writer of the twentieth century.[94]

To attribute the presence of dog-eared copies of *Animal Farm* and *Nineteen Eighty-Four* in homes and libraries scattered throughout the world after 1945 largely to the promotional efforts of Washington and London would naturally be absurd. Orwell in many respects could not have timed the novels' appearance better given the deterioration of East–West relations in the late 1940s, and it was this, together with the arrival in the 1950s of a new 'celebrity age' courtesy of television, the improved levels of literacy particularly in the developing world, and the continued presence of the Cold War itself, that facilitated the rapid circulation of words like 'vaporize', 'Big Brother', and 'Orwellian', not official propaganda. Yet it is difficult to escape the conclusion that the work of the IRD, USIA, CIA and others did much to lift Orwell's profile, particularly in the late 1940s and 1950s (for which official records are available). Western officials found *Animal Farm* and *Nineteen Eighty-Four* far more pliable than their Soviet counterparts, as the cinematic adaptations of the works show. Categorical evidence that this reconfiguring of Orwell produced the results they were looking for is lacking. What the reactions to these films tend to confirm, however, is the contribution that *Animal Farm* and *Nineteen Eighty-Four* made to the culture of the Cold War by helping to imprint in Western consciousness, above anything else, the fundamental link between communism and totalitarianism. More generally, the study has highlighted the central, long-term role played by the book in the Cold War propaganda conflict, and the paramount importance of linguistic issues – including the use and abuse of concepts such as freedom, tyranny, democracy and truth, as well as totalitarianism – within that conflict.

It remains to be seen whether Orwell's status dips as the Cold War recedes, and the sales and authority of *Animal Farm* and *Nineteen Eighty-Four* diminish as the books are deemed less 'relevant' politically. For the time being at least, the 'claiming' of his works continues. In October 1999 the US cable network TNT, makers of the acclaimed *Cold War* documentary series aired in the mid-1990s, broadcast the first made-for-television version of *Animal Farm*. Directed by the head of Jim Henson's Creature Shop in London, John Stevenson, and filmed on location in Ireland, the production featured state-of-the-art animatronic technology and a cast of hundreds of live animals. The end of this film also markedly diverged from Orwell's text. The sheepdog, Jessie, whose puppies have earlier been taken to become Napoleon's guard dogs, resolves to lead an escape attempt. In a flash forward, we see the few animals which managed to escape return to find that the rule of the pigs has been overthrown and that the former Animal Farm has collapsed into decay and pollution. In another flash forward we then see a happy American family driving through the farm gate in an open car, a version of *Blueberry Hill* playing on the radio. This new family – the perfect owners – will run the farm and a new generation of Jessie's puppies will live there in happiness. The message to the viewer would seem to be obvious: thank heavens for the end of communism, and for the return of the market economy and human rights. It appears that Orwell is as useful to some *after* the Cold War as he was *during* it.[95]

NOTES

1. Public Record Office, London (hereafter PRO) FO1110/189/PR1135/G, Minutes by Celia Kirwan, 30 March and 6 April 1949. That Orwell kept such a list was not news in 1996 to two of his biographers. See Michael Shelden, *Orwell: The Authorized Biography* (London: Minerva, 1991), p.468; Bernard Crick, *George Orwell* (London: Penguin, 1992), p.556. The list itself was published in 1998. See Peter Davison (ed.), *The Complete Works of George Orwell*: vol.xx: *Our Job is to Make Life Worth Living 1949–1950* (London: Secker and Warburg, 1998), pp.240–59.
2. Seamus Milne and Richard Norton-Taylor, 'Orwell Offered Blacklist', *The Guardian*, 11 July 1996, p.1; Ros Wynne-Jones, 'Orwell's Little List Leaves the Left Gasping for More', *The Independent on Sunday*, 14 July 1996, p.10; Tom Utley, 'Orwell is Revealed in Role of State Informer', *The Daily Telegraph*, 12 July 1996.
3. Frances Stonor Saunders, *Who Paid the Piper? The CIA and the Cultural Cold War* (London: Granta, 1999), p.300; Davison (ed.), *Our Job is to Make Life Worth Living*

1949–1950, pp.324–5; Timothy Garton Ash in Peter Davison (ed.), *Orwell and Politics* (London: Penguin, 2001), xvii; Robert Conquest, 'In Celia's Office: Orwell and the Cold War', *Times Literary Supplement*, 21 Aug. 1998, pp.4–5. For the most recent defence of Orwell's actions – on the grounds that the IRD was not involved in domestic surveillance, that Orwell was not motivated by personal gain, that nobody suffered as a result, and that, anyway, some of his suspicions turned out to be right – see Christopher Hitchens, *Orwell's Victory* (London: Penguin, 2002). For a critical response to Hitchens see Andy Croft, 'Ministry of Truth', *The Guardian*, 25 May 2002, p.9 (Review section).

4. John Rodden, *The Politics of Literary Reputation: The Making and Claiming of 'St. George' Orwell* (Oxford: Oxford University Press, 1989), pp.ix and 263ff.

5. See, for instance, George Orwell, 'Politics and the English Language', reprinted from George Orwell, *Shooting an Elephant and Other Essays* (New York: Harcourt, Brace and Company, 1946), in Robert Jackall (ed.), *Propaganda* (London: Macmillan, 1995), pp.423–37.

6. W.J. West (ed.), *Orwell: The War Commentaries* (London: Duckworth/BBC, 1985).

7. Crick, *George Orwell*, pp.455–6.

8. See also George Orwell, 'The Prevention of Literature', in George Orwell, *The Orwell Reader: Fiction, Essays and Reportage by George Orwell* (New York: Harcourt Brace Jovanovich, 1955), pp.367–79.

9. George Orwell, 'Toward European Unity', *Partisan Review*, July–Aug. 1947, reproduced in Sonia Orwell and Ian Angus (eds.), *The Collected Essays, Journalism and Letters of George Orwell*, vol. iv: *In Front of Your Nose 1945–50* (London: Secker and Warburg, 1968), pp.370–6.

10. For more on the 'Third Force' issue and the IRD's relationship to it see Christopher Mayhew, *A War of Words: A Cold War Witness* (London: I.B. Tauris, 1998), pp.14–47; Hugh Wilford, 'The Information Research Department: Britain's Secret Cold War Weapon Revealed', *Review of International Studies* 24/3 (1998), pp.353–69.

11. For the reviewers' 'wars' that greeted the publication of *Animal Farm* and *Nineteen Eighty-Four* see Crick, *George Orwell*, pp.488–92, 563–70, 603–4; Shelden, *Orwell*, pp.470–4; Donald McCormick, *Approaching 1984* (London: David and Charles, 1980), pp.12–13.

12. Crick, *George Orwell*, pp.450–52, 488; Jeffrey Meyers, *A Reader's Guide to George Orwell* (London: Thames and Hudson, 1975), p.131.

13. Gillian Fenwick (ed.), *George Orwell: A Bibliography* (New Castle, Delaware: St. Paul's Bibliographies, Winchester/Oak Knoll Press, 1998), pp.126–31.

14. Ibid., p.129; Crick, *George Orwell*, p.569; Davison (ed.), *Our Job is to Make Life Worth Living 1949–1950*, pp.134–6.

15. See Rodden, *The Politics of Literary Reputation*.

16. Ibid., pp.44–5. Publishing information about the sales of Orwell's books between 1946 and 1970 can be found in Fredric Warburg, *All Authors are Equal* (London: Hutchinson, 1973), pp.35–59, 92–121.

17. Crick, *George Orwell*, pp.488–92, 563–70, 603–4; Shelden, *Orwell*, pp.470–74; McCormick, *Approaching 1984*, pp.12–13; See Rodden, *The Politics of Literary Reputation* 4, *passim*.

18. Davison (ed.), *The Complete Works of George Orwell*: xix: *It is What I Think 1947–1948* (London: Secker and Warburg, 1998), p.23. A Hungarian edition of *Animal Farm* was eventually published in 1984. See Fenwick (ed.), *George Orwell*, p.118.

19. Davison (ed.), *It is What I Think 1947–1948*, pp.86–9.

20. Ibid., pp.211, 224; Letters from Orwell to Leonard Moore, 10 April 1947 and 24 July 1947, 11 Aug. 1947: Berg Collection, New York Public Library. On the political and diplomatic context of this work in Germany by the US High Commission and the British Foreign Office see Nicholas Pronay and Keith Wilson (eds.), *The Political Re-education of Germany and her Allies after World War Two* (London: Croom Helm, 1985).

21. On the IRD's establishment and activities in the late 1940s and 1950s see L. Smith, 'Covert British Propaganda: The Information Research Department, 1947–77', *Millennium* 9/1 (1980), pp.67–83; R. Fletcher, 'British Propaganda since World War Two – A Case Study', *Media, Culture and Society* 4/2 (1982), pp.97–109; W. Wark, 'Coming in from the Cold: British Propaganda and the Red Army Defectors, 1945–52', *The International History Review* 9/1 (1987), pp.48–72; W.S. Lucas and C.J. Morris, 'A Very British Crusade: The Information Research Department and the Beginning of the Cold War', in R. Aldrich (ed.), *British Intelligence, Strategy and the Cold War* (London: Routledge, 1992), pp.85–110; Foreign and Commonwealth Office Library and Records Department, *IRD: Origins and Establishment of the Foreign Office Information Research Department 1946–48* (London: Foreign and Commonwealth Office Library and Records Department, 1995); S.L. Carruthers, 'A Red Under Every Bed? Anti-Communist Propaganda and Britain's Response to Colonial Insurgency', *Contemporary Record* 9/2 (1995), pp.294–318; Paul Lashmar and James Oliver, *Britain's Secret Propaganda War* (Stroud: Sutton, 1998); Tony Shaw, 'The British Popular Press and the Early Cold War', *History* 83/269 (1998), pp.66–85; Wilford, 'The Information Research Department'; Tony Shaw, 'The Information Research Department of the British Foreign Office and the Korean War, 1950–1953', *Journal of Contemporary History* 34/2 (1999), pp.263–82.
22. PRO FO1110/221/PR1373/G, Minute by Leslie Sheridan, 12 May 1949; FO1110/221/PR1589/G, Ralph Murray to Christopher Mayhew, 10 April 1949; Lashmar and Oliver, *Britain's Secret Propaganda War*, p.98; Fenwick (ed.), *George Orwell*, pp.103–4, 136–7.
23. PRO FO1110/221/PR442 IRD circular, 4 March 1949.
24. PRO FO1110/221/PR1589/G Ralph Murray to Christopher Mayhew, 10 April 1949; FO1110/189/PR1135/G Minute by Celia Kirwan, 30 March 1949; FO1110/221/PR505G Ralph Murray to Christopher Warner, 28 Jan. 1949.
25. For the details of Ampersand and other companies that published IRD material between the early 1950s and 1977, when the IRD was closed down, see Lashmar and Oliver, *Britain's Secret Propaganda War*, pp.100–103.
26. PRO FO1110/264/1634/G June 1949; Davison (ed.), *Our Job is to Make Life Worth Living 1949–1950*, p.319.
27. PRO FO1110/373/PR8/27/51, Minute by C. Stephenson, 28 March 1951. Hyde had left the Communist Party in 1948 when he was news editor of the *Daily Worker*. Published by Heinemann, *I Believed* was a bestselling, sensational account of his work for the 'cause' and his conversion to Catholicism. *The God That Failed* was published in Britain by Hamish Hamilton and by Harper and Bros in the United States in January 1950. Its contributors were Ignazio Silone, André Gide, Richard Wright, Arthur Koestler, Louis Fischer and Stephen Spender. On the book's origins and impact see Anthony Howard, *Crossman: The Pursuit of Power* (London: Jonathan Cape, 1990), pp.142–3, and Saunders, *Who Paid the Piper?*, pp.64–6.
28. PRO FO1110/716/PR10111/31/G, Report on IRD work, 20 May 1955.
29. PRO FO1110/221, Ernest Main to Ralph Murray, 4 April 1949.
30. PRO FO1110/221/PR3361, letter (translated), V. Puachev to Orwell, 24 June 1949; FO1110/221/PR3361, correspondence between FO and IRD, 18 July 1949; FO 1110/221/PR3361 Celia Kirwan to Charles Thayer, 4 Nov. 1949; Davison (ed.), *It is What I Think 1947–1948*, p.473; Davison (ed.), *Our Job is to Make Life Worth Living 1949–1950*, p.153; Sonia Orwell and Ian Angus (eds.), *The Collected Essays, Journalism and Letters of George Orwell*, vol.iv: *In Front of Your Nose* (London: Secker and Warburg, 1968), p.567.
31. Rodden, *The Politics of Literary Reputation*, p.202; Walter Hixson, *Parting the Curtain: Propaganda, Culture and the Cold War, 1945–1961* (London: Macmillan, 1997), pp.123–4.
32. PRO FO1110/319/PR48/82/G, Roderick Parkes to Ralph Murray, 25 Oct. 1950; Minutes by Ralph Murray and Leslie Sheridan, 7 and 10 Nov. 1950.
33. PRO FO1110/365/PR127/9, Ralph Murray circular, 11 Dec. 1950. For details of the

production process see FO1110/392/PR32/14/51/G and FO1110/392/PR32/89/G.

34. PRO FO1110/392/PR32/41/51 IRD circular, 25 April 1951.

35. Cited in Rodden, *The Politics of Literary Reputation*, p.434.

36. US National Archives, Washington, DC, RG59 511.4121/6–2651, Acheson to US Embassy London, 26 June 1951.

37. Rodden, *The Politics of Literary Reputation*, p.434; PRO FO1110/373/PR8/78, John Rayner to Ralph Murray, 16 March 1951.

38. PRO FO 1110/738/PR121/68/G, Minute by IRD's Editorial Adviser, 21 Feb. 1955.

39. PRO FO1110/740/PR124/3/G, H.A.H. Cortazzi to Douglas Williams, 28 Jan. 1955.

40. On Orwell's enormous reputation in West Germany, including the efforts by *Der Monat*, during the Cold War see Rodden, *The Politics of Literary Reputation*, pp.288ff. For more on Lasky and the CCF's activities in general see Saunders, *Who Paid the Piper?* and Peter Coleman, *The Liberal Conspiracy: The Congress for Cultural Freedom and the Struggle for the Mind of Post-War Europe* (New York: The Free Press, 1989).

41. I. Anisimov, 'Enemies of Mankind', *Pravda*, 12 May 1950, p.3. Translated in *Current Digest of the Soviet Press*, 1 July 1950, pp.14–15.

42. Rodden, *The Politics of Literary Reputation*, p.202.

43. Ibid., pp.210–11; Arch Puddington, *Broadcasting Freedom: The Cold War Triumph of Radio Free Europe and Radio Liberty* (Lexington, Kentucky: The University Press of Kentucky, 2000), pp.12–13, 67; Scott Lucas, *Freedom's War: The US Crusade Against the Soviet Union 1945–56* (Manchester: Manchester University Press, 1999), pp.100–104, 253–5. On the part played by Secker and Warburg in promoting *The Captive Mind* as 'the first full-length story of the position of the intellectual behind the Iron Curtain', see Gordon Johnston, 'Writing and Publishing the Cold War: John Berger and Secker and Warburg', *Twentieth Century British History* 12/4 (2001), pp.451. On the influence and availability of *Animal Farm* and *Nineteen Eighty-Four* in Eastern Europe in later Cold War decades see also Timothy Garton Ash in Davison (ed.), *Orwell and Politics*, pp.xi–xii; Dan Jacobsen, 'The Invention of "Orwell"', *The Times Literary Supplement*, 21 Aug. 1998, p.3.

44. Rodden, *The Politics of Literary Reputation*, pp.82–9. As a schoolboy in Manchester, England in the 1970s, I can testify to this on both counts.

45. Peter Davison (ed.), *The Complete Works of George Orwell*: vol. xiii: *Animal Farm* (London: Secker and Warburg, 1998), pp.115–24; Rodden, *The Politics of Literary Reputation*, p.202.

46. Rodden, *The Politics of Literary Reputation*, p.273.

47. Nancy E. Bernard, *US Television News and Cold War Propaganda 1947–1960* (Cambridge: Cambridge University Press, 1999), pp.48, 115–31, 155–77. CBS, ABC and DuMont were the three other US television networks.

48. Rodden, *The Politics of Literary Reputation*, p.274; Philip Hamburger, 'Nineteen Eighty-Four', *The New Yorker*, 3 Oct. 1953, p.84.

49. Rodden, *The Politics of Literary Reputation*, p.274; Emma Lambert, 'Time, Inc. and the Cultural Cold War during the Eisenhower Administration', paper presented at the 69th Anglo-American Conference of Historians, Institute of Historical Research, London, 7 July 2000; Saunders, *Who Paid the Piper?*, pp.52, 146–7, 158, 266; Lucas, *Freedom's War*, pp.166–8.

50. Jason Jacobs, *The Intimate Screen: Early British Television Drama* (Oxford: Oxford University Press, 2000), pp.139, 151.

51. BBC Written Archives Centre, Reading (hereafter BBC WAC): AC T5/362/2 Television Drama *Nineteen Eighty-Four* (1954), File 2; BBC WAC Press Cuttings P6555, Book 14a Television Programmes, 1953–4; BBC WAC Transcript of *Panorama*, 15 Dec. 1954; Rodden, *The Politics of Literary Reputation*, p.275.

52. Paula Burton, *British Broadcasting: Radio and Television in the United Kingdom* (Minneapolis: University of Minnesota Press, 1956), pp.275–6.

53. BBC WAC T5/362/2 Television Drama *1984* (1954), File 2; BBC WAC Press Cuttings P6555, Book 14a Television Programmes, 1953–4; BBC WAC Transcript of 'Panorama', 15 Dec. 1954; Rodden, *The Politics of Literary Reputation*, pp.274–80.

54. 'BBC Repeats 1984 Despite Objections', *The New York Times*, 17 Dec. 1954, p.35; Jacobs, *The Intimate Screen*, p.155.
55. See Foreign and Commonwealth Office Library and Records Department, *IRD*, pp.17–18; Wilford, 'The Information Research Department', pp.364–6; Lashmar and Oliver, *Britain's Secret Propaganda War*, pp.57–65; Mayhew, *A War of Words, passim*.
56. Both the Honorary Secretary, Michael Goodwin, and General Secretary, John Clews, of the British Society for Cultural Freedom were IRD contract employees. Warburg, *All Authors are Equal*, pp.154–7; Saunders, *Who Paid the Piper?*, especially pp.109–11.
57. *Daily Express*, 14 Dec. 1954, in BBC WAC Press Cuttings P6555, Book 14a Television Programmes, 1953–4; Nigel Kneale, 'The Last Rebel in Airstrip One', *Radio Times*, 10 Dec. 1954, p.15. Kneale had created the immensely popular and critically acclaimed 1953 science-fiction BBC television serial, 'Quatermass'. This might help to account for the science-fiction feel of 'Nineteen Eighty-Four'.
58. '1984 and All That', *Daily Mail*, 14 Dec. 1954, p.1; '1984', *Daily Express*, 15 Dec. 1954; 'The Lesson of "1984"', *Daily Mail*, 18 Dec. 1954, p.1; Peter Black, 'Honest Orwell Did Not Write To Horrify, in Love with Freedom He wanted To Warn', *Daily Mail*, 14 Dec. 1954, p.4.
59. '1984', *The Times*, 15 Dec. 1954, p.5. Rodden, *The Politics of Literary Reputation*, writes: 'It is probably unusual that one can point to a single moment from which a writer's popular reputation is "launched", but in Orwell's case the date is clear: Sunday, 12 Dec. 1954', (p.274). On the huge sales of *Nineteen Eighty-Four* after the BBC play, see ibid., p.281.
60. These letters can be found in BBC WAC T5/362/2 Television Drama '1984' (1954), File 2.
61. *The Times*, 16 Dec. 1954; *New Statesman*, 18 Dec. 1954: BBC WAC Press Cuttings P6555, Book 14a Television Programmes, 1953–4; Isaac Deutscher, '1984 – Mysticism of Cruelty', reprinted in *Heretics and Renegades, and Other Essays* (London: Jonathan Cape, 1955), p.35. Susan L. Carruthers (Rutgers) has undertaken further analysis of the role of novels by Orwell and Arthur Koestler in the construction of Cold War perceptions of Soviet 'totalitarianism'. See, for example, '"More Dramatic than Fact": Cold War Fiction, Modernity and the Total State', paper delivered at the July 2001 conference of the Society for Historians of American Foreign Relations, Washington, DC, USA.
62. Contract for *Animal Farm* between RD-DR Corporation and Halas and Batchelor Cartoon Films Ltd., 19 Nov. 1951, Halas and Batchelor Collections, London; Letter from Borden Mace, President of RD-DR Corporation, during the making of *Animal Farm*, to author, 28 March 1998; *Daily Film Renter*, 28 Nov. 1951; Howard Hunt, *Undercover: Memoirs of an American Secret Agent* (London: W.H. Allen, 1975), p.70.
63. Evan Thomas, *The Very Best Men: Four Who Dared – The Early Years of the CIA* (New York: Simon and Schuster, 1995), pp.29–30, 32–3, 63; Harry Rositzke, *The CIA's Secret Operations* (New York: Reader's Digest Press, 1977), pp.149–54; John Ranelagh, *The Agency: The Rise and Decline of the CIA* (London: Sceptre, 1988), pp.198–202, 216–24.
64. Paul Wells, 'Dustbins, Democracy and Defence: Halas and Batchelor and the Animated Film in Britain 1940–1947', in Pat Kirkham and David Thoms (eds.), *War Culture: Social Change and the Changing Experience in World War Two* (London: Lawrence and Wishart, 1995), pp.61–72; Elaine Burrows, 'Live Action: A Brief History of British Animation', in Charles Barr (ed.), *All Our Yesterdays* (London: British Film Institute, 1986), pp.272–85; Letter from Borden Mace, President of RD-DR Corporation, during the making of *Animal Farm*, to author, 28 March 1998.
65. Notes on discussion of script changes, Sept. and Oct. 1951, and on changes made in dialogue and timing, September 1952, *Animal Farm* archive, Halas and Batchelor collection, Southampton Institute's International Animation Research Archive (SIIARA); Letter from Borden Mace to author, 28 March 1998; Review of *Crime of the Century* (British title of *Walk East on Beacon*), *Monthly Film Bulletin*, Sept. 1952.
66. Letter from John Halas to Warburg, 12 Nov. 1952, *Animal Farm* archive, Halas and

Batchelor collection, SIIARA; Crick, *George Orwell*, p.560, p.567. Secker and Warburg published an illustrated edition of *Animal Farm* based on the film in 1954. For more on the linkages between Secker and Warburg and the CCF see Johnston, 'Writing and Publishing the Cold War', pp.432–60.

67. *Foreign Relations of the United States* (hereafter *FRUS*), vol.i, 1951 (Washington DC, 1979), pp.178–80, paper approved by the PSB, 28 September 1951 – 'Role of PSB under 4/4/51 Presidential Directive'; Scott Lucas, 'Campaigns of Truth: The Psychological Strategy Board and American Ideology, 1951–1953', *The International History Review* 18/2 (1996), pp.279–302; Hixson, *Parting the Curtain*, pp.17–19.

68. Richard Hirsch, PSB, to Tracy Barnes, 'Comment on "Animal Farm" Script', 23 Jan. 1952, PSB Index Files 062.2., Harry S. Truman Library, Independence, Missouri. This emphasis on the simplicity of the propaganda message also surfaced in January 1952 during the PSB's consideration of an enhanced role for literature as an anti-communist weapon. Cleverly distributed, clearly written and effectively subsidized, 'a literature of counter-ideology' would spell out 'the lie inherent in Soviet propaganda'. Godel to Barnes, 14 Jan. 1952, *United States Declassified Document Reference System* (hereafter DDRS) 1991, 1113.

69. George Orwell, *Animal Farm* (Harmondsworth: Penguin, 1980), p.88.

70. Ibid., p.120.

71. Patrick Murray, *Companion to Animal Farm* (Dublin: The Educational Press, 1985), p.39; Crick, *George Orwell*, p.451.

72. Script change discussions, March and Nov. 1952, *Animal Farm* archive, Halas and Batchelor collection, SIIARA; Author's correspondence with Vivian Halas, Feb. 1998; Lucas, *Freedom's War*.

73. Sol Stein, ACCF Executive Director, letter to Paris Theatre manager, 5 Jan. 1955; Stein memorandum concerning discount coupons for *Animal Farm*, 11 Jan. 1955; Murray Baron circular to trade unions, 17 Jan. 1955; Borden Mace letter to Stein concerning MGM distribution, 14 Jan. 1955: Box 8, folder 2, ACCF archives, Tamiment Library, New York University.

74. PRO FO 1110/740/PR124/3/G, H.A.H. Cortazzi to Douglas Williams, 28 Jan. 1955; FO 1110/740/PR124/6/G, Information Section Saigon Embassy to Information Policy Department, 9 March 1955.

75. Cited in Rodden, *The Politics of Literary Reputation*, p.445.

76. Spencer Brown, 'Strange Things at Animal Farm', *Commentary* (Feb. 1955), p.157; David Sylvester, 'Orwell on the Screen', *Encounter* 4/3 (1955), pp.35–7.

77. *Catholic Herald*, cited in *Films and Filming* 1/6 (1955); *Daily Mail*, 12 Jan. 1955.

78. Hunt, *Undercover*, p.70; Hixson, *Parting the Curtain*, pp.87–119.

79. International newspaper cuttings scrapbook, *Animal Farm* archive, Halas and Batchelor collection, SIIARA; Rodden, *The Politics of Literary Reputation*, pp.382–98. For a fuller analysis of the 1950s' cinematic versions of *Animal Farm* and *Nineteen Eighty-Four* see Tony Shaw, *British Cinema and the Cold War: The State, Propaganda and Consensus* (London: I.B. Tauris, 2001), ch.4.

80. Saunders, *Who Paid the Piper?*, p.295.

81. *Daily Film Renter*, 23 Dec. 1954; *Daily Mail*, 22 Dec. 1954; *News Chronicle*, 4 July 1955; *The Daily Herald*, 5 Aug. 1955; Saunders, *Who Paid the Piper?*, pp.288–9, 295.

82. *Sunday Citizen*, 14 Oct. 1962.

83. Saunders, *Who Paid the Piper?*, p.289. Anti-communist movies with which Columbia was involved included *Walk a Crooked Mile* (Gordon Douglas, 1948), *Invasion USA* (Alfred E. Green, 1952) and aforementioned *Walk East on Beacon* (Alfred Werker, 1952).

84. Stein's letter to Rathvon, 31 Jan. 1955, Box 4, folder 11, ACCF archives, Tamiment Library, New York University; Stein's correspondence with author, 28 April 1998.

85. The ending of the film released in the United States corresponded with Orwell's book, with Winston and Julia estranged and the two of them having learned to love Big Brother. Owing to the lack of production records it is not entirely clear why two endings with different messages were made. For a (positive) review of the American

version see *The New York Times*, 1 Oct. 1956. For the decisions on the two endings see *The Times*, 10 March 1957, p.7.

86. *Sunday Citizen*, 14 Oct. 1962.

87. *The Daily Herald*, 2 March 1956; *Daily Mail*, 1 March 1956; *Sunday Express*, 4 March 1956; *Daily Mail*, 27 Feb. 1956.

88. Motion Picture Association of America spokesman, cited in Rodden, *The Politics of Literary Reputation*, p.445. Neither *1984* nor *Animal Farm* were listed during 1955–57 by *Variety*, which computes the box-office sales of all films that gross above $1 million.

89. Ironically, Redgrave was on Orwell's list of suspected crypto-communists and fellow-travellers given to the IRD in 1949. See Davison (ed.), *Our Job is to Make Life Worth Living 1949–1950*, p.254.

90. *Sight and Sound* 53/2 (1984); *New Statesman and Nation*, 10 March 1956.

91. *Daily Mail*, 27 Feb. 1956; *The Times*, 15 Nov. 1983. The second cinematic adaptation of *Nineteen Eighty-Four* appeared in 1984. Also titled *1984*, this was a British film directed by Michael Radford, produced by Virgin, and starring John Hurt (as Winston) and Richard Burton (as O'Brien). For more details of this film, which largely stayed faithful to the book, see in Rodden, *The Politics of Literary Reputation*, pp.285–7.

92. Rodden, *The Politics of Literary Reputation*, pp.202–4; FBI file: C.F. Downing to Mr. Parsons, 31 March 1959, 'Smear Campaign: Committee for a Return to the Homeland – Internal Security – Russia', http://foia.fbi.gov/orwell/orwell1.pdf. During the later stages of the Cold War domestic critics of the US government also saw *Nineteen Eighty-Four* as an analysis of 'Orwellian' aspects of the American social and political system, including the FBI, the CIA and advertising agencies, whose uses of language were often compared to newspeak. See Richard A. Schwartz, *Cold War Culture: Media and the Arts, 1945–1990* (New York: Checkmark Books, 2000), p.230.

93. PRO FO371/56912/N1221G/10772/38, Minutes by Pierson Dixon, 22 Aug. and 18 Sept. 1946; FO371/56912/N1221G/10772/38, Christopher Warner to Robert Bruce Lockhart, 2 Sept. 1946; FO1110/221/PR505/G, Ralph Murray to Christopher Warner, 28 Jan. 1949; Richard J. Aldrich, *The Hidden Hand: Britain, America and Cold War Secret Intelligence* (London: John Murray, 2001), pp.106–7, 139. A good example of the politico-scholarly veneration of Solzhenitsyn's work in the West during the Cold War is John Dunlop, Richard Haugh and Alexis Klimoff (eds.), *Alexander Solzhenitsyn: Critical Essays and Documentary Materials* (New York: Collier Books, 1975). On Solzhenitsyn's acknowledgement of the importance of Orwell in heightening awareness of the dangers of communism in the West see Joseph Pearce, *Solzhenitsyn: A Soul in Exile* (London: HarperCollins, 1989), p.106.

94. Rodden, *The Politics of Literary Reputation*, p.16; Timothy Garton Ash in Davison (ed.), *Orwell and Politics*, p.xi.

95. For further information on this film see: http://alt.tnt.tv/movies/tntoriginals/animalfarm/atf/info.html. For a critical reaction to it see: www.wsws.org/articles/1999/nov1999/anim-n12.shtml.

Abstracts

'The Man Who Invented Truth': The Tenure of Edward R. Murrow as Director of the United States Information Agency during the Kennedy Years, *by Nicholas Cull*

This study examines Cold War culture through the institutional history of an agency established specifically to shape that culture: the United States Information Agency, and particularly its best-known director, Edward R. Murrow. It looks at the divergence between Murrow's declared attitude to international information (his 'warts and all' approach) and the reality as experienced by his Voice of America journalists. Cases considered include: the Bay of Pigs; the Berlin Wall and Nuclear Testing issue; the Cuban Missile Crisis; representation of Civil Rights (during which Murrow went some way to redeem himself) and the Vietnam War. Although the article uncovers only a few points at which Murrow impacted on US foreign policy decisions, it argues that the achievements of his tenure are not to be found in overnight successes but in the cumulative flow of information and ideas. It notes the irony that the Cold War was won for the free market but – in terms of information at least – it was not won by free market media, but by the intervention of state-sponsored agencies like Murrow's USIA.

'Soviet Cinema in the Early Cold War': Pudovkin's *Admiral Nakhimov* in Context, *by Sarah Davies*

The article considers how the emerging Cold War shaped the development of Soviet thinking on the role and significance of cinema, which came to be regarded as a key weapon in what was presented from the outset as an ideological war. It focuses on the impact this had upon the making of the great Soviet director Pudovkin's *Admiral Nakhimov*.

Future Perfect?: Communist Science Fiction in the Cold War, *by Patrick Major*

Russian science fiction emerged from a prolonged period of censorship in 1957, opened up by destalinisation and real Soviet achievements in the space race, typified by Efremov's galactic epic,

Andromeda. Official communist science fiction transposed the laws of historical materialism to the future, scorning western nihilistic writings and predicting a peaceful transition to universal communism. Scientocratic visions of the future nevertheless implicitly critiqued the bureaucratic developed socialism of the present. Dissident science fiction writers emerged, such as the Strugatsky brothers with their 'social fantasies', problematizing the role of intervention in the historical process, or Stanislaw Lem's tongue-in-cheek exposures of man's cognitive limitations.

The Education of Dissent: The Reception of the Voice of Free Hungary, 1951–56, *by Mark Pittaway*

Recent years have seen considerable attention devoted to the cultural history of the Cold War. Within this cultural history some attention has been paid to the history of western broadcasting to Soviet bloc countries in Central and Eastern Europe. Most of this work has concentrated on the institutional histories of individual radio stations and their relationship to politics. Little or no systematic attention has, however, been paid to the reception of these radio stations in their target societies. This article, which concentrates on the reception of the Voice of Free Hungary in that country during the early 1950s, lays the foundations of an approach to the social history of western broadcasting towards the Soviet bloc.

The Debate over Nuclear Refuge, *by David Seed*

From the late 1940s onwards a heated debate took place in the USA over whether it was possible to take practical preventive measures against nuclear attack. This essay examines the participation of a number of novelists in that debate and in particular the different ways in which they dramatize the anticipated effects of fall-out and the panic which would follow such attacks. Writers such as Judith Merril questioned the reassuring orthodoxies put forward by the US government, and the descriptions of nuclear shelters in the fiction of the period tends to confirm the title of one of the earliest comments on this controversy, namely that there is no place to hide.

'Some Writers are More Equal than Others': George Orwell, the State and Cold War Privilege, *by Tony Shaw*

George Orwell's *Animal Farm* (1945) and *Nineteen Eighty-Four* (1949) are widely regarded as two of the best known and most influential novels in English of the Cold War. By 1989, the novels had sold almost 40 million copies in more than 60 languages, more than any other pair of books by a serious or popular post-war author. This article concentrates on the role official western propagandists played in lifting Orwell's profile during the first decade or so of the Cold War. It examines why *Animal Farm* and *Nineteen Eighty-Four* were appropriated by the British and American governments, what financial assistance was given to foreign publishers in order to make the books more accessible, and what changes the books underwent when they were transferred to the cinema and television screens in the 1950s in order to make them more 'understandable' to the non-literary public. The article therefore sheds light on domestic and trans-national cultural propaganda, and on the creation and distortion of cultural icons during the Cold War.

Notes on Contributors

Nicholas J. Cull is Professor of American Studies at the University of Leicester. He is the author of *Selling War: the British Propaganda Campaign against American 'Neutrality' in World War II* (1995). He is currently completing a complete history of the USIA and US information overseas for Cambridge University Press.

Sarah Davies is Senior Lecturer in History at the University of Durham. She is the author of *Popular Opinion in Stalin's Russia* (1997). She is currently working on Soviet cinema in the Cold War, and is also involved in a collaborative research project on Stalin's political values.

Patrick Major is Senior Lecturer in History at the University of Warwick. He is the author of *The Death of the KPD: Communism and Anti-Communism in West Germany, 1945–1956* (1997). He is currently completing a socio-cultural history of the Berlin Wall, as well as developing a comparative interest in the popular culture of the Cold War, East and West.

Rana Mitter is University Lecturer in the History and Politics of Modern China at the University of Oxford. He is the author of *The Manchurian Myth: Nationalism, Resistance, and Collaboration in Modern China* (2000). His current project explores the ways in which the war against Japan has shaped Chinese political culture from the 1930s to the present.

Mark Pittaway is Lecturer in European Studies in the History Department at the Open University. He has published on industrial communities in postwar Hungary, most recently 'The Reproduction of Hierarchy: Skill, Working-Class Culture and the State in Early Socialist Hungary' (*Journal of Modern History*) and is completing a book on the social history of Hungarian industrial labour between 1944 and 1958.

David Seed is a Professor in American Literature at the University of Liverpool. He has published *American Science Fiction and the Cold War* (1999) and is currently completing a study of fictional depictions of brainwashing.

Tony Shaw is Senior Lecturer in History at the University of Hertfordshire. He is the author of *British Cinema and the Cold War: The State, Propaganda and Consensus* (2001) and *Eden, Suez and the Mass Media: Propaganda and Persuasion during the Suez Crisis* (1996).

Index